MW01625174

MYSTERY READER'S WALKING GUIDE

WASHINGTON, D.C.

Praise for Mystery Reader's Walking Guide: Washington, D.C.

"Alzina Stone Dale's masterwork spotlights the mind-numbing multitude of fictional murders and villainy set in the nation's capital . . . a lesser treatment would not have done justice to the panoramic stage provided by Washington, D.C. Who would have thought the old town had so much blood in it?"

—Edward S. Gilbreth, Mystery Book Critic, *Chicago Sun-Times*

"Beneath Washington's layer of well-known history lies a secret but equally abundant layer of fictional history. Alzina Stone Dale has conducted a meticulous investigation into that realm to show that this city's reputation is not quite accurate: Rather than the murder capital, Washington should be called the Murder Mystery Capital. Any visitor would find it intriguing to follow in her footsteps."

—Phyllis Richman, author of *The Butter Did It*;
food critic, *Washington Post*

". . . A wonderful travel guide for mystery readers who have the ability, inclination, and opportunity to visit the locations of their favorite D.C. sleuths, or would rather just sit in their cozy armchair at home to rediscover the streets, buildings, stores, etc., mentioned in the authors' works."

—August P. Aleksy, Jr., owner, Centuries and Sleuths Bookstore

MYSTERY READER'S WALKING GUIDE

WASHINGTON, D.C.

Alzina Stone Dale

Agatha Award Winner, 1995

Maps by John Babcock

PASSPORT BOOKS

NTC/Contemporary Publishing Company

ISBN 0-7394-0562-4

Cover design by Nick Panos
Cover illustration by John Babcock
Interior maps by John Babcock

Published by Passport Books
An imprint of NTC/Contemporary Publishing Company
4255 West Touhy Avenue, Lincolnwood (Chicago), Illinois 60646-1975 U.S.A.

Printed in the United States of America
International Standard Book Number: 0-8442-0480-2

For Barby and Paul Garner,
whose hospitality made this book possible
and
For Malice Domestic, Inc.,
who made it worth doing.

CONTENTS

MAPS

ACKNOWLEDGMENTS

This book is dedicated to Paul and Barby Garner, who have been our hosts, and to the organization affectionately known as Malice Domestic, Inc.—its originators, officers, and volunteers as well as my fellow authors and the wonderful fans who come.

I had many, many helpers. First prize is a tie between Barbara Goetz Garner and William F. (Bill) Deeck. Without Barb's tireless book hunting, book-review watching, fact-finding, and hospitality, and the incredible riches of Bill's library, loaned and mailed unstintingly, this guide could never have been written. As longtime D.C. resident Barb helped me deal with the physical city, Bill invariably knew offhand who had won an Edgar for what story, or—sigh—recommended yet another author and lent me the book! The vast number of books mentioned can be blamed on him!

I also got books or the names of books from the Arsenic and Oolong Society, Eleanor Taylor Bland, Maureen Collins, Pat Carlson, Robert A. Carter, Dan Crawford, Barbara D'Amato, Beth Fedyn, Barbara Gauntt, Ed Gilbreth, Gar Anthony Haywood, Jeremiah Healy, Hugh Holton, Richard Klein, Barbara Lee, Nicole St. John, Rebecca Reynolds, Phyllis Richman, Kelsey Roberts, Joan Turchik, Sue Whittaker, and Bill Wooby of the Collector.

I had special help galore from Kathy Harig and Paige Rose

of Baltimore's Mystery Loves Company bookstore who not only carted books to Chicago for me but also shared their copyrighted Baltimore Mysteries book list, their Mystery Tour, and their expertise! I had additional aid and comfort from mystery bookstores like Mystery Bookshop: Bethesda, Chicago's Centuries and Sleuths, Fifty-Seventh Street Books, Scotland Yard, Ltd., Something Wicked, and Washington's MysteryBooks, while my favorite library continues to be the Bridgman Public Library and my favorite secondhand bookstore, The Book Rack, both in Berrien County, Michigan.

My invaluable reader-checkers worked hard catching my mistakes, which were legion. They were Maureen Collins, William F. Deeck, Barbara Goetz Garner, Barbara Gauntt, Kathy Harig, Richard Klein, Jean McMillan, Tina McGill, Martha Pennigar, Helen Lillie Marwick, Barbara Mertz, Patricia Moyes, and Bill Wooby. Thank you all.

My husband, Charles, not only walked the walks and read the guide, but proofread and spell-checked it, catching innumerable errors. Those that remain are my very own.

INTRODUCTION

How to Use This Guide

Washington, D.C., is the power capital of the world, and the mysteries set there, whether detective stories, police procedurals, or thrillers, reflect the city's special ambiance. Whether you do your sleuthing on foot or while relaxing in a comfortable chair, following its amateur detectives and PIs, as well as the Secret Service, FBI, Capitol Police, Metropolitan Police, and the CIA will give you an authentic sense of what makes D.C. tick.

Washington's mysteries describe its social history and popular culture as it rose from the foggy bottom of the Potomac River to become the capital of the world. R. B. Dominic (aka Emma Lathen) called it a city poised between past and future because what happens today shapes the tomorrows of millions of Americans, and presidents, ambassadors, and even typists grapple with the future in the shadow of the past.

Always check a mystery's publication date, because in D.C.'s detective stories the city changed from a sleepy, provincial southern town to a world-class city. A mystery's publication date is given in the text and included in the book lists for each walk in this book.

Historically, Washington, D.C., was born as the result of a deal between Alexander Hamilton and Thomas Jefferson that the South would pay the North's Revolutionary War debts if the capital were located below the Mason-Dixon Line. The original District of Columbia was a diamond-shaped ten-mile square that included Arlington National Cemetery and Old Town Alexandria, which is why they are included in this guide. With the exceptions of classy Georgetown and trendy Dupont Circle, D.C. mysteries have more scenes set in public places such as the White House, the Capitol, or the Mall than in residential neighborhoods or urban slums.

More D.C. mysteries' murders stem from grasping for power and influence than from private greed or malice, but since Watergate, with the exception of Tom Clancy's President Jack Ryan, there are few heroes there. Even in a cozy affair, Washington's major characters are still presidents, senators, bureaucrats, lobbyists, or media moguls.

Following the format of the earlier guides in this series, each of these eight walks begins with a historical introduction, followed by lists of places of interest and places to eat and a map of the walk. Most places to eat have a connection to a mystery, but many of the national museums and other public buildings have cafeterias and rest-room facilities that are open to the public. Special tours such as the annual Georgetown Garden Tour are noted, and suggestions for possible side trips appear at the end of the walks.

If you want to follow only Margaret Truman's sleuthing couple, Annabel Reed-Smith and Mac Smith, or Elliott Roosevelt's mother, Eleanor, or R. B. Dominic's Ohio congressman, Ben Safford, look the author up in the index. Many of the mysteries mentioned are out of print and hard to find. The best places to locate copies are your local library or secondhand bookstores.

Pierre L'Enfant's capital is elegant, but his street-numbering system—including diagonal avenues, north and south alphabet streets, and east-west numbered streets—begins at Capitol Hill and is confusing. To help you, maps of the individual walks are included and all the walks begin and end at a Metro subway station. At each Metro station, in addition to a systemwide wall map and ticket machines, you can get a pocket map of the system. There are reduced rates on the

Metro from 9:30 A.M. to 3:00 P.M., the prime time for D.C. sleuthing, but remember there are no rest-room facilities in any Metro Station! Your best alternatives are D.C.'s hotels, public buildings, or fast-food outlets.

To orient yourself to the entire city, take the Old Town Trolley Tours of Washington by day or by night. They pick up passengers at major points like Union Station, the Capitol, or Georgetown, and you can hop on and off and buy a ticket en route. The entire tour takes about two hours and the cost is $18. For more information call (202) 832-9800.

If you get tired midway or want to head to your hotel at the end of a walk, you can find a taxi easily and fairly cheaply, thanks to the zone fare system. Despite its reputation as a real-life murder capital, Washington is a safe place to walk by day if you use common sense, but a companion is always fun and a good idea. In Elaine Raco Chase and Anne Wingate's *Amateur Detectives: A Writer's Guide to How Private Citizens Solve Criminal Cases* (1996), they point out that, although the District of Columbia complies with the Brady Law, it is a "sick joke" to say that there is no illicit commerce in firearms within the District! So do take care. You can expect to be hassled, however, at the White House, where security is so tight you can hardly see your fellow tourists for the guards.

Enjoy your walks!

1

WHITE HOUSE/ DOWNTOWN WALK

BACKGROUND

Capital architect Pierre L'Enfant laid out Washington with its center on Capitol Hill, but in many D.C. mysteries the White House is the real source of power and prestige. L'Enfant planned to have the "President's house" a palatial mansion, surrounded by an eighty-acre private park, but his plan was not carried out. Even so, the John Adamses, its first inhabitants, hung laundry in the unfinished State Rooms of the three-story sandstone mansion and Thomas Jefferson thought the scaled-down version "big enough for two emperors and the grand Lama." Jefferson also returned the part of the grounds now called Lafayette Park to the people by dividing it from the White House with Pennsylvania Avenue—the broad avenue running from Georgetown to the Capitol used for ceremonial processions. Sadly today, the barricaded avenue and White House are more like the White Fort than the "People's House" and if D.C. mysteries are any clue, John Adams's wish "May none but honest and wise men ever rule under this roof" has long since been forgotten! Perhaps it really is time to try a woman president for a change.

When the British burned the city in 1814, the president's resourceful wife, Dolley Madison, managed to save important documents and the portrait of George Washington. Afterward, the sandstone Georgian building was rebuilt (the first of many times) and whitewashed to hide the smoke damage, but it was not until the term of President Theodore Roosevelt in 1900 that presidential stationery simply used "the White House" as its address.

There are three ways to visit the White House: line up for the daily public tours, contact your representative or senator for tickets to an early morning reserved tour, or be a VIP yourself and get invited there for coffee or a State Occasion. Otherwise, you must rely on the descriptions found in many a mystery or the occasional PBS show or presidential speeches from the Oval Office.

Mysteries by real insiders like ex-staffers or former First Children Margaret Truman and Elliott Roosevelt give you an insider's view at specific periods, showing the changes in its layout and usage. Other mysteries describe the areas you will not see unless you are on the staff: the West Wing and the First Family's private quarters on the second and third floors.

Across from the White House is Lafayette Park with its still constant flow of demonstrators, bureaucrats, and tourists across from historic St. John's Church and the Hay-Adams Hotel. Farther north there are government offices, institutions like the *Washington Post* and the *National Geographic*, and hotels like the Mayflower—often a rendezvous for mystery characters. To its west is the Victorian Executive Office Building (once the State, Army, and Navy Departments), and to the east, the Treasury, with its tunnel often used in mysteries to bring in secret White House "guests."

Beyond the Treasury is Federal Triangle with the Press Club, Old Post Office, Commerce and Justice Departments, City Hall, and the FBI. North of Pennsylvania Avenue is "Downtown," D.C.'s original commercial center with more hotels, museums, and theaters stretching to the Washington Convention Center.

LENGTH OF WALK: 3 miles

You can do this walk in one or two parts or make a day of it, stopping to eat at one of the many mysterious places mentioned. It divides naturally just past the White House at Hotel Washington (about 1½ miles). The second half to Metro Central is another 1½ miles. If you stop at Hotel Washington, you may want to get a taxi rather than walk to one of the nearest Metro stations, which are McPherson Square, three blocks north on 14th Street, or Federal Triangle Station, four blocks east on 12th Street.

See the map on page 7 for the boundaries of this walk and page 261 for a list of the books and detectives mentioned.

PLACES OF INTEREST

Blair House, 1651 Pennsylvania Avenue.

Commerce Department/National Aquarium, Pennsylvania Avenue between 14th and 15th Streets. Open daily 9:00 A.M.–5:00 P.M. Free. Call 482-2825.*

Corcoran Gallery of Art, 17th Street and New York Avenue. Open Mon., Wed., and Fri.–Sun. 10:00 A.M.–5:00 P.M., Thurs. 10:00 A.M.–9 P.M. Donation. Call 638-1439. (See also Cafe des Artists for Continental breakfast, lunch, English tea, or Sunday brunch.)

Decatur House, 748 Jackson Place. Open Tues.–Fri. 10:00 A.M.–3 P.M., weekends noon–4 P.M. Tours on the hour and half hour. Fee. Call 842-0920.

Ford's Theater, 511 10th Street. Lincoln Museum in the basement. Open daily 9:00 A.M.–5:00 P.M. (theater closed when rehearsals or matinees are in progress). Free. Call 426-6924. See also the Petersen House, 516 10th Street (across the street). Open daily 9:00 A.M.–5:00 P.M. Free. Call 426-6830.

Friendship Arch, H Street at 7th Street. Entrance to Chinatown.

*The telephone area code is 202 unless otherwise indicated.

Hotel Washington, 515 15th Street. Rooftop restaurant, bar, deli, lobby lounge. Call 638-5900.

J. Edgar Hoover Federal Bureau of Investigation Building, 10th Street and Pennsylvania Avenue. Tour entrance on E Street. Open for one-hour tours weekdays 8:45 A.M.–4:15 P.M., closed federal holidays. Free. Call 324-3447.

Lafayette Square, bounded by Pennsylvania Avenue, Madison Place, H Street, and Jackson Place.

Madison Hotel, 15th Street and M Street. Two restaurants, bar, parking (fee). Call 862-1600.

Martin Luther King Memorial Library, 901 G Street. Open Mon., Wed.–Thurs. 10:00 A.M.–7:00 P.M., Tues. 10:00 A.M.–9:00 P.M., Fri.–Sat. 10:00 A.M.–5:30 P.M. Free. Call 727-1111.

Mayflower Hotel (Stouffer Renaissance), 1127 Connecticut Avenue. Two restaurants, bar, parking (fee). Call 347-3000.

National Geographic Society, 17th Street and M Street. Open Mon.–Sat. and holidays 9:00 A.M.–5:00 P.M., Sun. 10:00 A.M.–5 P.M. Free. Call 857-7588.

National Museum of Women in the Arts, 1250 New York Avenue. Open Mon.–Sat. 10:00 A.M.–5:00 P.M., Sun. noon–5:00 P.M. Donation $3. Call 783-5000.

National Press Club Building (the Shops, a vertical mall with a bookstore, restaurants, and a food court), F and G Streets, 13th and 14th Streets.

Old Executive Office Building, Pennsylvania Avenue west of White House.

The Pavilion at the Old Post Office, 1100 Pennsylvania Avenue. Vertical mall inside Old Post Office with boutiques, restaurants, and a performing-arts stage with daily free entertainment.

Pension Building, F Street between 4th and 5th Streets. Mon.–Sat. 10:00 A.M.–4:00 P.M., Sun. noon–4:00 P.M. Tours weekdays at 12:30, weekends at 12:30 and 1:30 P.M. Free. Call 272-2448.

Renaissance Washington D.C. Hotel, Malice Domestic Convention, 1998. 999 9th Street across from Washington Convention Center. Five restaurants, parking (fee). Call 228-9898.

Renwick Gallery, Pennsylvania Avenue and 17th Street. Open daily 10:00 A.M.–5:30 P.M. Free. Call 357-2700.

St. John's Episcopal Church (Church of the Presidents), 16th Street and H Street. Open Mon.–Sat. 8:00 A.M.–3:00 P.M., tours Sunday after 11:00 A.M. service. Call 347-8766.

Treasury Building, 15th Street and Pennsylvania Avenue. Tours every Saturday, except holiday weekends, at 10:00, 10:20, 10:40, and 11:00 A.M. Call ahead one week and provide name, birth date, Social Security number; bring photo ID. Call 622-0896.

Vista International Hotel, 1400 M Street, complete with atrium and Caribe Restaurant on Level 2. Call 429-1700.

White House, 1600 Pennsylvania Avenue. Open Tues.–Sat. 10:00 A.M.–noon. Free. During March through September, stop at White House Visitor Center on the Ellipse for tickets for public tour. Other months, go directly to the Southeast Gate. Tickets for Congressional tours arranged in advance through your local representatives. Call 456-7041 ahead of time to be sure White House is not closed for an official function.

Washington, D.C., Convention Center, 1212 New York Avenue. Call 789-7000.

Washington Post, 16th Street and L Street. Tours.

Willard Inter-Continental Hotel, 1401 Pennsylvania Avenue. Lobby where President Grant coined the term "lobbyist," parking (fee). Call 628-9100.

Places to Eat

This walk includes many famous old hotels with coffee shops or restaurants that you may want to patronize because they appear in mysteries. Some do not open before lunch (11:00 A.M.) and some are not open on Sundays.

Le Lion d'Or, 1150 Connecticut Avenue (in basement). Reservations required. Call 296-7972.

Occidental Grill (in English basement of the Willard Hotel), 1475 Pennsylvania Avenue. Open daily. Reservations advised. Call 783-1475.

Old Ebbitt Grill, 675 15th Street. Popular with journalists and television reporters. Call 347-4800.

Pavilion at the Old Post Office, 12th Street and Pennsylvania Avenue. Restaurants and carry-out counters.

The Shops, National Press Building, F and G Streets between 13th and 14th Streets. Boston Seafood Company restaurant, top-floor Food Hall.

Vista International Hotel, 1400 M Street. Caribe Cafe on level 2.

Willard Room, Willard Inter-Continental Hotel, 1401 Pennsylvania Avenue. Reservations advised. Call 637-7440.

– WHITE HOUSE/DOWNTOWN WALK –

Begin your walk at the Farragut North Metro stop on the yellow line. Come out the K Street Exit and look across K Street at Farragut Square. In Mary Plum's *State Department Cat* (1945), young George Stair had just been released from a Japanese prison camp where his Foreign Officer father had died. Stair was trying to get into the F.O. himself and had passed the written exams. Now he walked to his orals all the way from Dupont Circle, through Farragut Square and down Jackson Place to Pennsylvania Avenue to reach the "architectural curiosity" occupied by the State Department (Old Executive Office Building).

Turn right to walk north up Connecticut Avenue. One block north at L Street there is a McDonald's that you may want to use for a pit stop/coffee break because you must remember that *no Metro stations have public rest rooms.* In William Safire's *Sleeper Spy* (1995), reporter Irving Fein met his CIA source to get a lead on a USSR sleeper spy at a McDonald's on the site of the famous restaurant Sans Souci at 726 17th Street.

Cross L Street to the Mayflower Hotel, the "Grande Old Dame" of Washington at 1127 Connecticut Avenue. Its grand marquee trimmed with flags reminds you of Claridge's in

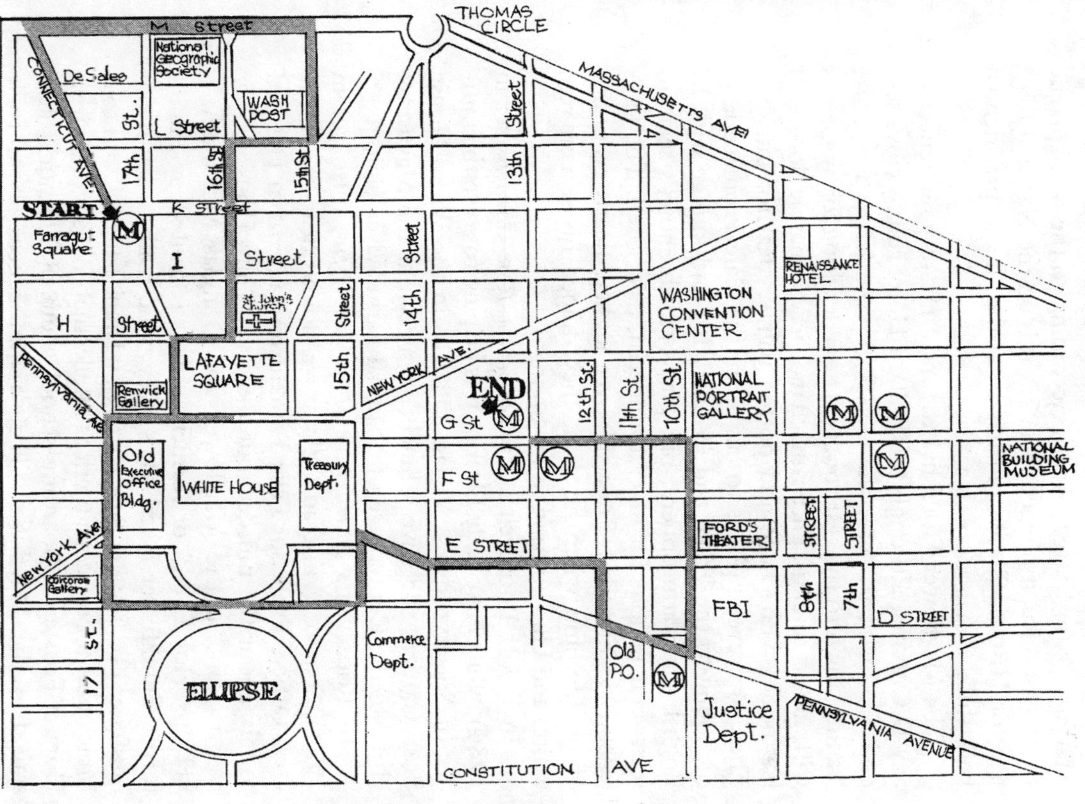

Walk 1: The White House and Downtown

London, one of the models for Agatha Christie's Bertram's Hotel (see *Mystery Reader's Walking Guide: London* [1996] Mayfair/Oxford Street Walk). According to the brass plaque by the entrance, it opened in 1925. It is on the National Register of Historic Places and has been the site of presidential balls since Calvin Coolidge.

The Mayflower Hotel has the most mystery references of any D.C. hotel, although the Willard Hotel runs a close second. Go inside to "case the joint." To your left is a staircase leading down to the rest rooms. The block-long lobby gleams with gilded ceilings, glittering chandeliers, a marble floor, and has nooks with chairs and potted palms, ideal for intrigue. There are several places to eat, from the Cafe Promenade in the lobby to the Town and Country bar and lounge with its English Club atmosphere, but Harvey's, the hotel's seafood restaurant famous for its crab imperial, has closed. The FBI's legendary Director J. Edgar Hoover ate here nearly every day of his life, and when he died, they draped his seat in red, white, and blue bunting in his honor.

In Elliott Roosevelt's *Murder in the Rose Garden* (set in 1934), while First Lady Eleanor was helping to solve the murder of Society hostess Vivian Taliafero in the White House Rose Garden, she gave a luncheon speech at the Mayflower Hotel to the Conference of National Farm Wives Union.

In Roosevelt's *Murder in the Oval Office* (also set in 1934), Senator Winstead Colmer was found dead inside the Oval Office. Professor Felix Frankfurter came from Harvard to talk about the murder, but the only White House staffer free to dine at the Mayflower was Douglas McKinney, a "Happy Hot Dog," or former student recruited by Frankfurter. Frankfurter asked McKinney if he read locked-room mysteries like *The Big Bow Mystery* by Israel Zangwill and told McKinney not to scorn them as intellectual challenges. British Horatia Fenster, a boarding-school chum of Eleanor's, also stayed at the Mayflower. Their reminiscences about their schoolgirl escapades gave Mrs. R. the clue to how murder was done "in a locked room."

In Elliott Roosevelt's *Murder in the Blue Room* (set in

1942), White House Press Room secretary Emily Ryan was found murdered in the Blue Room during a secret visit to D.C. by USSR Foreign Secretary Vyacheslav Molotov. It turned out that her only close friend was Peggy Shearson, a waitress at the Mayflower Hotel dining room. Eleanor Roosevelt's two Dr. Watsons—Secret Service Agent Dominic Deconcini and Metropolitan Police Department Chief of Detectives Ed Kennelly—went there to interrogate Peggy Shearson, who next turned up dead herself.

In Haynes Johnson and Howard Simons's *The Landing* (set in 1942), two Nazi spies were dropped off by submarine to assassinate President Roosevelt and start a D.C. race riot. Navy Lieutenant Harry Eaton, assigned to the investigation, took his girlfriend Constance Aiken to Harvey's for lunch. Constance was a confidential secretary at the FBI and the couple talked about J. Edgar Hoover, who was having Vice President Henry Wallace shadowed as a security risk.

In Eleanor Pierson's *Murder Without Clues* (1942), wartime Washington was in transition from a sleepy Southern town to the "Corridors of Power." While the police were searching John Hadley's law office for clues to the murder of his client, heiress Lila Donnelly, Hadley's young partner Ross Allen escaped to the Mayflower's cocktail lounge for lunch. But when Allen was spotted by other guests from the Hadley party where Lila was murdered, he was called over to tell all.

In *Death Before Bedtime* (1953), Edgar Box's (Gore Vidal) bright young Peter Cutler Sargeant III, hired to run the presidential campaign of Senator Les Rhodes, was staying at the senator's home when the senator was blown up. One of the other guests (and suspects) Camilla Pomeroy, had slept with Sargeant who asked her to lunch at the Mayflower where the food was good and there was a string quartet in a cocktail lounge perfect for assignations. Most of the customers were Society ladies like Leslie Ford's Grace Latham who dropped by after a hard morning of shopping or Red Cross work. Congressional figures did not lunch there, but came there to drink at about five.

In Helen MacInnes's *I and My True Love* (1952), Kate

Jerold, the young cousin of D.C. society member Sylvia Pleydel who was married to a coldly correct State Department bureaucrat, got a job as a tour guide at the new Berg Foundation for the Understanding of Contemporary Form in Painting and Sculpture. The Berg was housed across from the Statler Hotel in a new "matchbox" building with a heavy glass door and a praying mantis mobile in the hallway. Korean vet Lieutenant Bob Turner met Kate there and took her to the Mayflower Hotel bar. Kate was upset because she had discovered Sylvia Pleydel was secretly meeting Czech Communist Jan Brovic.

In Leslie Ford's *Washington Whispers Murder* (1953), widowed Grace Latham and her perennial beau Colonel John Primrose had lunch at the Mayflower lounge before she went to her hairdresser. (Grace commented that the colonel had never asked her to marry him and would be terribly embarrassed if she asked him.) The row between Congressman Hamilton ("call me Ham") Vair, a McCarthy type, and industrialist Rufus Brent had hit the headlines and the detecting duo were involved. Leslie Ford was a pet author of President Harry Truman; did daughter Margaret get hooked on crime by her dad?

In the Gordons' *Power Play* (1965), when FBI Director Byron O'Connell died, California Senator Ralph Donahue's administrative assistant Dyke Crandall wanted to put a puppet in as head of the agency. The other candidate was FBI second-in-command Tom Schuler. Schuler's support came from young black Congressman Glenn Holden of Gary, Indiana. When Holden met Dyke Crandall at the Mayflower cocktail lounge, Crandall offered Holden a big payoff appointment if he'd shut up.

In Ross Thomas's *Cast a Yellow Shadow* (1967), Michael Padillo had a small suite at the Mayflower, rented for him by Fredl, the German wife of his partner, Cyril McCorkle (the Mac of Mac's Place). As soon as Padillo arrived via a Liberian freighter, the FBI came by for a visit.

In Jeffrey Archer's *Shall We Tell the President?* (1977; rev. ed. 1985), when Ted Kennedy (EMK) was elected president in 1980, a U.S. senator plotted to assassinate him. (In the 1985 edition, the president was Florentyna Kane.) FBI Special Agent Marc Andrews met Dr. Elizabeth Dexter, daughter of suspect Senator Dexter, and her father at the Mayflower. R. B. Dominic's Ohio Congressman Ben Safford also filled in his time between murders and congressional affairs attending compulsory gatherings here.

In Ross Thomas's *Ah, Treachery!* (1994), the Little Rock crowd has gotten elected with help from rainmakers (fundraisers) like Millicent Altford. Altford had been robbed of over one million dollars that was not hers, so she hired ex-Major Edd "Twodees" Partain to ride shotgun for her. In Room 517 of the Mayflower Hotel there was a midnight meeting of the bad guys (Col. Millwed and Major General Hudson) to plot how to protect their asses and to scare Twodees and Nick, his ally at VOMIT (Victims of Military Intelligence Treachery). The result was that the two hired hit man Emory Kite to kill Partain.

In Marilyn Quayle and Nancy Northcott's *The Campaign* (1996), a splashy union event in the Mayflower Hotel Ballroom was attended by Attorney General Jonathan Hunter and Presidential Chief of Staff Eugene Corforth. Both White House insiders were also part of the Oval Office conspiracy to discredit Georgia's black Republican Senator Bob Grant and prevent his reelection so that he could not run for president.

After savoring the Mayflower Hotel's mysterious atmosphere, go back to Connecticut Avenue. Turn right and walk half a block to tiny De Sales Street, partly used as a parking lot but the modern-looking ABC-TV News Washington Bureau is here, too. Several murder suspects worked for ABC in Carey Roberts's *Pray God to Die* (1994). In Helen MacInnes's *I and My True Love*, Fargo Street (De Sales Street) was a tiny alley between Connecticut and 17th Street. Jan Brovic, a Czech member of a visiting mission, rented a safe house there. Brovic wanted to defect, but his family were being held hostage back home.

Cross De Sales Street, then cross Connecticut Avenue at the M Street corner to the Capitol Broadcasting Company building at 1150 Connecticut Avenue. Go inside the building and take the elevator to the basement. You will find a handsome wooden door with no sign, but around the corridor from the elevator you will see the name "Lion d'Or" on the service door to the alley. This is one of Washington's top restaurants: Le Lion d'Or.

In Margaret Truman's *Murder in the Smithsonian* (1983), British historian Dr. Lewis Tunney found out about a huge art scam being worked out of the Smithsonian. When Tunney came to the U.S. for the Bicentennial Fourth of July, he was murdered at a gala at the National Museum of American History. Then Tunney's fiancee Scottish Heather McBean who came over to help with the murder investigation, Metropolitan Police Department Captain Mac Hanrahan, and eccentric Chesterton-like Dr. Evelyn Killinworth, a Georgetown University professor, met here for lunch. (It was the kind of expensive place Dr. Killinworth liked.)

In Phyllis Richman's chef d'oeuvre about competing French chefs called *The Butter Did It* (1997), the murder victim was Laurence Levain, the French chef of Chez Laurence, which was named in the same breath as Le Lion d'Or. Levain was renowned for his tiny pasta squares called Les Quilts, but was also known to have a serious heart condition: le cholesterol.

Come out of Le Lion d'Or, after lunching there if you can afford it. Somewhere to your left "a few blocks north of K and west of Connecticut," was "Mac's Place" featured first in Ross Thomas's *Cast a Yellow Shadow* (1967) and later in *Twilight at Mac's Place* (1990). Barbara Gauntt thinks it may be based on Mike Palm's at Connecticut Avenue, but Maureen Collins has heard of other places, too! Mac's Place was a relic from an earlier American past with a bar and grill in a long narrow room, generous drinks, and a varied menu. Herr Horst, the maitre d', remembered everyone, even Granville Haynes whom he had not seen since Haynes's eighteenth birthday. The proprietors were Michael Padillo and Cyril McCorkle, the Mac of Mac's Place, who now had a bright daughter called Erika.

After ex-CIA soldier of fortune Steadfast Haynes's funeral,

the mourners came here. His mistress Isabelle Gelinet explained that they had been in D.C. for the trial of Oliver North, which Steady had thought would make a nice epilogue for his memoirs. Instead, Mac's Place became the headquarters for the hunt to find and sell Steady's memoirs.

Recross Connecticut Avenue and take M Street toward 17th Street. Cross 17th Street and go another block east to 16th Street, passing the National Geographic Society. At the corner of 16th Street cross M Street to your left and check out the elegant Jefferson Hotel. The entire Bush family "took over" the Jefferson for Bush's inauguration in 1989, but it is now infamous, Washington-style, as the place where top-ranked (and paid) political advisor Dick Morris hung out with his floozie, letting her in on secrets of Clinton's second campaign.

As guests of my old friend Rachel Goetz, we stayed there during the first Malice Domestic in 1988. It is an annual convention honoring the traditional or "cosy" mystery. In her introduction to the short story collection *Malice Domestic 6*, Anne Perry described them as tales drawn from all the material of human good and evil, domestic matters in the broadest sense of human relationships.

The first convention was held at Silver Spring, Maryland, and I took the Metro north, but after the banquet a female cabby drove me back to the Jefferson Hotel. That year the first Agatha Winners were: Best Novel: Carolyn G. Hart, *Something Wicked*; Best First Mystery: Elizabeth George, *A Great Deliverance*; Best Short Story: Robert Barnard, "More Final than Divorce."

There was no Lifetime Achievement Award and no Best Nonfiction Award in 1988, but by 1993 there were both. My *Dorothy L. Sayers: the Centenary Celebration* was a nominee, but lost out to roommate and fellow Chicagoan Barbara D'Amato's *The Doctor, the Murder, the Mystery.* During a session on Richard III run by Barbara Michaels (aka Elizabeth Peters), Carolyn G. Hart told me how much she had enjoyed *Mystery Reader's Walking Guide: London*, which she also quoted in *Southern Ghost* (1992).

The Jefferson's small lobby with a fireplace and comfortable chairs is hospitable to footsore mystery tourists. To your left are rest rooms and to your right is the dining room where the hotel serves afternoon teas in a perfectly "cozy" setting.

Come out of the Jefferson Hotel and look at the building next door, which was the National Rifle Association's headquarters with a shooting range for members. (Like a lot of mysteries, the NRA has moved to Fairfax, Virginia.) Across 16th Street is the brand-new, ugly National Education Association building, one of many powerful D.C. lobbies like the one in R. B. Dominic's *Epitaph for a Lobbyist* (1974).

Recross M Street to the National Geographic's Explorer's Hall and go inside if you have time. Then cross 16th Street (now known as Sakharov Plaza). As you cross 16th Street you can see Mrs. George Pullman's Beaux Arts mansion of brick and stone. It was purchased by the USSR in the 1930s for their embassy. As a result, it is the embassy featured in older mysteries like Eleanor Pierson's *Murder Without Clues* (1942). In it, a dashing young attaché was suspected of murder because his brand of Turkish cigarettes was found at the scene of the crime.

Continue walking along M Street past the large handsome redbrick Gothic Revival Union Bethel AME Church and cross 15th Street to the Madison Hotel (another Grande Dame of mystery scenes). Look inside where the lobby is decorated with many beautiful clocks and there are plenty of places to sit. There are rest rooms, too, and a lobby cafe.

In Richard Timothy Conroy's hilarious *The India Exhibition* (1992), ex-Foreign Officer Henry Scruggs, like Conroy, worked at the Smithsonian, handling cross-cultural events and international personnel. Scruggs was musical, drank tea, and was a gourmet cook. With the help of flower child/exhibit designer Violet Strauss, Scruggs set up an India Exhibition on K. V. Chandra, supposedly a VIP like Gandhi. Scruggs took Violet Strauss to the Madison Hotel, which was the kind of place Henry liked: quiet and civilized, where you could order Scotch safely and the main dining room had excellent food, perfect service, and elegant surroundings. But Violet told him "Jeezus, Henry, this is like a morgue."

In Margaret Truman's *Murder in the Smithsonian* (1983), Heather McBean stayed at the Madison Hotel, but while she was out, her hotel room was ransacked. When she met MPD Captain Mac Hanrahan at the hotel bar, Hanrahan wanted her to go back to England and let him solve the murders.

In James Grady's *Hard Bargains* (1984), PI John Rankin, an ex-investigator for Washington columnist Ned Johnson (aka Jack Anderson of "Washington Merry-Go-Round"), was hired to investigate a mysterious death of a trucker. On a tip, Rankin met some mobsters at the Madison Hotel lobby bar, "one of the city's classiest homes away from home." A big guy at the bar told Rankin to go upstairs to a suite. When Rankin did so he met a lawyer who warned him off the investigation, then told him to stay and order dinner but added that they'd never met.

One block east of the Madison Hotel at 14th Street and M Street is the Vista International Hotel (at the edge of Thomas Circle). In Hugh Holton's *Chicago Blues* (1996), Chicago Police Commander Larry Cole, investigating the murders of two Chicago mafia hit men who worked for Antonio de Lisa (aka Tony Accardo) teamed up with an old friend, ex-cop now FBI Special Agent Reggie Stanton. Stanton went to D.C. and checked into the Vista International Hotel with its atrium lobby to wait for a message from FBI Deputy Director Connors. The message was to meet there for breakfast, but the meeting was a setup. So Stanton engineered a major flood—of beer—in the atrium, which gave him a chance to kidnap Director Connors.

Come out of the Madison Hotel and turn left to walk down 15th Street. Across the street, stretching to 16th Street between M and L Streets are the buildings of the world-famous *Washington Post*. In addition to famous real and fictional reporters, its publisher-owner Katherine Graham is a model for mystery hostesses who hold power parties in Georgetown (see Walk 7).

Although most earlier mysteries used outdated or made-up names for newspapers, like the *Courier* in Keats Patrick's *Death Is a Tory* (1935), in Louisa Revell's *The Men with Three*

Eyes (1955), Ruth Gibson, the energetic young head of southeast Washington's Neighborhood House, told her guest Miss Julia that her board members only came to visit when the *Washington Post* was taking photographs for a feature.

The *Post* is the paper of record in most mysteries like Conroy's *The India Exhibition* where Henry Scruggs persuaded their reporter to "pop" for very expensive lunches and information.

James Grady's *Runner in the Street* (1984) was about the street murder of a D.C. hooker who came from Oregon and went to Harvard (one of the Brightest and the Best). The *Washington Post* actually published an obituary of Janet Armstrong, which led her dad to hire PI John Rankin to investigate her murder.

In Patricia Cornwell's *All That Remains* (1992), Abby Turnbull, a reporter friend of Chief Medical Examiner Kay Scarpetta who had left Richmond for a fancy job with the *Washington Post*, had a contract to write a book about the serial murders that were being investigated. But Abby was harassed by the FBI as she worked on her book because they were afraid the murderer was one of their own.

In Ron Nessen and Johanna Neuman's *Knight and Day* (1995), *Washington Post* "cub" reporter Jane Day yearned to make the big time by exposing someone important. Unfortunately her exposé of Senator Barton Jacobson, which got her a byline, backfired when her source was murdered after he appeared on the Jerry Knight talk show.

In Phyllis Richman's *The Butter Did It* (1997), the amateur sleuth tracking down the murderer of Chef Laurence Levain of Chez Laurence was Chas Wheatley, restaurant critic of the *Examiner* (fictional). Phyllis Richman, however, is the real-life restaurant critic of the *Washington Post* and her descriptions of the job are not only fun but revealing. Chas (short for Charlotte Sue) is a Washington walker who thinks nothing of walking from her Seventh Street loft to Georgetown at any hour of the day or night—a person after my own heart!

Another of Richman's colleagues on the *Post* is Nina King, the editor of *Book World*. Together with mystery buff Robin

Winks, King wrote *Crimes of the Scene* (1997), a resource guide for the international traveler. In it, King and Winks briefed the reader on each country's background, reviewed selected mysteries set in Europe, Africa, South America, and the Far East, then supplied lists of other mysteries set there. Anglo-American mysteries were not included unless set in foreign climes—like the British Raj.

Cross 15th Street at L Street and walk back along L Street to 16th Street. There are lots of places to stop and eat, but if you take advantage of the classy hotels, wait until you reach the Washington or Willard Hotels on the east side of the White House, where you can eat and drink in a specially mysterious setting.

Across 16th Street at the corner of L Street you can see the American Legion Headquarters. There are several other modern buildings nearby, including the *Christian Science Monitor*, that could be James Cain's fictional Institute of Biography in *The Institute* (1976). In this mystery, Cain, author of *The Postman Always Rings Twice*, had scholar-cum-football star Dr. Lloyd Palmer hunting for twenty-two million dollars to establish a national institute of biography, with him as director. Senator Hood of Nebraska, who owed him a big favor, introduced Palmer to financier Richard Garrett who saw the Institute as a dandy front for a corporate blackmail scheme. The Institute opened in a beautiful modern building of sandstone faced with black granite with two big bronze doors. It was named after Garrett's young wife Hortense, who fell for Director Palmer in a big way.

One block south at K Street is the Capitol Hilton Hotel (1001 16th Street at McPherson Square) where Hortense Garrett and Institute Director Palmer went to buy newspapers after Hortense had thrown a huge party to open "her" Institute, which the president and his wife attended. The opening occurred just before a Georgia senator opened hearings on the tax-exempt status of the Institute. Another classy old hotel, the Sheraton-Carlton, is on the other corner.

Cross K Street and continue down 16th Street to I (Eye) Street. Cross I Street and go one more block south to H

Street to St. John's Church on the corner just north of Lafayette Park. Known as the "Church of the Presidents," St. John's Church was the second Episcopal church built in D.C.—the first is Christ Church on Capitol Hill. It was designed in the shape of a Greek cross by Henry Latrobe in 1815; the steeple and portico were added later. An unpretentious yellow stucco with white trim, it reminds you of the simple eighteenth-century style of many of London's parish churches.

Every president since Madison has attended services at St. John's and by tradition Pew 54 is set aside for the president and his family. There are also kneelers embroidered with all of their names. President Ford is said to have prayed there before granting former President Nixon a pardon.

In Elliott Roosevelt's *The White House Pantry Murder* (set in 1941), British Prime Minister Winston Churchill had arrived for a top secret war parlay. Mrs. Roosevelt found him both charming and infuriating, given to wandering the halls at all hours, taking endless baths, and demanding brandy and cigars whenever the spirit moved him. Churchill went with President and Mrs. Roosevelt to church at St. John's on Christmas morning. He enjoyed the hymns, but told Eleanor he'd never heard "O Little Town of Bethlehem," so she explained it was written by American Phillips Brooks. Behind St. John's at 1525 H Street is the Parish Building, also known as Ashburton House, which used to be the British embassy. Among the ambassadors who lived there was novelist Edward Bulwer-Lytton, famous for *The Last Days of Pompeii.*

Leave St. John's Church to cross 16th Street to the elegant but snooty Hay-Adams Hotel at 800 16th Street. It was built in 1926 on the site of the H. H. Richardson–designed double house of Lincoln's secretary John Hay and Henry Adams. All three men had been Harvard classmates. The Richardson house was being built during Sarah Booth Conroy's *Refinements of Love* (1993), which is about the mysterious death of Clover Adams, Henry's wife in 1885. For the ordinary mystery tourist, the Hay-Adams Hotel staff has a very forbidding demeanor (much the way Clover Adams described her husband), and stray visitors are not encouraged in the small walnut-paneled lobby. So don't count on this hotel as a rest stop or a place to eat lunch.

Ross Thomas's elegiac *Twilight at Mac's Place* (1990) opened with the sudden death of Steadfast Haynes in an expensive suite at the Hay-Adams Hotel. Haynes died the night before the inauguration of the forty-first president (Bush), the first (and only) president to have been head of the CIA. Haynes's mistress Isabelle Gelinet proceeded to call the CIA and blackmail them into giving him a full military funeral at Arlington National Cemetery by threatening that she would publish his memoirs.

In Sarah Booth Conroy's *Refinements of Love* (1993; set in 1885), you get a magnificent picture of Gilded Age Washington, especially the Lafayette Park "Mafia" known as the Five of Hearts: H. H. Richardson, John Hay, Henry Adams, Henry James, and Augustus Saint-Gaudens. You also get an ingenious and plausible theory about the death of Clover (Marian) Adams, wife of Henry Adams who was a descendant of presidents and author of an odd autobiography called *The Education of Henry Adams.* Adams supposedly never recovered from Clover's suicide; he destroyed all her things and never spoke of her again. His Harvard chum, sculptor Augustus Saint-Gaudens, created a weird hooded figure called *Grief*, which was placed at her grave in Rock Creek Cemetery, and when Adams died in 1918 he was buried next to Clover.

In *Refinements of Love*, Conroy suggested that Clover wrote *Democracy*, a satiric novel about Washington in the Gilded Age that Adams took credit for. Henry James called Clover, who identified with the heroines of *Daisy Miller* and *Portrait of a Lady*, a "Voltaire in petticoats," but she was not mentioned in Edith Nalle Schafer's *Literary Circles of Washington* (1993), where Henry was made much of as a great historian. Both Henry Adams and his Harvard college crony diplomat John Hay also appear in Eric Zencey's *Panama* (1995). *Panama* is set during the 1892 Panama Canal scandal in France.

A century later in Margaret Truman's *Murder at the*

National Gallery (1996), curator Luther Mason, who set up the world-class Caravaggio Exhibition, which included a missing Caravaggio called *Grottesca*, addressed a group of George Washington University art history students at the Hay-Adams at lunch.

Turn right along H Street across from Lafayette Park to Jackson Place with brick sidewalks where the charming Federal houses have been turned into agencies and institutes. Jackson Place itself is a parking lot. At the corner is Decatur House, built for Admiral Decatur, the scourge of the Barbary pirates of Algiers. The house had other VIP tenants like Henry Clay and Martin Van Buren before it was donated to the National Trust for Historic Preservation.

Tour Decatur House, then turn left to walk down Jackson Place to Pennsylvania Avenue. Near the corner on Pennsylvania Avenue is Blair House with a canopy and the American flag displayed. It is really two houses, the Blair-Lee Houses, one painted white and one red. Lee House was built by a Custis granddaughter of George Washington and belonged to the powerful Lee family of Virginia. It was here that Robert E. Lee was offered, and declined, command of the Union troops at the beginning of the Civil War.

Blair House was purchased in 1942 as a Presidential guest house, supposedly at the behest of Eleanor Roosevelt who was tired of putting up potentates in the White House. (In Johnson and Simons's *The Landing* [1986; set in 1942], Winston Churchill was shown roaming the halls late at night looking for a drink.) President Truman and his wife and daughter, Margaret, lived there during the first major restoration of the White House when it was gutted and rebuilt with steel beams. In 1950 a group of Puerto Rican nationalists tried to assassinate President Truman in a daring attack in which a Secret Service agent was killed. (See also Walk 4.)

Walk along Pennsylvania Avenue to the corner of 17th Street where you come to the Renwick Gallery, a Second Empire style brick and sandstone mansion with corncob capitals, designed by James Renwick in 1859 to hold banker W. W. Corcoran's art collection. Corcoran's gallery opened in

1870 after the financier returned from European exile during the Civil War. This was the same year New York's Metropolitan Museum of Art opened. This collection included the shocking statue of the nude *Greek Slave*, mentioned by Clover Adams in *Refinements of Love*. Later the Corcoran Collection was moved to its new home at 17th and E Streets.

Leave Renwick House to turn left past the western side of Lafayette Park (in Clover Adams's day it was fenced in like a London square and only residents had keys). Since the '60s it has been the site of demonstrations, sit-ins, sleep-ins, etc. but it had earlier visitors like the suffragettes who chained themselves to the White House fence.

D.C. architect Pierre L'Enfant had intended Lafayette Park to be the President's Park to match the President's House, but Thomas Jefferson chose to share it with the country instead. Inside Lafayette Park you can enjoy the energetic equestrian statue of President Andrew Jackson, waving his cocked hat. The statue was made from cannon Jackson captured in the War of 1812. Then look around for the bench with the plaque reading "The Bernard M. Baruch Bench of Inspiration," which Safire's reporter Irving Fein sat on in *Sleeper Spy* (1995), while killing time before his date with his CIA source at McDonald's. According to Safire, President Truman became irritated by Baruch's well-publicized advice.

The park was the site of a famous true-life crime on February 27, 1859. Representative Daniel Sickles shot and killed U.S. District Attorney Barton Key in a duel because the younger Key was having an affair with Sickles's wife. Key was the son of Francis Scott Key, who wrote "The Star-Spangled Banner" (See Walk 7).

In Margaret Truman's *Murder on the Potomac* (1994), Annabel Reed-Smith became a member of the Board of the National Building Museum. Its chairman Wendell Tierney was also a sponsor of Tri-S (or Scarlet Sin Society), a group of actors who staged historical reenactments and the group were currently "doing" the deadly duel between Sickles and Barton Key.

In Mignon G. Eberhart's *The Man Next Door* (1942),

young Maida Lovell had come to wartime Washington with her boss Steve Blake who was running a new hush-hush department. At that time, passersby could see Cordell Hull, that great and benign statesman, walking quietly, without fanfare, across the park to his office in the State Department (Old Executive Office Building) while Bernard Baruch sat thoughtfully on a bench feeding the fat squirrels with peanuts, talking quietly to those who came to him. To Eberhart, scenes like these showed the real Washington with its lack of ostentation and true homely dignity.

In Helen MacInnes's *I and My True Love* (1952), secret lovers Sylvia Pleydel and Czech Jan Brovic discovered that her husband was trying to make her appear mentally ill. Terribly upset, Sylvia wandered to Lafayette Park where a sympathetic cabby picked her up and offered to show her the sights, starting with the White House. He told Sylvia it was being repaired because the floors were sagging like a canvas tent.

In Charlotte Armstrong's *Alibi for Murder*, originally published as *The Dream Walker* (1955), actress Cora Steffani was hired to discredit John Paul Marcus, a Bernard Baruch type who liked to sit on a bench in Lafayette Park and offer wise words. A Cold War spy set up a carefully worked out plot where Steffani "dreamed" that she met a man in Washington who asked her to give an envelope to Marcus "from Ray," discrediting Marcus.

Spiro Agnew's *The Canfield Decision* (1976) opened with an idealistic group demonstrating in front of the White House by Lafayette Park. They were being used by a master spy Yoram Halevy who posed as an Israeli but was really a Chinese-Iranian agent. Halevy also "manipulated" Vice President Canfield who thought he was in charge of Halevy's campaign to discredit the president.

In Lawrence Sanders's *Capital Crimes* (1989), John Tollinger, executive assistant to President Hawkins's Chief of Staff, had a secret meeting in Lafayette Park with ex-FBI agent Martin Lindberg. The two men sat on a bench in their overcoats, discussing how to get enough information to discredit Brother Kristos, a Rasputin-like phony who had become the president's chief advisor since he helped the president's hemophiliac son George.

After walking through Lafayette Park, return to Pennsylvania Avenue directly across from the White House. You will notice that not only has Pennsylvania Avenue been turned into a blockaded cement-barricaded mall usable only by pedestrians, roller-bladers, and bikers, but there are flashing police cars at either end of Lafayette Park, MPD police on guard outside, and inside the fence not only regular Secret Service types but men in full SWAT uniform, black from head to heel, armed with Uzis. The White House has become the White Fort, guarded like a Middle Eastern palace and armed like a German bunker, hardly the "Peoples' House" presidents and press still piously call it.

Turn right to walk past the White House Guard House toward Executive Avenue, which is no longer open to anyone, but fenced off as a parking lot. You are passing the West Wing—the office part of the White House—and may see TV cameras set up on the lawn, using it as a backdrop for a news break.

During the twentieth century the White House has been the real center of the city for mysteries set there. Almost every sleuth, public or private, goes to the White House or refers to it as a power source. In mysteries, as elsewhere, the term "the White House" stands not only for the president but for the whole executive branch of government. Among the security forces there are a number of code words used for the incumbent president like "Julius" or "Ranger." The most common one is POTUS for President of the United States.

In recent Washington mysteries the president is often a knave or a fool, while the writers are often former "insiders." In Marilyn Quayle and Nancy Northcott's *The Campaign*, distraught First Lady Estelle made a tearful tour of the White House after realizing that everyone knew about POTUS's infidelities. She ended in the State Dining Room with Lincoln's portrait above the mantelpiece and below it President John Adams's words "I Pray Heaven to Bestow the Best of Blessings on THIS HOUSE and on all that shall hereafter Inhabit it. May none but Honest and Wise Men ever rule under this Roof."

Adams's successor Jefferson thought the place was too big, but he enjoyed landscaping it. Each president since has planted something. The James Madisons' flight when the British torched Washington in 1814 is described in Charles Goodrum's *The Best Cellar* (1987), and a necklace belonging to the resourceful Dolley who cut Washington's portrait out of its frame is part of the plot of Barbara Michaels's *Shattered Silk* (1986).

The mansion was painted white to hide the burn marks but the name "the White House" only became official under Theodore Roosevelt, who built the offices in the West Wing. He organized other major renovations of the White House, which had to be redone by President Truman in the 1950s. A third renovation of the White House, begun under President Carter, has been completed under President Clinton.

As a tourist, you see only the Red Room, the Blue Room, the Green Room, the East Room, and the State Dining Room. It's better to get VIP tickets from your congressman, but you still won't see the Rose Garden or many of the rooms mentioned in mysteries, such as the Cabinet Room, the Lincoln Bedroom (Sitting Room), the West Wing, the Situation Room, or the Oval Office.

But mysteries can take you "inside"; some even have maps like Elliott Roosevelt's *Murder in the Oval Office* (set in 1934) or William Safire's *Full Disclosure* (1987). Since the floor plan of the White House has changed over the years, you must note the date of each mystery mentioned.

If every mysterious White House reference were included, this walk would be too long, and if you stand and stare at the White House you may be arrested. Thanks to the omnipresent media, the Secret Service has had to cope with the intruder problem on a daily basis.

These mysteries are named in chronological order. The first White House mystery I came across was P. M. Carlson's short story "The Father of the Bride" in Greenberg and Nevins's *Mr. President, Private Eye* (1989). It took place at the time of the wedding of President U. S. Grant's daughter Nellie in 1874. Irish Bridget Mooney and her Aunt Mollie came from St. Louis to tell the president about a government scam there, hoping to help Bridget's chances for an acting career. Aunt Mollie was murdered in their boardinghouse, but Bridget met the dapper English scoundrel Algernon Charles Frederick Sartoris, whom the president's daughter was to marry, and ended up as a maid at the White House, where she saw President Grant sobbing in his daughter's bedroom after the ceremony.

In Sarah Booth Conroy's *Refinements of Love* (set in 1885), Clover and Henry Adams were invited to a dinner party by President Grover Cleveland and his sister Rose. The guests included Henry James, whose dinner partner was Washington VIP Frances Hodgson Burnett, author of *Little Lord Fauntleroy* and *The Secret Garden*. The company assembled in the East Room which Clover thought looked like a jungle of potted plants.

In Elliott Roosevelt's *Murder in the Rose Garden* (set in 1936), Vivian Taliafero, a seductive D.C. hostess and the daughter of a former senator, was found murdered in the Rose Garden. She turned out to be blackmailing Washington VIPs. First Lady Eleanor investigated her murder with Secret Service agent Stan Szcygiel and Lieutenant Edward Kennelly of the District police, ending with a roundup of suspects in the Cabinet Room. Eleanor also took time to have dinner in the private dining room with Harry Hopkins and Mary McLeod Bethune, her source on Negro problems and politics, and Bethune brought young prize fighter Joe Louis (Barrow) there to meet her.

In Roosevelt's *Murder in the Oval Office* (set in 1934), Alabama Senator Winstead Colmer was found dead inside the Oval Office. He had been called there by an usher during a formal White House state dinner. The Secret Service and District police let Mrs. Roosevelt see his body, then removed it, not telling the president or the press until morning! Busy Mrs. Roosevelt took time to investigate and held a final session in the Oval Office with FDR, and her buddies, Baines of the

Secret Service, and Kennelly of the District police. Both President and Mrs. Roosevelt disliked J. Edgar Hoover and his FBI, so he was never included. (FDR liked to annoy Hoover by calling him "John Edgar.") In these Roosevelt mysteries the pool built for FDR in the colonnade to the West Wing was a major meeting place, while Eleanor's White House Office was the room traditionally known as the Lincoln Bedroom.

In Roosevelt's *A First Class Murder* (set in 1938), First Lady Eleanor Roosevelt agreed to travel to France on the maiden voyage of the French line's queen ship, the *Normandie*. Among her companions were the Jack Bennys, Charles Lindbergh, Josephine Baker, and college student Jack Kennedy, who helped her solve a shipboard murder.

In *The White House Pantry Murder* (set in 1941), Winston Churchill was visiting secretly, wandering the halls at all hours, demanding brandy and cigars and baths. In the midst of serious talk about a second front a murdered German was found in the pantry, greatly upsetting the housekeeper, Mrs. Nesbitt. In *Murder in the Blue Room* (set in 1942), a "Mr. Brown"—aka USSR Foreign Secretary Molotov—was the secret guest when two black White House ushers found Emily Ryan, who worked for Press Secretary Steve Early, shot in the Blue Room.

In Haynes Johnson and Howard Simons's *The Landing* (set in 1942), Nazi spy Gunther Haupt, landed on a secret mission by a German sub, came to the White House where there were antiaircraft guns on the lawns and roof, air-raid sirens sounding, heavy chains over the gates, and every few feet behind the fence an American soldier posted (as there is now). Churchill was there on his secret visit, staying up all night and upsetting the staff. Haupt got into the White House by pretending to be a Jewish refugee who hoped to give FDR some rare stamps. In John Lee's *The Ninth Man* (also set in 1942), the Nazis had secretly landed spies to kill FDR. Dietrich, the ninth Nazi, got into the White House dressed as a White House policeman and shot FDR's guard near the swimming pool, then dragged FDR underwater in an attempt to drown him.

During the Cold War, in Allen Drury's *Advise and Consent* (1959), after the scandal about Senator Brigham Anderson had played out to its sad conclusion, the president asked Senator Orrin Knox of Illinois to come see him at the White House. They were very different politicians who wanted the same prize, but now the president told Senator Knox that the Russians had just beaten the Americans to the moon. As a result, he wanted to recruit his old rival to be vice president. Knox agreed, but the president suddenly died in office. Drury wrote that men all around the globe were shaken because so much power had resided in that one heart in that one house.

In William F. Buckley, Jr.'s *The Story of Henri Tod* (1984; set in 1961), Blackford Oakes, assigned to find out USSR intentions about the Berlin Wall brought his best German contact, Henri Tod, to a top-level meeting with President John F. Kennedy and his advisors in the basement Situation Room. In spite of Oakes—and Kennedy—the Wall went up.

In Fletcher Knebel and Charles W. Bailey's *Seven Days in May* (1962), the Chairman of the Joint Chiefs of Staff, "Gentleman" James Scott, disapproved of the mutual disarmament treaty President Jordan Lyman signed with the USSR. He and his conspirators planned a coup d'etat on a May Saturday during a practice red alert (instant mobilization). Marine Col. Martin Casey, on duty at the Pentagon, discovered the plot and for seven days in May the president and a few trusted advisors tried to stop the coup. Finally the president faced General Scott one on one in the Oval Office and made him resign.

In the Gordons' *Power Play* (1965), when FBI Director Byron O'Connell died, Senator Ralph Donahue's ruthless administrative assistant Dyke Crandall plotted to put in a puppet as head of the FBI. In a final confrontation at the White House Dyke Crandall still wouldn't admit he used Mob money to try to buy the FBI directorship.

In Robert J. Serling's thriller *The President's Plane Is Missing* (1967), President Jeremy Haines was facing the menace of Red China and needed a secret meeting with the USSR. He found a double to play POTUS, only to have Air Force One crash while he was away. Then the vice president terrified the Cabinet by insisting on a preemptive nuclear strike against the Chinese.

In Sam Greenlee's *The Spook Who Sat by the Door* (1969), Dan Freeman was the first black to make it through CIA training, but quit, tired of being "the CIA's nigger." But he had to report to the White House so the president could tell him goodbye. Freeman had been present when the president gave a rebel yell in the Taj Mahal, upsetting the Indians, but Freeman had managed to calm them down.

In Ross Thomas's *The Porkchoppers* (1972), "those people over in the White House" needed alcoholic Don Cubbin reelected head of his big labor union, so they hired Walter Penry, whose firm specialized in skullduggery, to steal the election. Cubbin's son Kelly, who had demonstrated for McCarthy in Chicago and later joined the D.C. police department, came along to ride shotgun for his dad.

In Nick Carter's *Death of the Falcon* (1974), Nick Carter (aka AXE's Agent N3) was driven to a White House meeting with the president, secretary of state, and his boss Hawk. They told him his new assignment was to keep ex-queen Sherima (the Silver Falcon) wife of Shah Hassan of Adabi, who was visiting D.C., safe from the terrorist group called the Silver Scimitar.

In Robert Travers's *The Apartment on K Street* (1972), after programmed (brainwashed) John Keefer, who was in charge of an atomic bomb capable of blowing up D.C., was shot dead, there was a top secret conference with the president at the White House. POTUS was as much concerned about the danger of rumors as the actual bomb.

In Vice President Spiro Agnew's *The Canfield Decision* (1976), urbane USSR Chairman Dradadov and President Walter Hurley got along very well at a state dinner, much to the annoyance of hawkish Vice President Canfield. But Canfield was the dupe of a China agent with Iranian connections posing as an Israeli activist.

In William Safire's *Full Disclosure* (1987), President Sven Ericson was blinded in an assassination attempt, but it was the fact that President Ericson had not "fully disclosed" an earlier blind spell that pushed him into resigning.

In Jeffrey Archer's *Shall We Tell the President?* (1977), Ted Kennedy was elected president in 1980 by beating Governor Jim Thompson of Illinois. Then a senator organized a conspiracy to assassinate EMK, which was discovered by the FBI. Director H. A. L. Tyson decided he and Special Agent Marc Andrews would handle the job by themselves, but at each stage of the hurried investigation, the key question was: Shall we tell the president?

John Ehrlichman's *The Company* (the CIA's nickname) (1977) opened in the Oval Office, which was a shambles with its furniture moved out for TV equipment. President Esker Scott Anderson then told the nation that he would not seek reelection. He had succeeded President William Arthur Curry who was killed in an airplane crash. After Anderson's surprise announcement, everyone scrambled to protect himself. This was especially true for CIA Director William Martin, who had obeyed a personal order of Curry's to have Father Julio Benitimes, leader of a South American invasion force, killed, so that the invasion failed.

In Richard Himmel's *Lions at Night* (1979), Undersecretary of State Lowell Callender used a new Cuban conspiracy to make himself look like a "new" Teddy Roosevelt Rough Rider. Callender first paid his respects to the President in the Oval Office, then ignored his orders not to run a counterattack using his State Department "Callender Commandos."

Margaret Truman's Washington mystery series began with *Murder in the White House* (1980). Secretary of State Lansard Blaine had been found taking big bribes, but when told to resign, he tried instead to blackmail President Webster. Soon after that, the secretary was found garroted in the Lincoln Sitting Room.

In Frederick Forsyth's *The Devil's Alternative* (1980), there was a terrible wheat crop failure which caused a power split in the Kremlin, with one group pushing for a sudden attack against Western Europe. Ukrainian separatists took advantage of the crisis by seizing an oil tanker which they would blow up to contaminate European shores unless their message was broadcast. British superspy Adam Munro (of the Firm, le Carré's "Circus") was flown over and brought by tunnel from the Old Executive Building to the Oval Office, where he told President William Mathews and his top advisors that they faced the Devil's Alternative: kill one group of men or another to save the world from nuclear war.

In Tom Clancy's first thriller, *The Hunt for Red October* (1984), Dr. Jack Ryan was a bright CIA researcher who helped figure out what the captain of the Russian supersub was doing. During the multinational chase/hunt there were continual meetings at the White House, asking Russian ambassador Arbatov to explain why the USSR was carrying on war games in the Atlantic. There was also a meeting on how to shut up liberal Senator Donaldson, who often leaked secret information from his committee.

In James Grady's *Hard Bargains* (1984), Detective Nick Sherman drove past the White House on Pennsylvania Avenue just as the front-end loaders moved the last of the waist-high concrete barriers in place. The White House grounds were already surrounded by a six-foot black steel picket fence but a new gray barrier covered the center strip in the street to block a car bomber.

In Lawrence Sanders's *Capital Crimes* (1989), President Hawkins came under the influence of "Brother Kristos," who seemed to help his hemophiliac son George. Chief of Staff Henry Folsom and his executive assistant John Tollinger met secretly in the basement Situation Room to discuss their fear the media would discover Kristos's undue influence, which was leaked by the vice president. Meanwhile, the President and First Lady arranged for Brother Kristos to spend the night in the Lincoln Bedroom and hold a prayer breakfast in the East Room. The prayer breakfast guests then went to the Cabinet Room where Brother Kristos sat in the presidential chair and preached about a massive giveaway of all federal surplus food.

In Tom Clancy's *Clear and Present Danger* (1989), the president (known by the code name "Wrangler") intervened in a drug war in South America without informing Congress.

The Chiefs of Staff came to the Oval Office to tell him Operation Showboat was under way, but they were not certain it represented a real clear and present danger to the country.

In Martin Greenberg and Ed Gorman's *Danger in D.C.: Cat Crimes in the Nation's Capital* (1993) there are several cat tales featuring the White House. In John Lutz's "The President's Cat Is Missing," Roy Smathers kidnaped Boots (aka Socks) from the White House, using a van full of cats. He took Boots to a secluded farmhouse outside D.C. belonging to his chum Norman's Aunt Agatha, but they couldn't tell which cat was the real Boots! In the meantime, the mobster Belinski Brothers turned up to capture Boots, then the White House SWAT team appeared with dogs.

In Carole Nelson Douglas's "Sax and the Single Cat," Midnight Louie of Las Vegas came to D.C. as a result of a message from Kitty Kong, top cat, telling him that presidential cat Socks was missing. Louie found Socks hiding behind the Justice Department. He told Louie he wanted to be home in Arkansas but Louie persuaded him not to be the only First Feline in history to leave the White House to the dogs.

Larry Beinhart's *American Hero* (1993) is a '60s-style satire on the Gulf War with footnotes to document "sources" such as *Rolling Stone* magazine. In it, Republican publicist Lee Atwater, dying of a brain tumor, suggested that if the polls were bad, Hollywood be hired to "do" a war for President Bush. The idea was embraced by the president and secretary of state (shown as boyish WASPS) and implemented by big-time Hollywood producer David Hartman, who was Jewish. Hartman arranged for Saddam Hussein to invade Kuwait for a stiff price, then headed back to the White House to report in person. As Hartman arrived, in spite of his rather cynical behavior, he mused to himself that "in spite of time and weather, fire and smoke, additions and reconstructions, the White House remains an elegant expression of the aspirations that motivated the age of revolution and rationalism."

In Ann Ripley's *Mulch* (1994), President Jack Fairchild wanted to recruit Peter Hoffman, an inventor-arms trader cum defense contractor for a top job at the Defense Department "minding" the dovish secretary. But Hoffman still had to pass a security clearance and to help that along, he killed his current mistress.

In E. J. Gorman's *The First Lady* (1996), Claire Hutton had been secretly visiting an old college chum, David Hart. Hart had been one of a foursome made up of (President) Matt Hutton, Claire, and superreactionary talk-show host Knox Stansfield. After Hart blackmailed Claire for "a fresh start" he was found shot with Claire's gun.

In *Absolute Power* (1996), David Baldacci quoted Lord Acton's dictum, "Absolute power corrupts absolutely." Absolute power was wielded by President Alan Richmond, a compulsive kinky womanizer whom his Secret Service guards had to protect by shooting his "date" Cindy Sullivan at her Middleburg mansion. Later in the Oval Office with Cindy's husband Walter Sullivan, the president promised to stay on top of investigating her murder, but he was caught by Jack Graham, a young D.C. defense lawyer, and Seth Frank, a Virginia detective, and arrested during a Cabinet meeting.

In Charles McCarry's *Shelley's Heart* (written in 1995 but set in the future), at 2 A.M. on Inauguration Day ex-President Franklin Mallory secretly came to see President-Elect "Frosty" Lockwood via the alley door at the rear of the Treasury Annex. Met by Chief of Staff Julian Hubbard, Mallory was taken by tunnel into the cellar of the East Wing and by elevator to the Lincoln Sitting Room. The ex-president and the new president then discussed Mallory's offer to let Lockwood resign because his election had been stolen electronically, but Lockwood chose to be sworn in regardless.

In Gar Anthony Haywood's *Bad News Travels Fast* (1995), retirees Dottie and Joe Loudermilk, who drove their beloved Airstream trailer to D.C. to see the sights, passed by the Presidential Palace which they found "unmistakable" but somehow "unspectacular." Viewed from the Pennsylvania Avenue side it looked surprisingly small, like a dollhouse. But it was still a special sight: the playground of kings, queens, movie stars, and Nobel Prize winners.

In syndicated columnist Jeff Greenfield's *The People's*

Choice (1995), the elected president was killed accidentally before the Electoral College met. The electors voted for the vice president-elect, Theodore Pinckney Block, a WASP of the WASPS (rich and stupid but honorable and upright). But President Ted Block decided that the "people had not chosen him." *Primary Colors* (1996) by Anonymous, actually *Newsweek*'s Joe Klein, is also about a presidential campaign but has almost no D.C. settings.

Marilyn Quayle and Nancy Tucker Northcott in *The Campaign* (1996) have black Georgia Senator Robert Hawkins (Bob) Grant—Newt Gingrich crossed with Clarence Thomas—running for reelection in the face of a presidentially orchestrated power play to keep him from winning because he might be a presidential contender. During the campaign, Senator Grant's administrative assistant Cynthia Novitsky had lunch with her old friend the First Lady at the White House. They ate from Lady Bird Johnson's china, in a room created by Jackie Kennedy to be cozy with antique hand-painted paper with scenes from the American Revolution.

In Margaret Truman's *Murder at the National Gallery* (1996), Annabel and Mac Smith were invited to the formal White House dinner for the opening of the National Gallery's Caravaggio exhibition. Annabel Reed-Smith was a college roommate of the vice president's wife Carole Aprile and at her request was serving on the gallery's committee in charge of arrangements.

Mary Higgins Clark's *My Gal Sunday* (1996) has short stories about former President Henry Parker Britland IV, a forty-something WASP charmer and his new bride, Congresswoman Sandra O'Brien Britland. In "They All Ran After the President's Wife," Britland got a call from the new president in the Oval Office, telling him the terrible news that Sandra had been kidnaped coming home from a session of Congress. In general, mysteries reflect the fact that living at 1600 Pennsylvania Avenue has not been a very safe occupation in the twentieth century.

Leave the White House to go right on Pennsylvania Avenue past West Executive Drive which is closed to the public and used as a parking lot. Walk along Pennsylvania Avenue, "America's Main Street," past the Old Executive Office Building to 17th Street.

The Old Executive Office Building was constructed in 1871–88 in an unabashedly Victorian design, in total contrast to D.C.'s classical public buildings; outspoken outrage over this "decorated wedding cake" continued for years. The building originally housed the Departments of War, Navy, and State, but all three had moved out by 1947. It was renovated under President Kennedy to house executive offices such as the vice president's.

In Diplomat's *Murder in the State Department* (1930), State Department Undersecretary Harrison "Handsome Harry" Howard was found murdered at midnight on a black March night in his State Department office. Harrison, who was preparing the final draft of a treaty allying the British, the Americans, and—believe it or not—the Japanese, was sitting at the mahogany desk, once used by Lincoln's secretary John Hay, when he was stabbed with a steel filing spike. The mystery was investigated by the debonair Dennis Tyler, Chief of the Bureau of Current Political Intelligence (CPI), a branch of the Secret Service, which answered to the secretary of state. What Tyler uncovered was a former czarist spy posing as Clovis Brown, leader of the American Anti-Imperialism Association. This was a pacifist-front organization to which many VIPs like Supreme Court justices, senators, and other Know-Nothings belonged. Brown's real plans were to take over the country with a coup, using bootleggers, gangsters, and the unemployed. Tyler foiled Brown by ordering a "practice" general mobilization of the armed forces to keep order.

In Van Wyck Mason's *The Washington Legation Murders* (1935), Captain Hugh North of G2 met at the State Department with the Chief of Staff and Senator Phineas B. Babcock. The senator believed that international agents were "passé" and that there were plenty of laws on the books to handle peacetime espionage. He refused to support catching a superspy called the Guardsman who stole American military secrets.

In Eleanor Pierson's *Murder Without Clues* (1942), Vladimir Lorshi, a second or third secretary at the Russian embassy, was a suspect in the murder of socialite Lila Donnelly because he smoked Russian cigarettes. Because of Lorshi's diplomatic status, the State Department was in charge. To question him young lawyer Ross Allen went to Old State, which bristled with obsolete cannons and columns, its halls dimly lit by an occasional light bulb, looking just the way a State Department should, grim and slow-moving, set in its ways.

In Mary Plum's *State Department Cat* (1945), young George Stair went to the State Department's architectural curiosity to take his orals. The building with its dimly lit high ceilings reminded him of the reign of Queen Victoria. George thought he might meet John Quincy Adams, who came to work at 5 A.M., about the time easygoing Henry Clay ended his card parties. Instead, George met Trouble, a tawny-colored cat, and a girl named Nancy Coleman.

By 1977, in Spiro Agnew's *The Canfield Decision*, the vice president's office was at Old State; Vice President Canfield retired there to lick his wounds when accused of treason.

In *Faithfully Executed* (1992), Michael Bowen quotes the Constitution: "the President shall . . . take Care that the Laws be faithfully executed." After the first federal execution in decades Major Alex Cunningham demanded an autopsy because he believed the man was dead before he got the lethal injection. When ex-Foreign Officer Richard Michaelson was asked to investigate, he was issued the credentials to get into the Old Executive Office Building and the need-to-know access codes to make documents pop up on his computer screen.

In Lawrence Sanders's *Capital Crimes* (1989), when it became clear that President Hawkins was under the spell of Brother Kristos, Vice President Samuel Trent, a nasty Boston Brahmin, authorized his personal aide Michael Oberfest to leak the story to the media.

Cross 17th Street at Pennsylvania Avenue and turn left to walk south to G Street. The entrances to the Executive Office

Building are heavily guarded so no one can go inside without security clearance.

In Pat McGerr's *Pick Your Victim* (1946), the office of the not-for-profit Society to Uplift Domestic Service was located to the right on Pennsylvania Avenue between G and H Streets. In 1944 Pete Robbins, SUDS's former public relations person, was stationed in the Aleutians with a group of bored GIs who would bet on anything. When a Christmas box arrived with a partial clipping saying his ex-boss Stetson had murdered someone at SUDS, the guys had Pete make a list of suspected victims, then laid bets while waiting for the next letter from home.

Cross G Street and keep walking down 17th Street to F Street. Cross F Street and keep going along 17th Street to New York Avenue. Cross New York Avenue to the Corcoran Gallery, built in 1897 to replace the outgrown building now known as the Renwick Gallery. It has a handsome Beaux Arts exterior and a famous interior rotunda.

In Haynes Johnson and Howard Simons's *The Landing* (written in 1986 but set in 1942), Nazi superspy Gunther Haupt went to the Corcoran Gallery. He saw a ponderous mass of white marble, more like an ancient sarcophagus than a modern repository for great art. When he found that the museum had only American art, which he despised, he left again.

In Charles McCarry's *Shelley's Heart* (1995), newly appointed Chief Justice Archimedes Hammett met President Lockwood's Chief of Staff Julian Hubbard here in front of Samuel F. B. Morse's *The Old House of Representatives*, a painting that does not ordinarily attract crowds of art lovers. They were both members of the secret Shelley Society.

Come out of the Corcoran and walk to E Street, which runs behind the White House just north of the Ellipse. Take E Street past the golden monument to the Army Expeditionary Forces of World War I. The Washington and Jefferson Monuments are to your right and the White House Truman balcony and South (Easter egg) lawn is to your left.

Usually you can walk along outside the White House railings and talk through the fence with the SWAT troops inside who wear black and carry automatic rifles. If there are VIP guests inside or the president will be leaving, you may be hustled along by the MPD officers.

Directly south of the White House on your right is the Ellipse. In the center are the Zero Milestone—shades of Imperial Rome—and the national Christmas tree, planted during President Carter's term. Neither tourists nor citizens are allowed to turn left up East Executive Drive to Hamilton Drive by the Treasury, so stay on E Street to 15th Street.

Cross 15th Street, where the huge Commerce Department and National Aquarium are on your right, taking up a block. Then turn left at Pershing Park to cross 15th Street to meet Pennsylvania Avenue again.

You are at the back of the Treasury Building, the oldest governmental office building and the largest Greek Revival structure in the world. President Andrew Jackson insisted that it be put there, destroying L'Enfant's sweeping vista from the White House to the Capitol (and making Pennsylvania Avenue begin to zigzag confusingly).

The Treasury is home to its T-Men and the Secret Service who guard the president. Reading mysteries you are well aware that D.C. has continual turf wars over the jurisdictions of the Metropolitan (District) Police Department, the FBI's G-Men, the Secret Service, the Capitol Police, the Treasury's T-Men, and the CIA, which until recently was supposed to have no role in internal affairs.

In Barbara D'Amato's *Killer.app* (1996), computer genius Dean Utley of SJR Systems planned to take control of the world by killing the president because "He who controls the flow of data controls everything," a very scary thought! The president was coming to Chicago, prompting anxious security memos from the Secret Service.

Cross 15th Street and Pennsylvania Avenue to Hotel Washington. The hotel has a pleasant lobby with places to sit, rest rooms, and a bar. Take the elevator and punch R (for rooftop) to reach the open-air restaurant that overlooks both the Treasury and the White House. In bad weather you can eat inside, but we sat by the parapet under the awning having lunch and watching an entourage of closed limousines and panel trucks move out of the White House. There are rest rooms on the top floor, too.

In Ross Thomas's *If You Can't Be Good* (1973), syndicated D.C. columnist Frank Size hired Decatur Lucas to find out why rich Senator Robert F. Ames blew his own career by accepting a $50,000 bribe, then resigning. On the rooftop deck of Hotel Washington, Lucas made a deal with the Senator's daughter Carolyn to get secret information, but she was murdered first.

In Richard North Patterson's Edgar-winning *The Lasko Tangent* (1979), Chris Paget of the Economics Crimes Commission was trying to get the goods on a White House crony, wheeler-dealer William Lasko, without being terminated himself. Told to report to Mary Carelli "upstairs," he took her for a gin and tonic on the deck of the Hotel Washington. Paget felt the view had an odd unreality, like the Washington imagined by tourists, in spite of the knit-suited bureaucrats all about them drinking gin with tight mouths.

In George P. Pelecanos's *Down by the River Where the Dead Men Go* (1995), bartender-cum-PI Nick Stefanos, Jr., took his girl Lyla to have a drink on the roof of the Hotel Washington, a "corny thing" to do, but lovely when the city was lit up at night. An obnoxious TV personality had a table nearby, and Lyla winged a peanut toward him. She missed, but got a round of applause from others sitting nearby. At Hotel Washington you have gone 1¾ miles and are now in historic Downtown, once the major shopping area, now being restored and renovated.

Leave Hotel Washington and turn left on Pennsylvania Avenue to the Willard Hotel, arguably the most famous hotel in all Washington. You come first to the Occidental Grill. There are really two restaurants: the Occidental itself and the Occidental Grill below at ground level.

In Louisa Revell's *The Men with Three Eyes* (1955), Miss Julia and her niece's chum, Ruth Gibson, who ran a settlement house, spent Ruth's day off "doing" Downtown D.C. They shopped at Garfinckel's and Woodward & Lothrop, saw sights on the Mall, lunched at the Occidental, and had tea at the Mayflower Hotel.

In Richard Conroy's *Mr. Smithson's Bones* (set in 1972), Smithsonian liaison Henry Scruggs and his lover, Phoebe Casey, had lunch at the Occidental whose nineteenth-century grandeur with its vast pillars, etched glass, dark paneling, crimson drapes, and velvet booths they both enjoyed. They were guests of *Washington Post* reporter Carl Harrison, who wanted to pump them about the killing fields of the Smithsonian where half a dozen curators had been murdered. (See Walk 2.)

In Ross Thomas's *Ah, Treachery!* (1994), the "Little Rock crowd" had gotten elected with the help of fund-raisers like Millicent Altford, a rainmaker. When she was robbed of $1.2 million, Altford hired cashiered Major Edd "Twodees" Partain to protect her. They came to D.C. where Altford met some Clintonites at the Occidental Grill, which tried to look old with photos of politicians, scalawags, and statesmen from the past. Clinton's staffers threatened to haul Altford into a subcommittee hearing on Clinton's agenda for reforming campaign funding!

Explore both the Occidental and its Grill, then go next door to the Willard Hotel past its outdoor fountain and an indoor-outdoor cafe called the Capitol Grounds. It may be where Detective Fiona FitzGerald and her partner Cates waited for their boss. The ebony-colored Eggplant was at a meeting in the mayor's office in the Municipal Building across Pennsylvania Avenue in Warren Adler's *Immaculate Deception* (1991).

There have been hotels on this site since 1816. By 1850 the Willard brothers were running one, and during the Civil War so many VIPs stayed there that war correspondent Nathaniel Hawthorne suggested it was the real seat of Union government. Julia Ward Howe wrote the "Battle Hymn of the Republic" there, and it was President Grant who noticed the people lurking about the plant-filled lobby to catch government officials and named these sneaky creatures "lobbyists." The hotel's block-long arcade known as Peacock Alley is also the place where FBI agents learn to shadow suspects.

In Elliott Roosevelt's *Murder in the Rose Garden* (set in 1936), the night D.C. hostess Vivian Taliafero was murdered in the Rose Garden, Republican Senator Cranshaw of Maine had a drink with FDR at the White House. Then he left by the South Portico and walked to the Willard where he met Burton Oleander, president of the Coal-Fired Utilities Association, for supper.

In Keats Patrick's *Death Is a Tory* (1935), syndicated gossip columnist Sally Shaftoe was buttering up Congressman Gil Lightfoot by driving him to his hotel, the Willard. Lightfoot, who was a murder suspect, went into the hotel, ordered cold chicken and a bottle of wine, remembered it was Sunday and changed his order to scrambled eggs and coffee. Then he strolled out the F Street entrance and caught a cab to the home of Homer Huddleston, another of the reporters on the case.

In Ross Thomas's *Twilight at Mac's Place* (1990), Granville Haynes, son of dead spy and con artist Steady Haynes, was heir to his father's memoirs which were proving too hot to handle. Granville took a room at the Willard Hotel on the advice of McCorkle, the proprietor of Mac's Place, who told him it had been renovated in Second Empire style but had kept the old ladies in the lounge who were there when he arrived in D.C. in 1950. Shades of Agatha Christie's *At Bertram's Hotel*!

When Granville Haynes checked in, he noticed the block-long arcade called Peacock Alley and the lobby's comfortable chairs and near jungle of potted palms. His room had a view of the National Press Building across 14th Street.

There was a lot of action at the Willard, too. After a night at his dad's Virginia farm spent hunting for the memoir manuscript with Erika McCorkle, Haynes returned to the Willard and found MPD Detective Sergeant Darius Pouncy waiting for him in the lobby. They went to the Willard's glittering Espresso Cafe to discuss the murder of Isabelle Gelinet in her own bathtub. Another time, McCorkle saw an IRA hit man in the Willard lobby. McCorkle and the guy hired to protect Granville got into a shooting match that ended with one of them dead. Detective Sergeant Pouncy then met with McCorkle at the Expresso Cafe to have lentil soup and a ham sandwich. Eventually Mr. and Mrs. Pouncy ate at Mac's Place, too (see Walk 5).

In Carey Roberts's *Pray God to Die* (1994), after Caroline McKelvey who worked for Congressman Jim Woodward was murdered, Homicide Detective Anne Fitzhugh went to a Woodward party at the Willard. The Woodwards left the Willard to go to the Sky Roof of the old Hotel Washington next door for a private party, then to their Willard suite where TV reporters got Gertrude Woodward to admit crooked deals about money. Gertrude then jumped out the Willard's tenth-floor window.

In Margaret Truman's *Murder at the National Gallery* (1996), curator Luther Mason took his young staffer/mistress Lynn Marshall there for dinner to tell her he was not going to recommend her for promotion or get her a show for her own work. In revenge she took up with his son Julian and stole the Caravaggio original which Mason had found for his exhibit at the National Gallery.

Come out of the Willard Hotel and go to 14th Street. Pennsylvania Avenue jogs south here to form Federal Triangle, the area that goes all the way to 4th Street along Constitution Avenue.

After crossing 14th Street make sure you are on E Street. This is a good corner to pause, remembering that all the Inaugural Day parades and presidential funeral processions come this way, en route either to the Capitol Steps or to Union Station. In Allen Drury's *Advise and Consent* (1959), it was the route taken by the president's funeral procession after he died suddenly in the Oval Office during Senate confirmation proceedings for Robert Leffingwell, his nominee for secretary of state.

Across E Street is National Place, a vertical mall with over a hundred shops and places to eat. There is a bookstore up the central escalator where I tried unsuccessfully to get a second copy of Truman's *Murder at the National Gallery* (1996)—sold out—but did buy Congresswoman Barbara Mikulski and Marylouise Oates's *Capitol Offense* (1996). The building is really a group of historic structures, including the National Theater and the 1927 National Press Club building.

Keats Patrick's *Death Is a Tory* (1935) was a humorous description of the (print) media and the politics of the very new New Deal. Patrick commented that Washington was a spending city, and the country worked for it. He added that presidential press conferences did not depend on what the president wanted to say but on the questions the reporters asked him. Working here, D.C. reporters Homer Huddleston and "Tom" Collins, whose real name was Arthur, got a call from Department of Agriculture's Marshall Rich, who said that he had just shot his wife and her lover. Syndicated gossip columnist Sally Shaftoe tailed the other two to get an exclusive, but by the time they returned, their offices were jammed with other reporters so it looked as if the whole National Press Building had moved in for a pre–Gridiron Club dinner party.

In Leslie Ford's *The Murder of a Fifth Columnist* (1940), the nickname "the Fifth Columnist" had been bestowed on know-it-all columnist J. Corliss Marshall, who wrote "Marshalling the Facts," by columnist Pete Hamilton, who wrote "The Capitol Calling." Marshall was found dead at a party attended by the widowed Grace Latham; the murder was investigated by her beau, Colonel Primrose and his sidekick Sergeant Buck.

In Drury's *Advise and Consent* (1959), when a reporter leaving the Press Club spotted powerful Senator Orrin Knox arriving at the White House, he passed the word along, emptying the Press Club bar and driving the presidential press secretary up the wall.

In Leigh James's *The Capitol Hill Affair* (1975), Tony Baylor, who ran a little Washington "poop sheet" from a one-room office in the National Press Building suddenly found himself being used by the CIA to ferret out something smelly about the Senate Armed Services Committee.

Come out of National Place and walk to 13th Street. Cross 13th Street and stay on E Street another block to 12th Street. To your right is the Victorian clock tower of the Old Post Office, restored, thanks to Lady Bird Johnson, and filled to the brim with stores and offices. Known as the Pavilion at the Old Post Office, it is a good place to take a pit stop or a coffee break. (If you want to stop now for the day, turn right on 12th Street to go to the Federal Triangle Metro Station.)

The FBI's Washington (D.C.) field offices used to be in the Old Post Office. In Jeffrey Archer's *Shall We Tell the President?* (1977, rev. ed. 1985), when the FBI discovered a plot against the newly inaugurated president, the investigation was first handled by Nick Stamos, the head of the FBI's field offices, until he was murdered.

Cross 12th Street and turn right to walk one block to Pennsylvania Avenue and go past the Old Post Office Pavilion and Internal Revenue to 10th Street. The Justice Department is on Pennsylvania Avenue between 10th and 9th Streets across Pennsylvania Avenue from the J. Edgar Hoover Building. In Margaret Truman's *Murder in the White House* (1980), when the secretary of state was found murdered at the White House, Ron Fairbanks, whose mentor was Supreme Court Justice William G. Friederich, was appointed by President Webster to investigate the murder. Fairbanks was given an office at the Justice Department where he and his staff could interview the Washington VIPs suspected of the murder.

Cross 10th Street and go left to the J. Edgar Hoover Building. The FBI is known as "the Bureau"; the CIA, as "the Company." The basic rationale was the FBI handled internal affairs, the CIA, foreign affairs, but then the FBI crossed over because the CIA has had a history of moles, spies, and other problems. Now the FBI does, too.

The 1974 building occupies the entire block from 10th to 9th Street. Built with massive sandstone-colored concrete walls in a style Truman calls "Brutalism," it looks like a prison, but its daily one-hour tours are still among D.C.'s most popular. The heavily guarded entrance is on 10th Street.

In Elliott Roosevelt's '30s and '40s mysteries about FDR,

neither the President nor the First Lady could stand the Director, whom FDR called "John Edgar" to his face. In Haynes Johnson and Howard Simons's *The Landing* (set in 1942), pompous J. Edgar Hoover claimed to have caught all the Nazi submarine spies when there were really several still at large. FBI confidential secretary Constance Aiken became involved in the effort to stop those Nazi spies through her boyfriend, Naval Intelligence Lieutenant Henry Eaton.

In the Gordons' *Power Play* (1965), Hoover's memory was still venerated. (Gordon Gordon had been an FBI special agent.) According to the Gordons after Hoover took over the FBI, instead of playing gangsters, American kids wanted to grow up to be G-Men. In their mystery, when FBI head Byron O'Connell died Dyke Crandall, the power-hungry administrative assistant of figurehead Senator Ralph Donahue, hatched a plot to put in a puppet as head of the FBI.

The FBI were not admired by Rex Stout in *The Doorbell Rang* (1965). Most of the action took place in and around Nero Wolfe's New York brownstone, but this time Wolfe took on the unusual task of scaring the FBI into dropping an investigation. They were harassing Mrs. Rachel Bruner, who had read *The F.B.I. Nobody Knows* and was so upset she bought lots of copies and sent them to VIPS.

In Jeffrey Archer's *Shall We Tell the President?* (1977; rev. ed. 1985), Special Agent Marc Andrews told the Director about a plot against the president's life. The Director formed a tight committee of the two of them to discover the details before March 10. One of Archer's advisors was Clarence Kelley, a real Director of the FBI.

In Robert Ludlum's *The Chancellor Manuscript* (1977), the murder of J. Edgar Hoover was carefully planned and carried out by a group known as Inver Brass, who feared Hoover's unethical use of his private files. Mission accomplished, however, the conspirators found that half the files (M through Z) were missing!

In Margaret Truman's *Murder at the FBI* (1985), tourist Harry Jones's brother-in-law, impressed by Harry's description of the FBI tour, brought his family to stand in the long line outside the E Street entrance. Jones thought the building looked like a huge toaster with two slices of bread on top. Inside, his son's water pistol was confiscated. They took the tour which included the most popular firing range demonstration where the target was a crude figure of a man drawn in black with a small circle for the heart. The special agent doing the demonstration used three weapons—revolver, shotgun, and automatic rifle. All his shots went into the heart, but when he turned the lights off to show off his shooting, the body of Special Agent George Pritchard pitched forward, shot dead.

Zach Adams's *Pursuit* (1986) is an FBI procedural with most of the action outside D.C. The small son of FBI agent Martin Walsh, who had put a child-killer behind bars, was part of an attempted mass kidnaping that led the Bureau to a terrorist ring where satanists bought kids to brainwash them. In the book Adams quoted an FBI comment about President Nixon and the Watergate scandal, that "Contrary to popular belief, it was an FBI leak that had put Woodward and Bernstein on to the investigation of Richard Nixon's administration. . . . The investigation had been going on for a year before line one even appeared in *The Washington Post.*" (See also Walk 6.)

In former Senator William Cohen and Thomas B. Allen's *Murder in the Senate* (1993), when Senator Julia Bristow was found with her throat slit in the Senate underground train, a huge jurisdictional dispute erupted between the Capitol police, the MPD, and the FBI. Jeff Fitzgerald, a former FBI Special Agent, now Chief of Capitol Police, met with FBI tape expert Kyle Tolland at the Hoover Building, but still had to wait in the visitors lobby and be vouched for. If he and Tolland did not leave together, an alarm would sound.

To your right behind the FBI Building on 9th Street is the old Atlas Building, where many Washington, D.C., artists have studios, including some who exhibited at Bill Wooby's former The Collector Gallery and Restaurant in the Dupont Plaza Hotel (see Walk 5). Two artists, Judy Jashinsky, who lost many portraits in the Atlas Building fire on June 7, 1995, and Virginia Daley told me funny stories about how uptight the FBI was about security when their new headquarters went up.

Margaret Truman's researchers had visited the Atlas Building to talk with the artists and met a restorer who was working on a piece of a painting he thought was a Caravaggio. Other artists who helped advise Margaret Truman at a meeting set up at the Dupont Plaza Hotel by Bill Wooby are all mentioned by name in Truman's mystery *Murder at the National Gallery* (1996). Eight of them autographed the copy Bill Wooby gave me when we met.

Cross E Street and walk up 10th Street past the Hard Rock Cafe to Ford's Theater. Built during the Civil War and still used as a theater, it is most famous as the site of President Lincoln's assassination by Southern actor John Wilkes Booth. The Lincolns were attending a gala performance of *Our American Cousin*, in celebration of General Robert E. Lee's recent surrender at Appomattox, and the presidential box was draped in victorious red, white, and blue. Booth shot Lincoln at close range, then jumped to the stage, breaking his leg, and supposedly shouted "*Sic semper tyrannis!*" before mounting his horse, hidden in the alley, and galloping off. Today it is a working theater, with a small Lincoln museum in the basement. The same government agency runs the Petersen House, pale red brick with green shutters, directly across the street, where Lincoln died.

In G. J. A. O'Toole's *The Cosgrove Report* (1979 but set in 1867), Nicholas Cosgrove, the Pinkerton agent hired by Secretary of War Edwin Stanton to make sure that Lincoln's assassin John Wilkes Booth was dead, went to Ford's Theater to review the evidence from the killing. Booth's left boot, cut from his broken leg, was there, but the detective realized that if the buried body had no right boot, it was not Booth. Not long afterward he helped dig up the body secretly buried at Fort McNair near the Washington Navy Yard but the coffin held only a pile of stones!

In Barbara Paul's story "Close but No Cigar," a yellow tomcat appeared at a Ford Theater rehearsal for a new play.

When the cat jumped from the balustrade onto the stage just as John Wilkes Booth had done, he was adopted by Justine, one of the actors, who named him "Abe," but the very next day the cat Abe found the leading actor dead.

Continue up 10th Street to F Street, passing by massive old (1792) St. Patrick's Church. One block to your right at 9th Street you would find the National Museum of American Art and the National Portrait Gallery, both housed in the old Patent Office Building. During the Civil War the building was an army hospital where Clara Barton and Walt Whitman ministered to the wounded. The two museums are part of the Smithsonian Institution.

Five blocks to your right on F Street between 5th and 4th Streets you would find the National Building Museum, originally the Pension Building. Known as architect Meigs' Old Red Barn, it is the world's largest brick building. Designed like Michelangelo's Palazzo Farnese, its Great Hall with its gigantic columns has been used for many important events, including nine inaugural balls.

In Margaret Truman's *Murder on the Potomac* (1994), Annabel Reed-Smith was asked to join the National Building Museum's board, which was dedicated to preserving D.C. architecture. Annabel had only attended one meeting there—at which she was much annoyed to be introduced as Mac Smith's wife—when murder and mayhem broke out in the family of Board Chairman Wendell Tierney.

In Phyllis Richman's *The Butter Did It* (1997), D.C.'s important chefs gathered at the National Building Museum for City-Tastes, a cooking contest-cum-feast begun by famous Chef Laurence Levain as a benefit for the homeless. This year City-Tastes was covered live by the media because Levain had been found dead the night before; his former lover, *Washington Post* restaurant critic Chas (Charlotte Sue) Wheatley, had to attend right after writing Levain's obituary.

South of you between 5th and 4th Streets from F Street to Constitution Avenue is Judiciary Square, with D.C.'s Courthouse and the Metropolitan Police Headquarters, located in the Municipal Center. Like London's Scotland Yard, or Chicago's 11th and State, it is visited by most MPD officers in the course of a mystery, as well as by occasional murder suspects like Gar Anthony Haywood's retirees Joe and Dottie Loudermilk in *Bad News Travels Fast* (1995). Go take a look if you have extra time.

Walk one more block north on 10th Street to G Street. Across G Street on 10th Street is the Martin Luther King Library, the only D.C. building designed by Mies van der Rohe.

In George P. Pelecanos's *Down by the River Where the Dead Men Go* (1995), the night after he heard the murder by the Anacostia River, PI Nick Stefanos went to the Martin Luther King Memorial Library to read up on local history in the Washingtoniana Room. Pelecanos also thanked the library's staff for their help researching *The Big Blowdown* (1996), set after World War II.

Straight ahead of you at 10th and H Streets is the Washington Convention Center. It has four exhibition halls and forty meeting rooms, which until recently held yearly conventions like the ABA (American Booksellers Association).

In Robert A. Carter's *Final Edit* (1994), publishing CEO Nicholas Barlow came to the ABA from New York. As soon as Barlow checked in at the Shoreham Hotel he took a cab to the Convention Center to check on their booth. Sales manager Mary Sunday reported that neither their catalogs nor their books had arrived and she hated their booth location near the university presses. Their bank had refused to give them more credit and their business manager Mort Mandlebaum said to bring back a bestseller instead of the prestige books senior editor Parker Foxcroft bought. The next day Barlow arrived at the booth to find Foxcroft yelling at Andrew Phelps, a book reviewer for the *Washington Post*! The shouting match was remembered when editor Foxcroft was found murdered in the firm's New York office.

Malice Domestic is an annual convention that "salutes mysteries of manners." Established in 1989 and held each spring, in 1998 Malice Domestic moved downtown to the Renaissance Hotel at the corner of New York Avenue and 9th

Street near the Washington Convention Center, making it a handy starting point for taking these mysterious walks.

To your right on H Street at 8th Street is the Friendship Arch marking the entrance to D.C.'s Chinatown. In Haynes Johnson and Howard Simon's *The Landing* (set in 1942), Navy Intelligence Lieutenant Harry Eaton and Negro MPD Detective Leon Thomas had to meet in Chinatown to compare notes on some black murders because it was the only place in segregated D.C. where the two men could meet publicly.

Turn left to walk west on G Street. This used to be a big department store area. Now the opera is moving here from the Kennedy Center because it needs more room. Walk two more blocks to 12th Street to end your walk at Metro Central Station.

Possible Side Trips

These mystery sites may be reached by Metro or car.

Howard University: Take the Metro Green Line to the Shaw–Howard University Station. Howard University is straight north on 7th Street, which becomes Georgia Avenue at T Street. Its most famous building is Howard Hall, the home of General Oliver Howard, the founder of Howard University and a commissioner of the Freedmen's Bureau. The nation's most famous African-American university, its law school is the alma mater of many of the lawyers who spearheaded the Civil Rights movement, including Supreme Court Justice Thurgood Marshall.

In Sam Greenlee's *The Spook Who Sat by the Door* (1969), CIA trainee and token black Dan Freeman spent weekends in Washington on U Street just south of Howard University. He refused to enter Washington's black society, considering it a group of Uncle Toms.

Thirty years later, in Hugh Holton's *Chicago Blues* (1996), FBI Special Agent Reggie Stanton (a former Chicago cop), working with Chicago Commander Larry Cole, kidnaped FBI Deputy Director William Connors and hid him in the home of Howard University Professor Ronald Hakim.

Rock Creek Cemetery: on North Capitol Street, just west of Catholic University. Inside the cemetery on Rock Creek Church Road you can find the Adams Memorial known as *Grief*, the bronze monument Henry Adams commissioned from his old college friend Augustus Saint-Gaudens after the death of his wife, Clover. It was greatly admired by Soames Forsyte, Galsworthy's protagonist in *The Forsyte Saga*, who mused that it was the best thing he had come across in America.

But in *Refinements of Love* (set in 1885), Sarah Booth Conroy proposes that Henry Adams murdered his wife Clover. Adams did destroy all Clover's work and never spoke of her again, but according to Eric Zencey in *Panama*, Adams also had enjoyed both life and fame until he finally died in 1918 and was buried at Clover's side.

2

THE EAST MALL

Museums Walk

BACKGROUND

The Mall is the country's oldest park. Although it was planned by Pierre L'Enfant to be a grand avenue stretching from the Capitol to the Washington Monument, development along the Mall was not begun until ground was broken for the Washington Monument in 1848. Later, after the Civil War, much-needed drainage was carried out under "Boss" Shepherd, but there was still a maze of walks and fashionable drives across the area, and a railroad station with tracks leading to it stood where the National Gallery of Art stands today.

In 1902 the McMillan Commission finally created a comprehensive plan for the Mall, but managed only to move the railroad station to the newly built Union Station north of Capitol Hill and designate the far western end of the Mall as the future site of the Lincoln Memorial, which was finally finished in 1922.

During World War I the Mall was lined with temporary barracks and offices, but beginning with FDR's New Deal in the 1930s, the federal government finally began to put up the gleaming public offices on Constitution and Independence Avenues that make Washington "the city beautiful," or a modern replica of Imperial Rome. The Jefferson Memorial at the Tidal Basin was begun in 1934.

This walk, which covers only the eastern half of the Mall, is really a tour of the Smithsonian Museums, most of which are spread along the north and south sides of the Mall from 15th Street to Capitol Hill. The entire collection numbering over 140 million objects, housed in fourteen different museums, began with the odd $500,000 bequest in 1829 of Britisher James Smithson, the illegitimate son of the Duke of Northumberland. Smithson willed his estate to the United States "to found at Washington . . . an Establishment for the increase and diffusion of knowledge." Known affectionately as the "nation's attic" the Smithsonian was finally allowed by Congress to begin collecting and accepting other objects, which were first housed in the redstone Castle where Smithson is entombed. It is now the Smithsonian Information Center and the best place to get information about all the collections. Don't plan on doing more than going inside to check out mystery sites, museum by museum, or you will be walking the Mall for a week. Instead, decide which museums you want to revisit later or do the walk over several days.

LENGTH OF WALK: About 2 miles

See the map on page 55 for the boundaries of this walk and page 265 for a list of the books and detectives mentioned.

PLACES OF INTEREST

I. SMITHSONIAN MUSEUMS ON THE MALL

Call Dial-a-Museum at 357-2020 for recorded information on museum activities or 357-2700 for separate Smithsonian Museums.* All museums are free but are closed December 25.

Arthur M. Sackler Gallery, 1050 Independence Avenue. Open daily 10:00 A.M.–5:30 P.M.

Arts and Industries Building, 900 Jefferson Drive. Open daily 10:00 A.M.–5:00 P.M.

*The telephone area code is 202 unless otherwise indicated.

Enid A. Haupt Garden, 10th Street and Independence Avenue. Open daily Memorial Day–Labor Day 7:00 A.M.–8:00 P.M., rest of year 7:00 A.M.–5:45 P.M.

Freer Gallery of Art, Jefferson Drive and 12th Street. Open daily 10:00 A.M.–5:30 P.M.

Hirshhorn Museum and Sculpture Garden, Independence Avenue and 7th Street. ***Museum*** open daily 10:00 A.M.–5:30 P.M. Free docent tours daily at noon. ***Sculpture Garden*** open daily 7:30 A.M.–dusk.

National Air and Space Museum, between 4th and 7th Streets. Open daily 10:00 A.M.–5:30 P.M. Call 357-1686 for IMAX tickets. Ninety-minute tours given at 10:15 A.M. and 1:00 P.M.

National Museum of African Art, 950 Independence Avenue. Open daily 10:00 A.M.–5:30 P.M.

National Museum of American History, between 12th and 14th Streets off Constitution Avenue. Open daily 10:00 A.M.–5:30 P.M.

National Museum of Natural History, between 9th and 12th Streets off Constitution Avenue. Open daily 10:00 A.M.–5:30 P.M. Tours given at 10:30 A.M. and 1:30 P.M. Self-guided audio tour also available.

Smithsonian Information Center: Renwick's Castle, 1000 Jefferson Drive. Open daily 9:00 A.M.–5:30 P.M. See especially James Smithson's crypt and the Great Hall.

II. OTHER SITES MENTIONED IN WALK

Department of Agriculture, Jefferson Drive from 14th to 12th Streets.

National Archives, Constitution Avenue between 7th and 9th Streets. Open daily September–March 10:00 A.M.–5:30 P.M., April–Labor Day 10:00 A.M.–9:00 P.M. Free. Call 501-5400.

National Gallery of Art, West Building and East Building, between 7th and 3rd Streets with entrances at Constitution Avenue and Madison Drive. (This gallery is not an official part of the Smithsonian complex.) Open daily Mon.–Sat. 10:00 A.M.–5:00 P.M., Sun. 11:00 A.M.–6:00 P.M. Closed December 25 and January 1. Free.

West Building, 7th to 4th Streets. Free highlight tours and audio tours available.

East Building, 4th to 3rd Streets.

National Sculpture Garden/Ice Rink, 7th Street and Constitution Avenue. (site of Charles Goodrum's fictional Werner-Bok Library)

PLACES TO EAT

Most Smithsonian museums have places to eat; the trick is to try for an "off hour" so you don't have to stand in a long line.

National Air and Space Museum: Call 371-8750.

Flight Line, Independence Avenue at 4th Street. Self-service buffet on main floor.

The Wright Place. Full-service restaurant on top floor.

National Gallery: Call 347-9401.

West Building:

Garden Cafe. Full-service restaurant.

East Building:

Terrace Cafe. Full-service restaurant.

Connecting corridor:

The Buffet or ***The Cascade Cafe:*** Overlooking indoor waterfall with tables among potted palms. Espresso/cappuccino/wine bar with sandwiches, salads, and desserts.

National Museum of American History: Cafeteria and rest rooms available to public.

National Museum of Natural History: Off the Rotunda there are a cafeteria and rest rooms.

On the Mall there are also fast-food kiosks where you may buy something to eat in the ***Hirshhorn Museum's Sculpture Garden***.

EAST MALL: MUSEUMS WALK

Begin your walk at the Federal Triangle Metro Station on 12th Street just south of the Old Post Office. (If you want to

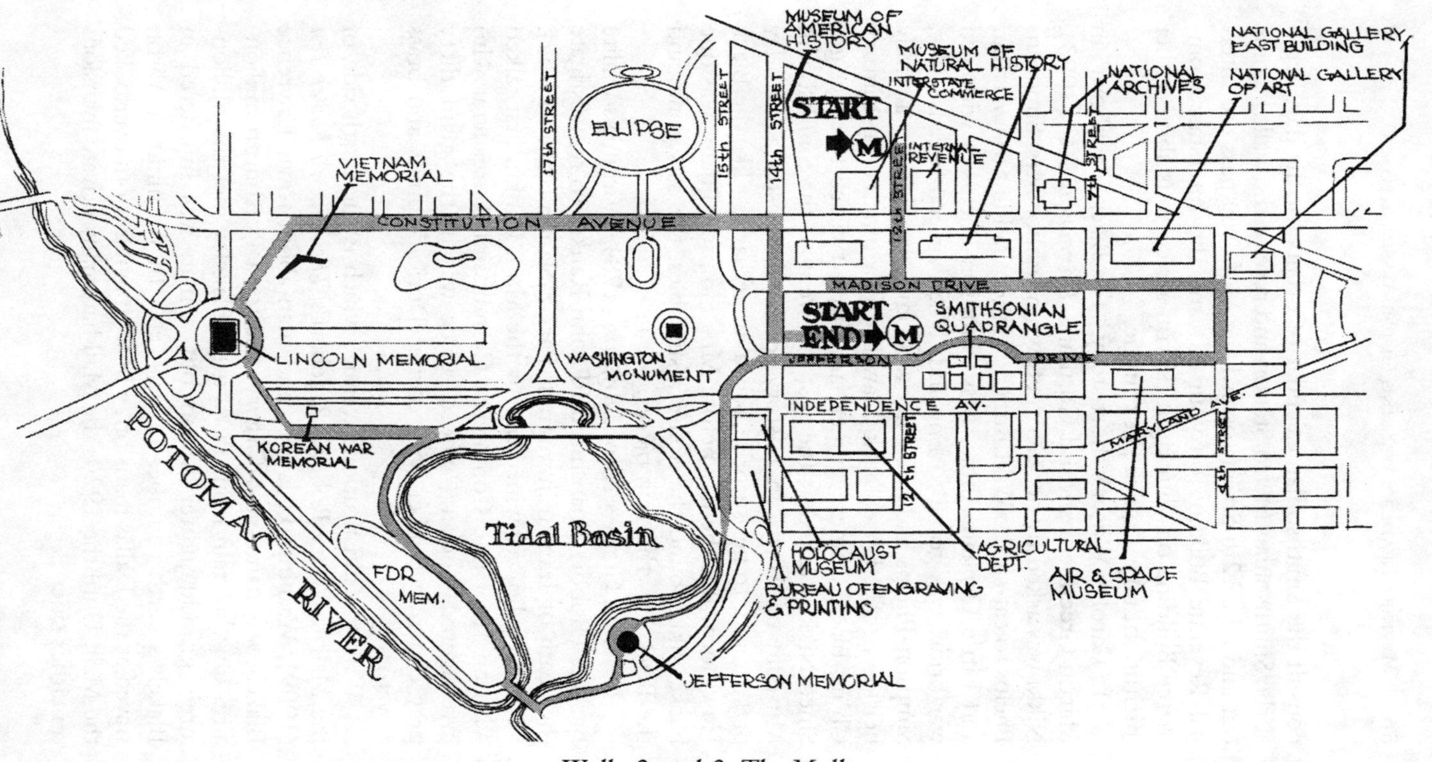

Walks 2 and 3: The Mall

consult the Smithsonian calendar of events for the day, begin at the Smithsonian Metro Station and reverse the walk.) Come out and take 12th Street toward the Mall. You pass the Internal Revenue Building on your left and the Interstate Commerce Building on your right. If you are curious about either institution, take a quick peek inside.

In Carolyn Wheat's short story "The Black Hawthorn" in Martin Greenberg and Ed Gorman's *Danger in D.C.* (1993), Nikki was asked by her Georgetown neighbor Mrs. Simpson-Phelps to cat-sit the Wild Bunch: Tigger, Paddington, Arthur, and Little Orphan Annie. Mrs. Simpson-Phelps, a widowed war bride, was going to England. Nikki agreed because Mrs. Simpson-Phelps had made her welcome, showing her a family heirloom called the Black Hawthorn, a nineteenth-century Ch'ng black Chinese ginger jar with a twisted-tree design. Since Nikki worked at the IRS, she went to the Smithsonian Museum of American History to buy her sister a birthday present and, to her surprise, saw a ginger jar just like the Black Hawthorn. But the day before Mrs. Simpson-Phelps was due back, Nikki found the house a shambles, the cats gone, and the Black Hawthorn in pieces.

In James Grady's *Hard Bargains* (1984), Virginia socialite Barbara (Bobbi) Sloan hired PI John Rankin to reinvestigate the death of Iranian immigrant Parviz Naderi (called Pasha), a trucker who was wiped out by the Mob. Rankin first talked with an Interstate Commerce Commission bureaucrat who investigated truckers, whose office was in the giant dirty gray concrete bunker with corner Doric columns and brass elevators.

Walk to Constitution Avenue, which is the north side of the Mall. In Mary Roberts Rinehart's *The Man in Lower Ten* (1909), Washington lawyer and man-about-town Lawrence Blakely was handling a forgery case for a Pittsburgh millionaire. On the train from Pittsburgh Blakeley met the millionaire's granddaughter Alison but a man was murdered in Blakely's berth (number Lower Ten). In Washington Alison stayed at the Dallas mansion, whose drawing room overlooked the Mall. Until the 1920s the Mall had many private mansions on either side.

Cross Constitution Avenue and take 12th Street to Madison Drive. Turn right on Madison Drive to the National Museum of American History (whose original name was the National Museum of History and Technology). This museum was established to display popular national icons like the "Star Spangled Banner" (the flag that flew over Fort McHenry), the first Model T Ford, Archie Bunker's slippers, and the First Ladies' gowns. Suspended in front of the Star Spangled Banner on the second floor is a Foucault pendulum, which demonstrates the earth's rotation by swinging back and forth across a compass rose design on the ground floor.

In Margaret Truman's *Murder in the Smithsonian* (set in 1976), when British Dr. Lewis Tunney, a historian friend of the vice president, came to America he was stabbed to death with Thomas Jefferson's sword in front of two hundred guests at a gala. Tunney fell down on top of the Foucault pendulum's compass rose as his murderer hid in the First Ladies' gown exhibit. The Medal of Harsa (aka Order of Cincinnati) was also stolen that evening, but it or a copy turned up in a Smithsonian garbage can. Later when Tunney's fiancee Heather McBean ran back from the National Gallery through the Fourth of July Bicentennial crowd on the Mall, she met a Smithsonian curator near the Foucault pendulum who tried to murder her, too.

In Richard T. Conroy's *Old Ways in the New World* (set in 1976), the secretary of the Smithsonian held a rooftop staff party here on the Bicentennial Fourth of July. But her party was water-bombed by fire helicopters trying to save the Castle, where some German mountain climbers, having made it to the top, started a bonfire to celebrate. Foreign Officer liaison Henry Scruggs and Miss Fontana of the Smithsonian Folklore Committee headed for the second floor where they discovered that the K'ng-Gui's ancestors, the Laok'u and Paok'u (red and black bugs) were eating "Old Glory." The ancestral bugs then ate the First Ladies' gowns, and in no time had eaten every kind of cloth in D.C.

In Conroy's *The India Exhibition* (1992), an exhibition about a K. V. Chandra, supposedly as important a person as Gandhi, was set up here in the main hall. But the whole operation was really an insurance scam worked by an Indian envoy. The museum's storeroom had a trap door which let thieves dump the phony gold statue of Chandra and the body of exhibit designer Violet Strauss into the underground river called the Tiber Creek tunnel. The statue turned up just beyond 12th Street, while Violet Strauss's body turned up in the Potomac River.

Come out of the museum and go left along Madison Drive back to 12th Street. Cross 12th Street and walk to the entrance to the Smithsonian's National Museum of Natural History. Opened in 1911, it was the third Smithsonian museum. It houses objects from the natural world, from a huge African elephant to the Hope Diamond.

In Conroy's *Mr. Smithson's Bones* (1993), Henry Scruggs walked a minor foreign VIP to the Natural History Museum, bringing along a skull they had found. Scruggs told the VIP how the Smithsonian began as a bequest to the young nation from James Smithson, the bastard son of the Duke of Northumberland, who never visited America, but whose body now rested in state in a sarcophagus in the Smithsonian Castle. Scruggs and his VIP ended up in the Physical Anthropology laboratory, where they learned from the computer that the skull they had found was actually James Smithson's skull. Someone had added his skeleton to the collections!

Accompanied by Security and Assistant General Counsel Phoebe Casey, Scruggs hurried to find out who was in Smithson's tomb. They discovered the freeze-dried body of Smithsonian General Counsel William Wright, known as "Bill of Rights," who was Phoebe's boss. Later in the Anthropology Department they found another curator eaten by beetles; his bones were clean as a whistle. The Smithsonian Institution Libraries (SIL) were on the museum's ground floor. SIL was run by huge Dr. Haas who was doing a little interlibrary loan drug trafficking, but she, too, came to a sticky end (see Walk 5).

In Truman's *Murder in the Smithsonian* (1983), the day after Dr. Tunney's murder, the staff was weighing the Hope Diamond with new equipment in the Hall of Gems. It is the largest blue marquis diamond in the world and supposedly carries a curse. Its first owner was Marie Antoinette, the guillotined queen of France, but more recently it was the proud possession of Evalyn Walsh McLean, one of D.C.'s famous society queens. When her husband Edward, owner of the *Washington Post*, went bankrupt and insane, the *Post* was sold to the father of present-day publisher Katherine Graham. (Most D.C. mysteries have a media mogul involved in the plot, but many do not call the newspaper by a real name.) In Max Allan Collins's mystery about the Lindbergh baby kidnaping, *Stolen Away* (1991), Nate Heller was sent east to help with the investigation and took on the role of chauffeur-cum-lover to Evalyn McLean.

The opening scene in Tony Hillerman's *Talking God* (1989) took place in the office of Catherine Morris Perry who had represented the Smithsonian in a row over burying the Native-American bones in their collection. The row was created by conservator Henry Highhawk, who was part Navajo. Highhawk was also replicating ceremonial Navajo masks for an exhibit, or perhaps to substitute his replicas for the real ones. When Perry opened a crude brown box on her desk, it turned out to contain the bones of her grandparents. Later on when both Navajo Tribal Police Lieutenant Joe Leaphorn and Officer Jim Chee came to Washington working on a murder back home, Highhawk himself turned up in one of the museum's collection drawers.

In Dan Brawner's "A Taste for the Good Life" in Greenberg and Gorman's *Danger in D.C.* (1993), Henry had a Siamese cat called Carnegie who ate jewels, then eliminated them. They worked together, and were planning to heist the Hope Diamond from the Smithsonian Hall of Gems. Henry let Carnegie out in front of the Natural History Museum, but Carnegie knocked over an old lady as he dashed inside. Henry parked his Lincoln in front to wait but an MPD cop, led by the old lady, brought back Carnegie, who had gotten sick inside the museum and spit up the Rosser Reeves star ruby. In spite of being surrounded by flashing squad cars, Henry was delighted to know that Carnegie still had such good taste.

Come out of the Natural History Museum and cross 9th Street to the open area between 9th and 7th Street on Madison Drive. In winter it is an ice rink and in summer an outdoor cafe. You are also at the location of the mythical Werner-Bok Library, invented by Dr. Charles Goodrum, a director of research at the Library of Congress. But to "see" it you need to check out the Library of Congress, which it marvelously resembles. (See Walk 4.)

In Goodrum's *Dewey Decimated* (1977), nasty anonymous letters received by publicist Betty Crighton Jones insisted that rare books in Werner-Bok's collection, like a Gutenberg Bible or Dead Sea Scrolls, were counterfeits. Poor Crighton felt that it was bad enough that the Werner-Bok averaged three bomb scares a week, on a par with the National Gallery and ahead of the Museum of Natural History! It is alarming how many bomb scares occur on the Mall in mysteries, so keep a sharp eye out and don't pick up any brown paper bags!

Turn left on 9th Street to walk back to Constitution Avenue. Then cross 9th Street to the National Archives, whose documents are hopefully all real! Built in 1937 as a strongbox for the nation's most precious official and historical records, the collection includes letters, documents, photographs, videos, and sound recordings, and runs the gamut from letters to presidents to Matthew Brady's Civil War photos to the photograph albums of Hitler's girlfriend Eva Braun. Historic documents like the Constitution are displayed in dim aquamarine light with a faint odor of chlorine, making them very hard to read. Every night they are lowered for security into a vault twenty feet below ground.

Leave the National Archives Building and, turning left on Constitution Avenue, walk to 7th Street. Go right on 7th Street back to Madison Drive, then turn left to the West Building of the National Gallery of Art, which stretches from 7th Street to 4th Street. It is connected to the East Building by an overpass and underground corridor across 4th Street.

This building is on the site of the Victorian Baltimore & Pacific Railroad Station where President Garfield was assassinated by a disappointed job seeker in 1881. Before the 1870s "clean-up" of the Mall by "Boss" Alexander Shepherd, Governor of the Territory of Washington (D.C.), railroad tracks led across the Mall both to this station and the Pennsylvania Railroad Station. They were replaced in 1904 by the massive Union Station (See Walk 4).

The National Gallery was created by one man, Pittsburgh industrialist Andrew Mellon, who with his friend Henry Clay Frick traveled to Europe to collect paintings. Opened in 1941, the museum was Mellon's gift to the country, but other wealthy collectors also donated works, among them Chester Dale, Joseph Widener of Boston, and Samuel Kress of New York City. Its standing collection of masterpieces that trace the history of Western art from medieval times to the early twentieth century is one of the greatest in the world. Its companion, the East Building, focusing on modern art, with its slablike, quirky angles is popular with tourists and one of the most visited art galleries in the world.

In Haynes Johnson and Howard Simon's *The Landing* (set in 1942), Nazi superspy Gunther Haupt left the Corcoran Gallery in disgust to walk to the new National Gallery to see the Kress Collection of Italian art. Gunther admired the statue of Mercury in the black-columned central rotunda, appreciating the fact that some of the art was booty stolen from Italy by Napoleon to decorate Paris, because now the Germans were looting Paris to endow Berlin. But Gunther really lost himself in Raphael's *Alba Madonna*, which you can admire on the main floor in Gallery 20.

Margaret Truman loves to cause murder and mayhem in this museum. Her favorite murder site is the fountain waterfall in the basement corridor between the West and East Buildings. In *Murder in the Smithsonian*, Scottish Heather McBean, here because of the murder of her fiance Dr. Lewis Tunney, walked from the Madison Hotel the length of the East Mall to reach the West Building of the National Gallery. Heather went inside to the marble-columned rotunda, then went to the Venetian section (Galleries 16–28 on the main floor) to look at Bellini, Gorgione, and Titian, stopping to admire Leonardo da Vinci's portrait of Ginevra de Benci, which you can also view in Gallery 20.

She then walked across the cobblestoned lower-level courtyard past the fountain waterfall when someone came up behind her and smashed her with a cane and ripped off her large purse. Heather fell against the sheet of water but some tourists saw her and called for help. Later in the museum's Garden Cafe MPD Lieutenant Joe Pearl, wearing a tan safari suit and pink shirt, watched Smithsonian staffer Janis Dewey and eccentric Dr. Evelyn Killinworth. Pearl was so obvious his victims complained about him to his boss, MPD Captain Hanrahan.

In Charles Goodrum's *Dewey Decimated* (1977), Yale librarian Edward George visited the National Gallery with another Werner-Bok staffer to "refresh" themselves before their police interrogation about a murder involving the replacement of rare books with inferior copies. They went to look at Vermeer and Holbein, preferring the well-ordered Dutch over early Italians. (Galleries 46–50 on the main floor.)

In Goodrum's *Carnage of the Realm* (1979), murder among high-priced coin collectors reunited the Werner-Bok Library sleuths: Yale librarian Edward George, PR person (Betty) Crighton Jones, and history Ph.D. candidate Steve Carson. They met at the National Gallery to compare notes on their research on coin and silver robberies in Washington, D.C., neighborhoods and George was startled to find that the National Gallery now served food.

In Goodrum's *The Best Cellar* (1987), the same sleuths teamed up to solve a murder related to Thomas Jefferson's gift—for which Congress reimbursed him handsomely—of his personal library to replace the Library of Congress holdings burned in 1814. During their investigation the three went to eat a quick quiche at the National Gallery.

In Truman's *Murder at the National Gallery* (1996), you get a Grand Tour behind the scenes. Director Courtney Whitney III explained to Annabel Reed-Smith that New York's

Metropolitan Museum is a museum while the National Gallery just collects pictures and some sculpture. But his staff of primadonna curators still went in for backbiting and jockeying for position. The executive committee for the Caravaggio exhibition, which included Annabel, met on the seventh floor of the East Building near Whitney's office. Annabel, who was the college roommate of the vice president's wife Carole, had been asked by her to keep an eye on the Caravaggio exhibition and its curator. Curator Luther Mason had not only set up the Caravaggio exhibition but found a new painting called *Grottesca* for the exhibit.

The opening reception for the Caravaggio exhibition was held in the rotunda on the main floor, with bars and hors d'oeuvres and a string quartet. There was a formal dinner at tables in the West Sculpture Hall and West Garden Court. The Caravaggio exhibition was hung in the West Building because curator Luther Mason threw a fit when told it would be in I. M. Pei's 1978 contemporary East Building. Mason secretly planned to indulge his pipe dream of making copies of the new Caravaggio so he could take the original to a Greek island worlds away, but a shove into the National Gallery fountain broke his neck.

You have gone about one mile, so this is a good place to stop for refreshments or a pit stop. Try one of the two restaurants or the Cascade Cafe in the basement where you can see the fountain—but don't go too near the water.

Come out of the East Wing of the National Gallery of Art and turn right to walk back to 4th Street. Then turn left to walk across the Mall (enjoying the view of the Capitol on your left and the Washington Monument on your right) to Jefferson Drive and the Air and Space Museum. The south side of the Mall tends to be loaded with tour buses and MPD cops on bikes and there are many cabs, making it easy to decide you have had enough for one day.

The National Air and Space Museum is a large modern building made of glass and granite blocks; it opened in 1976 for the Bicentennial. Inside, this modern museum are the

Wrights' *Flyer*, Lindbergh's *Spirit of St. Louis*, space capsules including *Apollo 11*, planes, balloons, helicopters, rockets, the Einstein Planetarium, and IMAX's Langley Theater.

In Jeremiah Healy's *The Staked Goat* (1986), Al Sachs, an old 'Nam buddy of PI John Cuddy was found "ritually" murdered on Boston's Beacon Hill. Deducing that Al Sachs's murder was not gay-bashing but related to his Vietnam service, Cuddy asked a mutual 'Nam chum named Colonel J. T. Kivens at the Pentagon for a look at Sachs's files. J.T. set up a "casual" meeting at the Air and Space Museum. Cuddy found it difficult to consider it a "museum" because it was filled with things he remembered as current events, but he spotted J.T. in uniform underneath Lindbergh's *Spirit of St. Louis.* After some protesting, J.T. gave Cuddy his card and told him to call. The next day Cuddy was allowed to see Al Sachs's files at the Pentagon.

In Gar Anthony Haywood's funny chase through D.C., *Bad News Travels Fast* (1995), retirees Dottie and Joe Loudermilk came to D.C. to sightsee but found themselves trying to get their activist son Eddie out of jail on a murder rap. After an exhausting search through Georgetown, not to mention another visit to District Headquarters, Dottie insisted that they take a break by eating a late lunch in the cafe at the National Air and Space Museum. Getting to the cafeteria, where the food was standard American, took them past the most impressive collection of historic aircraft and spacecraft in the world, and made Joe's day. Take time yourself to admire the Wright Brothers' *Flyer*, Lindbergh's *Spirit of St. Louis*, and *Apollo 11* as the Loudermilks did. If you're tired, take in one of the movies being shown.

Come out of the Air and Space Museum and turn left to walk along Jefferson Drive to the Hirshhorn Museum with its sunken Sculpture Garden. A doughnut-shaped concrete building reminiscent of New York's Guggenheim Museum, it opened in 1974 and has a collection of over four thousand contemporary paintings and drawings and over two thousand sculptures, including the largest group of Henry Moore works in the United States. The original collection was donated by immigrant Joseph H. Hirshhorn in 1966.

In Anne Morice's *Murder in Mimicry* (1977), British Tessa Crichton, the actress wife of Chief Inspector Robin Crichton of Scotland Yard, came to D.C. with a play opening at the Kennedy Center. The first day she was in D.C. Tessa went to see the new Hirshhorn Museum, affectionately known as the Bagel, and found it was an impressive circular building in a paved courtyard with sculptures ancient and modern. She was surprised, however, to find Rose, the star's companion-understudy, sitting in the Sculpture Garden with stage manager Terry Rack looking very miserable.

In Goodrum's *Carnage of the Realm* (1979), when Betty Crighton Jones and Steve Carson needed to compare notes on the coinage murders, he got them two box lunches from the Hirshhorn Museum of Art to eat in the Sculpture Garden, which is outdoors but below ground level. Steve said the Hirshhorn belonged to local Washingtonians the way all the other museums belonged to the tourists.

In Conroy's *Old Ways in the New World* (set in 1976), the Hirshhorn Museum's auditorium was the only place big enough for the official representatives of the White House, Commerce, Interior, Agriculture, State, the EPA, the armed forces, the Board of Trade, the ambassadors from Mexico and Canada, and the Smithsonian's own ABC Committee to meet. They had to decide how to handle the "fallout" from the Folklore Festival, especially the red and black bugs that were eating all the cloth in D.C. But the White House took over and announced that they were going to spray the city with DDT as soon as they had evacuated all the babies, birds, and dogs.

In Barbara D'Amato's short story "Freedom of the Press" in *Danger in D.C.* (1993), freelance Chicago reporter Cat Marsala had an interview with Representative Peggy Nicklis, the first woman elected from a conservative northwestern Chicago district. Nicklis had a shabby old office with a plush blue cat bed and litter box for her cat Mugum (MGM) who went everywhere with her. Nicklis had to cut the first interview short, but made another appointment for the next day. Before coming back for the second interview, Cat went to look at the Hirshhorn Museum and Sculpture Garden.

In Wendi Lee's short story "Indiscreet," after a murder of the madam of a high-class D.C. brothel the madam's cat was missing. The cat, called Miss Kitty, was an eighteen-pound Maine coon with tortoiseshell coat and white leggings. Suspicious, Louise, a *Washington Sun* reporter who had done a piece on the brothel, followed one of the "girls" called Holly to the Hirshhorn Museum. In the Sculpture Garden Holly met a man who slipped her an envelope. Louise followed him to the Yugoslavian embassy where she talked her way in and found the missing Miss Kitty.

After looking at the Hirshhorn and the "hidden" sculpture garden, continue on Jefferson Drive to the Smithsonian Quadrangle between 7th and 11th Streets station.

The Smithsonian Quadrangle was the brainchild of Smithsonian Director S. Dillon Ripley and was opened in 1987, but some of its buildings, like the "Castle," had been put up during the nineteenth century.

The first building you come to is the Arts and Industries Building, built in 1881 and decorated with an Arts and Crafts motif. It was the Smithsonian's first "official" national museum, built to house those 1876 Philadelphia Centennial exhibits for which the Castle had no space.

In Conroy's *Old Ways in the New World* (set in 1976), a huge international folk festival was being sponsored by the Smithsonian. Henry Scruggs was in charge of getting artists into the country and was blamed for everything they did. Scruggs was transferred to Arts and Industry's OOFS (Office of Folklore Studies) to share an office with (Prince) Cedric Mahute, a womanizing African ethnomusicologist from Aganga. In one of the tunnels under the Mall Mahute was deep-sixed with an animal tranquilizer gun, then frozen stiff.

In Truman's *Murder in the Smithsonian* (set in 1976), the Smithsonian bomber left a warning note by the Jupiter, a wood-burning passenger locomotive, then managed to set off a bomb in the *Philadelphia*, a single-masted square-rigged gunboat that was part of Benedict Arnold's flotilla on Lake Champlain.

Come out and walk along Jefferson Drive to the turreted red sandstone Castle, completed in 1855. Designed in Gothic Revival style by James Renwick, it has nine medieval towers and a Great Hall. To your left as you come in there is a small crypt which contains the tomb (sarcophagus) of James Smithson, who willed his fortune to the United States in 1829 to "found an Establishment for the increase and diffusion of knowledge among men." Beyond his small chamber-tomb, the Great Hall, with huge columns and Romanesque arches, is now a multimedia Visitors Information Center. The other rooms are closed to the public.

In Conroy's *The India Exhibition* (1992), Scruggs remarked that the Castle had been modeled after the ancestral castle of Dukes of Northumberland. His regular office was in the (main) Tower on the second floor near the secretary of the Smithsonian's parlor and Scruggs had the odd habit of counting the steps (sixty-two) every time he went up or down.

Directly south of the Castle is the Enid A. Haupt Garden, a restful spot with nineteenth-century garden benches and lampposts. It is a four-acre garden on the original site of the National Zoo, which included a small herd of buffalo. Their popularity led to federal efforts to preserve the remaining herds. Take one of the internal pathways across the quadrangle to see it.

In Lawrence Sanders's *Capital Crimes* (1989), when President Hawkins came under the spell of a modern-day Rasputin, Brother Kristos, the White House Chief of Staff's executive assistant John Tollinger waited on a wooden bench in the Enid Haupt Garden to meet with ex-FBI agent Martin Lindberg. Tollinger had hired Lindberg to collect information on Kristos (aka Jacob Everard Christiansen).

The Haupt's sandstone-and-iron gateway leads to the two underground museums: the Arthur M. Sackler Museum, whose Oriental art collection was donated in 1982, and the National Museum of African Art, moved here from the home of Frederick Douglass behind Capitol Hill. Visit them both if you have time, then walk to the Freer Gallery of Art at 12th Street and Jefferson. The nation's first art gallery, built in 1923, was donated by Detroit railroad magnate Charles Lang Freer, who collected Asian art as well as American paintings, particularly those of his friends James McNeill Whistler (including *Whistler's Father*) and John Singer Sargent.

In Ross Thomas's *The Brass Go-Between* (1969), Philip St. Ives was hired by the Coulter Museum to buy back the brass Shield of Kompareen, which had been stolen from a Pan-African collection on loan to the museum. On his way to a meeting with the top brass, St. Ives admired the elegant looks of the Coulter Museum, which was given to the country by an eccentric millionaire and located in the space occupied by the Freer Gallery of Art.

After visiting the Smithsonian museums, come out on 12th Street at Jefferson Drive. One block south across Independence Avenue there are more government buildings, including the Forrestal Building, the Energy Department, and the U.S. Postal Service. Another block south across L'Enfant Promenade at D Street is L'Enfant Plaza with a shopping mall and Metro station.

In Stephen Coonts's *Under Siege* (1990), Captain Jake Grafton rushed from a high-level security meeting to the L'Enfant Plaza Metro Station where a vicious terrorist attack had shot down scores of Christmas shoppers. President Bush's helicopter had been shot down near Camp David and Vice President Quayle had called up the National Guard to defend the capital. Captain Jake Grafton and his sidekick Toad Tarkington brought along *Washington Post* reporter Jack Yocke to teach him about "real life."

Ordinarily, this neighborhood south of the Smithsonian is simply another bastion of bureaucracy like the Department of Agriculture, a building complex built between 1904 and 1908 that stretches from 12th Street to 14th Street along Independence Avenue.

In Keats Patrick's *Death Is a Tory* (1935), skinny little Marshall Rich was a Department of Agriculture brain-trust botanist on loan from Southwestern Agricultural. Rich was doing experiments near Arlington Cemetery, trying to produce drought-free crops for the Dust Bowl. But one evening Rich called his reporter friend "Tom" Collins to tell him he had just shot his wife and her lover and was going to shoot himself next.

In addition to murder, the Agriculture Department represents the ever-burgeoning federal bureaucracy.

According to my college classmate Chuck Valsing, a department lawyer, an early secretary of agriculture went out on the Mall to observe the department's zoo and was struck dead by a bolt of lightning. His example has encouraged Agriculture's employees not to overdo devotion to duty.

In Bruce Holland Rogers's short story "Enduring as Dust" in *Danger in D.C.* (1993), the secretaries at CAP (Coordinating Administration for Productivity), housed in a drab little building near the Department of Agriculture, used a twenty-year-old memo letting them keep a cat called Dust as an excuse to keep replacing the original cat. No one knew or cared.

In Dan Crawford's short story "Under Separate Cover" in *Alfred Hitchcock's Magazine* (1990), D.C. staffer Elliott was told to find out about "Zimiamvia" so his agency, INTAD, could file a report before INDIST, a rival agency, did. Elliott took the back stairs to INDIST's offices to get into the office of his counterpart at INDIST. He was photographing the report when the other guy returned, but Elliott knocked him out, then calmly finished the job of stealing information from a fellow agency housed in the same building.

Contemplate the relentless, rising cost of government, a point well made by Barbara Michaels in her political mystery *Smoke and Mirrors* (1989), then take 12th Street to the Smithsonian/Mall Metro Station to end your walk.

3

THE WEST MALL

Monuments Walk

BACKGROUND

This walk covers the national monuments that stretch west along the Mall from the Washington Monument at 15th Street and Jefferson Drive to the Lincoln Memorial at 23rd Street and Independence Avenue. Designer Pierre L'Enfant intended the Mall to be a grand avenue from Capitol Hill to the Washington Monument, and did not extend it farther west because the Potomac River and the Tiber Creek, which ran along what is now Constitution Avenue, often flooded the entire area. After a bad flood in 1881 Congress finally appropriated funds to drain the marshes south and west of the Mall, creating Potomac Park, where the 1900 McMillan Commission placed the Lincoln Memorial.

Its southern boundary was extended when the Jefferson Memorial went up in the late 1930s on the shores of the Tidal Basin and in 1997 the long-planned Franklin Delano Roosevelt Memorial, located on West Potomac Park opened, too. In the meantime, despite the temporary buildings erected here during both World Wars I and II, the Mall slowly became the city's tree-lined playground and the place Washingtonians assume you mean when you want to take a walk!

Since the District began, the Mall has also been the place where ceremonies and celebrations, demonstrations, marches, and protests took place. The Fourth of July traditionally has been celebrated there, and a gigantic fireworks display was held on the nation's Bicentennial in 1976. During the War of 1812 the British used the Mall as a parade ground and in the Civil War the Army of the Potomac used it for a campsite and drill ground. The old veterans returned there in 1892 for the last big reunion of the Grand Army of the Republic.

Other Mall marchers and demonstrators have included Coxey's Army of the Unemployed in 1894, the Ku Klux Klan in 1925 (marching without their white sheets), and the 1932 Bonus Army of World War I veterans. Civil Rights demonstrators first heard Marion Anderson sing at the Lincoln Memorial on Easter 1939, thanks to First Lady Eleanor Roosevelt, then listened to Martin Luther King, Jr., give his "I Have a Dream" speech there at the climax of the 1963 March on Washington. Thereafter, Vietnam protesters, Gay and Women's Rights advocates, the Million Man March, all have occupied its wide territory with its green grass and dusty, tree-lined walks on either side.

Before starting this walk, remember that the only rest rooms are inside the public buildings and there are no restaurants along the Mall. If it is hot or rainy, there is very little shelter. Near the Washington Monument, however, there are fast-food stands and places to buy souvenir T-shirts.

LENGTH OF WALK: About 2 miles

You might consider using the blue and white Tourmobiles, which will allow you to hop on and off at all these sites. Call 544-5100* for more information. See the map on page 55 (the same map as Walk 2) for the boundaries of this walk and page 267 for a list of the books and detectives mentioned.

PLACES OF INTEREST

Bureau of Engraving and Printing, 14th and C Streets. Open weekdays 9:00 A.M.–2:00 P.M. Thirty-minute guided tours. Free. Rest rooms. Call 874-3019.

*The telephone area code is 202 unless otherwise indicated.

Franklin Delano Roosevelt Memorial, West Potomac Park south of the Tidal Basin. Four open-air rooms featuring each presidential term. Opened Spring 1997.

Japanese cherry trees, usually in flower in early April along the north side of the Tidal Basin. A gift of the Japanese in 1912 with the first one planted by First Lady Helen Taft. Centerpiece of D.C.'s Cherry Blossom Festival held each spring.

Jefferson Memorial, on Ohio Drive. Park rangers on duty 8:00 A.M.–midnight daily. June–September, twenty- to thirty-minute programs are presented by rangers. Free. There are a bookstore and a snack kiosk at the Tourmobile stop. Rest rooms. Call 426-6822.

Korean War Veterans Memorial, just north of Independence Avenue between 21st and 23rd Streets, south and east of the Lincoln Memorial. Privately funded, it was dedicated on July 27, 1995, the 45th anniversary of the Korean War Armistice.

Lincoln Memorial/Reflecting Pool, at western end of Potomac Park/the Mall, at 23rd Street and Independence Avenue. Park rangers on duty 8:00 A.M.–midnight daily. Free. Call 426-6895.

Lock Keeper's House, only remaining monument to the City/Tiber Canal, at 17th Street and Constitution Avenue.

Tidal Basin, part of the Potomac River until 1882. Paddleboats for rent for $8 per hour at the boathouse on the east side near the Bureau of Engraving.

United States Holocaust Memorial Museum, 100 Raoul Wallenberg Place (15th Street) near Independence Avenue. Open daily 10:00 A.M.–5:30 P.M. Free. Reserved tickets are required for a specific time. (Call Protix 1-800-400-9373 to reserve them ahead of time for a small service charge.) Closed Yom Kippur and December 25. Rest rooms. Call 488-0400.

Vietnam Veterans Memorial (the Wall), by Constitution Gardens at 23rd Street and Constitution Avenue. Names of more than 58,000 Americans etched on the dark granite face of the Memorial in the order of their deaths, with directories at either end listing the names in alphabetical order. Rangers on duty 8:00 A.M.–midnight. Free. Ranger programs June–Labor Day. Call 634-1568.

Washington Monument, directly south of the White House at 15th Street and Constitution Avenue. Open daily Easter Sunday–Labor Day 8:00 A.M.–11:45 P.M., rest of the year 9:00 A.M.–4:45 P.M. Closed December 25. Open July 4 until noon. Free, or get advance tickets for $1.50 via TicketMaster (call 1-800-505-5040). Climbing up the 897 steps is forbidden, but tours down the steps are given by the Park rangers weekends at 10:00 A.M. and 2:00 P.M. Rest rooms. Call 426-6839.

PLACES TO EAT

There really are none except for the fast-food street vendor stands located at almost every corner.

The Snack Bar, just west of Constitution Gardens Lake near the Lock Keeper's House sells hot dogs, other snacks, and drinks.

Jefferson Memorial, at the Tidal Basin Tourmobile stop has a snack bar (and rest rooms).

— WEST MALL: MONUMENTS WALK —

Begin your walk at the Smithsonian Metro Station. In *Black Widower* (1975), Patricia Moyes described a perfect day on the Mall when the Japanese ornamental cherry trees around the Tidal Basin had burst into pink blossoms, delighting the crowds of tourists, the Lincoln and Jefferson Memorials had never looked more Grecian, the Washington Monument more monumental, or the White House whiter, and to crown it all was the Capitol, looking like a gigantic wedding cake.

Come out of the station and take Jefferson Drive west to 15th Street and turn left to walk to the Washington Monument. Lit up like the Capitol, it dominates the cityscape by day and night. Originally it was to be in an exact line with the White House and the Capitol but that site was too swampy, so it was moved about three hundred feet south and east. Designs for the monument changed, ending up with the simple obelisk which was begun in 1848 but not completed until 1885. The elevator today is a high-tech model that whisks you up fast, unlike the original which was so temperamental that women and children were forbidden to use it. You may prefer to take the elevator up and walk down to admire the 188 stones donated as memorials.

In Haynes Johnson and Howard Simons's *The Landing* (set in 1942), Nazi superspy Gunther Haupt, put ashore by submarine to subvert D.C., recalled that during a visit before the Depression, D.C. still had trolley tracks and wooden platforms for the streetcars running down the center of Pennsylvania Avenue, but the temporary buildings from World War I, and the saloons and rooming houses on the south side of the Mall, had been demolished during the New Deal to make room for a burgeoning bureaucracy. Walking along, disguised as a foreign service officer on leave, Gunther was stopped by a Norwegian officer in uniform and together they rode to the top of the Washington Monument. Up there, Gunther killed the Norwegian and left his body looking at the view. There is another version of the secret landing of a Nazi "kamikaze" group planning to assassinate FDR in John Lee's *The Ninth Man* (also set in 1942).

In James Grady's *Six Days of the Condor* (1974), on Tuesday morning after the shoot-out on Capitol Hill, Malcolm (aka Condor) was on the run from everyone including his bosses at the CIA when he saw an ad in the *Washington Post* saying "Condor Call Home." Malcolm mailed information about his situation to the FBI, the CIA, and the *Post*. Then he spent the rest of the day in the long line at the Washington Monument while security and law-enforcement agencies all over the city were hunting him. By 4:15 P.M. Malcolm stole a car from Kentucky American Legionnaire Alvin Phillips, in D.C. for the National Conference on Youth and Drugs, who had been given a pass to go to the head of the line at the Washington Monument.

In Bill Crider's short story "Code Red: Terror on the Mall" in Greenberg and Gorman's *Danger in D.C.* (1993), terrorists known as the Bloody Swords of Allah took over the

Washington Monument along with the president's cat. It was still too early to kidnap tourists when the president drove up carrying an M16 rifle. He wanted to prove his manhood by fighting for his cat so he insisted on accompanying the FBI agents who climbed the 897 stairs. After several Secret Servicemen (guarding him) were shot by the terrorists, he led the charge and helped capture the rest of the gang, including the one that the cat jumped.

In Gar Anthony Haywood's D.C. "travelogue" called *Bad News Travels Fast* (1995), the senior Loudermilks, trying to track down the real killer so that their son Eddie would be released from custody on a murder rap, headed for the Mall where Eddie told them they could find one of the conspirators called Ahmed. Ahmed had a stand and sold souvenir T-shirts by the Washington Monument. The Loudermilks, on their first visit to D.C., had been on the Mall before but didn't know what it was called. They now decided that nothing drew your attention faster or held it longer than the Washington Monument. When they found Ahmed, he first offered them a deal on T-shirts, then gave them an address on 14th Street less than a mile from Howard University which turned out to be a crack house.

Admire the monument yourself, then return left on 15th Street, passing the Sylvan Theater, where open-air productions of musicals, drama, and dance are performed, to Jefferson Drive. Turn right on Raoul Wallenberg Place (actually 15th Street). At the corner is the U.S. Holocaust Memorial Museum, which opened in 1993. There are no mystery references to this very moving exhibit about the fate of the Jews in Hitler's Nazi empire, but it is certainly about mass murder. The street was renamed for the Swedish diplomat stationed in Budapest who tried to save Hungarian Jews and lost his own life in the process.

In Van Wyck Mason's *The Washington Legation Murders* (1935), Captain Hugh North of Army's G2 Intelligence and his old crony at the British Embassy, Major Bruce Kilgour, were pursuing an elusive international spy known as the Guardsman, who was selling intelligence secrets to the highest bidder. The Guardsman's spies murdered Swedish Count Erich Oxenstahl of the Swedish legation who was working with them.

Leave the Holocaust Museum to go left to the Bureau of Engraving. It is not a murder site in mysteries, but the presses which turn out $450 million per day would inevitably appeal to certain criminal types.

In Elliott Roosevelt's *Murder in the Rose Garden* (set in 1936), President Franklin D. Roosevelt routinely was driven from the White House to the railroad sidings near the Bureau of Engraving to board his presidential car without nosy reporters watching. His crippled state—the result of polio—was carefully hidden as much as possible during his terms of office. But there is considerable flak from the disabled because his memorial does not show FDR in a real wheelchair, only a chair with a small wheel on each leg.

In *Full Disclosure* (1977), his mystery about President Sven Ericson, who suddenly became blind in office, William Safire commented that with TV coverage, even FDR could not have kept his polio hidden as he did, but would have been an object of pity.

Continue on Wallenberg Place to East Basin Drive along the edge of the Tidal Basin. The Tidal Basin was created in 1882 from the Potomac River, which used to flood the White House south lawn on occasion. It helps to control the river's height and protects the reclaimed land of Potomac Park. It was first made famous as a "recreational spot" by Representative Wilber Mills's evening escapade with call girl "Fanne Foxe." When Fanne Foxe jumped out to avoid Mills's attentions, Mills drove his car right into the Tidal Basin. Mills retired from Congress two years later in 1974. Many congressmen and senators seem to engage in similar pursuits in D.C. mysteries, from Congressman Dirksen in Elliott Roosevelt's *The White House Pantry Murder* (set in 1939), to William Cohen and Thomas Allen's dead Senator Charles Bristow in *Murder in the Senate* (1993). Power certainly has its perks.

From the '60s on, running and jogging around the Mall

monuments has been a popular exercise in mysteries. In James Grady's *Runner in the Street* (1984), PI John Rankin, a former legman for syndicated columnist Frank Size (aka Jack Anderson) lived in a third-floor apartment on Pennsylvania Avenue east of the Capitol. (See Walk 4.) Rankin regularly ran west past the Capitol, down the Hill, and over the Mall to the Washington Monument, on to the Reflecting Pool and the Lincoln Memorial, and all the way back home again.

In Krandall Kraus's *The President's Son* (1986), Elaine, the wife of the president's gay son D.J., and her old friend Jessica went jogging near the Tidal Basin. They had come from the White House, followed by two Secret Service agents whom Jessica tried to make time with. D.J. and Elaine's marriage, orchestrated by D.J.'s ruthlessly ambitious mother Claudia, was known to White House insiders as "the Arrangement." Inevitably, the Arrangement did not work out.

In David Baldacci's *Absolute Power* (1996), Commonwealth attorney Kate Whitney, burglar Luther Whitney's daughter and lawyer Jack Graham's ex-girlfriend ran along the Mall from the Air and Space Museum to the Tidal Basin in her Georgetown University Law School sweatshirt. Jack Graham "accidentally" bumped into Kate who twisted her ankle. Graham then drove her home and ended up defending her burglar father Luther against the president of the United States.

Follow the pathway to the Jefferson Memorial, built in 1934 to resemble the Roman Pantheon, whose design Jefferson had admired. In Barbara Michaels's *Patriot's Dream* (1976), Jefferson's important mentor, George Wythe of Williamsburg, who taught both Jefferson and future Chief Justice John Marshall at the College of William and Mary, was called the "forgotten man of the American Revolution." There is no memorial to Wythe here nor to George Mason of Alexandria who also "put words in Jefferson's eloquent mouth."

In Noel Hynd's *Truman's Spy* (set in 1950), as the intelligence community, including the FBI and the new CIA, tried to come to grips with the Cold War, D.C. had the coldest winter in a dozen years. The cherry trees were hung with ice and there was a mantle of snow on the Jefferson and Lincoln Memorials.

In Margaret Truman's *Murder on Capitol Hill* (1981), Lydia James, a lawyer doing a special investigation on the murder of Senator Cale Caldwell for the Senate, met his son Cale Caldwell, Jr., at Hogate's at 9th and Maine Streets to pump him about the family. Hogate's, a fancy waterfront seafood restaurant, was just past the Washington Marina and the Capitol Yacht Club to the south of the Jefferson Memorial. If you want to take time out, go back left and find Maine Avenue and follow it south along the Potomac River to 9th Street past the Washington Marina to sample the crab cakes.

In Carey Roberts's *Pray God to Die* (1994), MPD homicide detectives Anne Fitzhugh and Don Dakota went back to the MPD Municipal Building after checking on their current murder case and ended up going on a drug bust during which Dakota accidentally shot a young woman while chasing the suspect. That night Anne went down Maine Avenue past the Jefferson Memorial and across the 14th Street Bridge to the Washington Marina where Dakota had his houseboat moored.

Cross the Inlet Bridge beyond the Jefferson Memorial past the Japanese cherry trees, which were donated long before Pearl Harbor. In the mysteries by Diplomat, *Murder in the State Department* (1930) and *Murder in the Embassy* (1930), the Japanese were our friends and allies in preserving western civilization.

One of the most bizarre episodes occurred in reporter Bill Goode's *The Senator's Nude* (1947), where a dead young woman was found in Senator Caleb Casper Smudge's bed. In protest, the "Girls of Seventy-Six," singing their marching song that began "From the Hall of Constitution," jumped poor park policeman Hubert Hornblow and chopped down scores of the cherry trees.

Admire the cherry trees (if in season) and continue westward along West Potomac Park. The Mall's newest monument, the FDR (Franklin Delano Roosevelt) Memorial has been in the works ever since Roosevelt's death in office in 1945. Funding for the monument was finally obtained by Florida's Senator Claude Pepper, senior citizen advocate extraordinaire. This particular location was a place Capital architect Pierre L'Enfant had reserved for a monument when he first planned the city. (It was also the last location where one could be built to harmonize with the existing ones.)

In Ron Nessen and Johanna Neuman's *Knight and Day* (1995), a caller to Jerry Knight's talk show taunted guest Drake Dennis, an environmentalist, with playing on the Big Green Machine in the Public Interest Softball league in West Potomac Park. Accused of bashing softballs, then of murdering his friend, environmentalist Calvin Davenport, Dennis went ballistic on the air.

Follow West Basin Drive around the Tidal Basin to Independence Drive near the western end of Kutz Bridge. As you turn left to walk along Independence Drive toward the Lincoln Memorial, you pass the newly dedicated Korean War Veterans Memorial. This is the first memorial to the conflict which was the "hot war" of the Cold War period and is now often called the "forgotten war."

In Helen MacInnes's *I and My True Love* (1952), the Korean War had just ended but its aftermath was affecting official Washington. One of her characters was returned Korean vet Lieutenant Robert Turner who had little time for the D.C. pols and media moguls who now made chums of the Chinese.

In Leslie Ford's *Washington Whispers Murder* (1953), the two sons of Rufus Brent, under consideration for a very important government post, had died within a day of one another in Korea. A bright young blackmailer who worked for Congressman Ham Vair (aka Joseph McCarthy), having stolen their letters, tried to pretend he had been their college chum so he could marry their sister and get the family fortune.

Look at the Korean War Memorial and then walk on to the Lincoln Memorial which is located at the far western end of the Mall in front of the Reflecting Pool. This memorial, designed to resemble the Parthenon in Athens despite arguments that it was pretentious for an American born in a log cabin, contains Daniel Chester French's monumental marble statue of a seated, brooding Lincoln and the texts of his Second Inaugural Address and the Gettysburg Address. Completed in 1922, it was the site of the historic concert given by African-American Marian Anderson in 1939 and the "I Have a Dream" speech of Martin Luther King, Jr., made to the participants in the 1963 March on Washington.

In Diplomat's *Murder in the State Department* (1930), pompous little Undersecretary of State Robert K. Pelton rollerskated down the corridor at State the night his archrival, Undersecretary of State Harrison Howard, was found stabbed to death at his desk with a steel filing spike. When the alarm was raised, Pelton beat it outside and threw his skates in the Lincoln Memorial.

The most exciting encounter here was the episode the newspapers labeled "Pyscho Grandma on Drugs Visits the Lincoln Memorial" in Gar Anthony Haywood's hilarious *Bad News Travels Fast* (1995). As the last effort by retirees Dottie and Joe Loudermilk to clear their son Eddie of a murder rap, they made a date with the real killer at the Lincoln Memorial with its big crowds and park rangers. They had promised to hand over a very newsworthy diary of a senator's love life but the killer, who claimed to have Eddie, took off down the Mall. Big Joe (an ex-cop) chased him while Dottie created a diversion to get the attention of the security guard by yelling out, "I saw his eyes move!" She dashed about, trying to drag other tourists to look at Honest Abe, with the security guard chasing her, until two MPD officers came and handcuffed her and led her away to a squad car with Joe trailing sheepishly after her.

George P. Pelecanos's *The Big Blowdown* (1996) is a grim look back in time at 1940s postwar Washington, D.C., which described its returned vets, facing segregation, mafia-like police and gangsters, and fighting to make a living and retain control of their city from the increasing hordes of bureaucrats. Greek Pete Karras and his lifelong buddy Italian Joe Recevo considered themselves real Washingtonians, who had nothing to do with those government types who were permanent tourists! Recevo scornfully asked Karras if he'd ever visited the Capitol or taken the White House tour, and Karras told him he went to the Lincoln Memorial one night to make out.

Walk past the Lincoln Memorial to your left and take Harry Bacon Drive to the Vietnam Veterans Memorial Wall, usually just called the Wall. It is a stark V-shaped black marble wall inscribed with the names of all those who died or were listed as missing in the Vietnam War, and its design caused the most controversy of any monument in Washington. It was dedicated in 1982 and has become one of the city's most visited sites.

Benjamin M. Schutz's *A Tax in Blood* (1987) opened at the Wall where PI Leo Haggerty and his girlfriend Samantha had gone with Haggerty's sidekick, 'Nam vet Arnie Kendall. Haggerty noticed that the Wall appeared suddenly, the way Stonehenge does in the English fields. To get to it you have to walk past the statue of the men guarding their dead comrades but Haggerty felt that not going past them would be "sneaking in."

He began to read the names, but there were too many names and they multiplied as he walked along. Ahead of him Arnie stood and snapped a salute; he had found a friend. A little boy named Jimmy, there with his mother, told Arnie that the name of his uncle, for whom he was named—James Tucker Calhoun—was on the Wall, and Arnie lifted him up to touch it. Later that same day a terrorist group set off a bomb at the Wall that killed nineteen innocent people, among them Jimmy and his mother, and scarred the Wall itself.

In Peter Crowther's short story "Dumb Animals" in *Danger in D.C.* (1993), redneck Sonny Curtis was leaning against the memorial with a cat in a basket beside him. He had come to Washington to be with Clinton in Camelot 2, but he had stabbed a man in a bar who wanted his fancy shirt, then run out with the cat. The stranger's friends tracked him to the Wall where he asked them to let the cat go, which they did after shooting him.

In Richard T. Chizmar's short story "A Capital Cat

Crime" from the same collection, another homeless man called Michael Flowers also went to the Vietnam Wall "to visit some friends." Next he went to an abandoned house near the river where he found a group of cats in a glass box. They were part of a secret CIA investigation which resulted in his being terminated, too.

In Jeremiah Healy's *Rescue* (1995), Boston PI John Cuddy came to Washington en route to Florida to rescue a boy named Eddie who was being victimized by a sect because of his birthmark (the Mark of Cain). Before he flew out of D.C., Cuddy took a cab to the Vietnam Memorial. He told the cabby he couldn't see it, but the cabby told him it was there, word of honor! He also recommended starting with the cluster—the bronze statue of three soldiers in fatigues. Cuddy was surprised to find the monument was not made of black marble but granite. He walked the length of the Wall once, just to get used to it.

In Maryland Representative Barbara Mikulski and Marylouise Oates's *Capitol Offense* (1996), newly appointed Senator Eleanor Gorzack's husband, John Joseph Gorzack, was a Vietnam MIA. Once she became a senator her chief concern, beyond learning the ropes and trying to handle her inherited staffers, was to get on the Select Committee on MIAs and push for more information about them. She managed to get the appointment, then went to Vietnam where the authorities gave her her husband's ring and identification including dog tags and rings from sixteen other MIAs. Back home, she gave Jack a proper Arlington Cemetery military funeral, then Senator Gorzack, who liked to sit near the Vietnam Memorial, went there with a slip of paper on which she had printed "Capt. Jack Gorzack, USMC." When a park ranger asked if he could help her copy a name, she said she was adding a name and tucked it into the flowers left at the base of the Wall.

Leave the Wall to take the path to your right past the Constitution Gardens beside an ornamental lake, whose resident ducklings kept disappearing. When the lake was drained, it turned out that the ducklings were being eaten whole by giant catfish.

Continue on the path to your left to reach Constitution Avenue at 17th Street. At the southwest corner of 17th and Constitution Avenue you come to the Lock Keeper's House, once used as a weighing station for barges when they transferred from the C&O Canal to the Canal of Tiber Creek (see Walk 7). It is now used to store landscaping equipment. Tiber Creek Canal was planned by L'Enfant to carry presidents (and supplies) by water to the Capitol. But the canal became a muddy sewer and obsolete when railroads could carry goods more easily, and by 1870 Boss Shepherd, busy improving the Capital, covered it over.

In Richard Conroy's *The India Exhibition* (1992), the Smithsonian's Henry Scruggs put together an India exhibit which turned out to be an insurance scam worked by a wily Indian diplomat. Exhibit designer Violet Strauss also disappeared, and it turned out she had been murdered and her body tossed through a trapdoor in the ground floor of a storeroom at the National Museum of American History into the Tiber. (See Walk 2.)

Go right on Constitution Avenue to 15th Street and take 15th Street to Jefferson Drive to return to the Smithsonian Metro Station to end this walk.

4

CAPITOL HILL WALK

BACKGROUND

This walk covers not only Capitol Hill but the neighborhood behind it with important institutions like the Library of Congress, the Supreme Court, and Union Station. This is clearly the place where R. B. Dominic's tart comment in *There Is No Justice* (1971) that D.C. was preeminently a city of talkers applies the best.

Capital planner Pierre L'Enfant chose Jenkins Hill for the Capitol because it was a "pedestal waiting for a monument," and he made sure that all major avenues lead to it, not the White House. The numbering/lettering system of Washington's streets also begins at the Capitol, so there is a 1st Street in front of the Capitol and a 1st Street behind it, as well as two A Streets on either side of East Capitol Street.

Although Capitol Hill is one of the highest points in Washington, no one may put up a building taller than the Capitol. George Washington laid the cornerstone in 1793, and the first session of Congress was called to order here on November 22, 1800. In 1814 when the British burned Washington, they torched the Capitol, but despite its swamps and weather, the building was rebuilt in the same place. During the Civil War troops were quartered there and it served as a military hospital, but the work on the Capitol's dome was finished in 1863, and President Lincoln ordered that the construction of its two wings continue as a "sign that we intend the Union shall go on."

The City Canal, filled by Tiber Creek, flowed along what is now Constitution Avenue, but instead of being a scenic water route from the White House, it was a muddy, smelly ditch. D.C. "Boss" Shepherd covered it over as part of his city improvement program, then in 1874 Frederick Law Olmstead, the famous landscape architect who created New York's Central Park, laid out the grounds, adding the East and West Terraces and the West Front's marble stairway.

Although the public is always allowed free access to the Capitol, what you can see depends on whether or not Congress is in session. At any time nowadays you will find Capitol Police all over the Hill. They are the Congressional police force like the Secret Service that guards the President.

The Library of Congress was established in 1800 for the use of Congress. Originally kept at the Capitol, by 1897 the rapidly growing collection needed more room so its elaborate Beaux Arts Jefferson Building was built, followed later by the Adams and Madison buildings nearby. By law, it receives a copy of every book published in the United States.

Across East Capitol Drive is the starkly white neoclassic Supreme Court Building, a comparative newcomer to Capitol Hill. After the Court had used various chambers at the Capitol, Chief Justice (and former President) William Howard Taft persuaded Congress to allocate funds for this building, which was completed in 1935. Court sessions are open to the public on a first come, first served basis.

The neighborhood behind the Capitol, which stretches east to the Eastern Market at D and 9th Streets and south to Fort McNair and the Navy Yard where the Potomac and Anacostia Rivers meet, was where L'Enfant expected D.C. to live. But the city moved westward toward the White House instead, partly because taxes were lower there. Southeast Washington has brick-paved streets with rows of nineteenth-century townhouses that are being gentrified but it still does not have the cachet of a Georgetown, Foggy Bottom, or Alexandria, and in many mysteries it is described as a ghetto or a slum.

The massive Beaux Arts Union Station at Massachusetts Avenue was built in 1907, replacing several railroad stations located on the Mall. (See Walk 2.) Chicago's Daniel Burnham was its architect, borrowing its grand designs from the Roman Baths of Diocletian and the Arch of Constantine. The station grew shabby in the '50s but has been rejuvenated with 100 shops, restaurants, a Metro station, and fast trains like the Metroliner which runs up and down the Eastern corridor.

Length of Walk: About 2½ miles

It is 1½ miles to the Capitol, another mile to Union Station. The walk is divided into two parts, which you can either do in a day or do separately. Unless Congress is in special session, the time to do this walk is on a weekday when everything is open.

See the map on page 91 for the boundaries of this walk and page 269 for a list of the books and detectives mentioned.

Places of Interest

Bartholdi Fountain, 1st Street and Independence Avenue. Frédéric-Auguste Bartholdi who designed the Statue of Liberty created the fountain for the country's 100th birthday in 1876, celebrated in Philadelphia.

The Capitol, on Capitol Hill's sixty-eight acres. Free. Open daily 9:00 A.M.–4:30 P.M. (Tours 9:00 A.M.–3:45 P.M.) Summer hours may vary but Rotunda and Statuary Hall typically open daily 9:00 A.M.–8:00 P.M. Closed Thanksgiving, Christmas, and New Year's Day. For guide service call 225-6827.* To watch Congress in session you need a gallery pass from your senator or representative. Call 224-3121 or ask a Capitol police officer. In its column "Today in Congress" the *Washington Post*, which acts as America's "court circular," carries a daily listing of committee meetings.

*The telephone area code is 202 unless otherwise indicated.

Eastern Market, 8th to 9th Streets at D Street. An 1873 building housing D.C.'s last open market, now the center of a group of small shops and restaurants.

Folger Shakespeare Library, 201 E. Capitol Hill Street. Mon.–Sat. 10:00 A.M.–4:00 P.M. Closed federal holidays. Free. Call 544-7077.

House Office Buildings: Rayburn, Longworth, and Cannon, C Street from 1st Street to 1st Street. Open when Congress is in session.

Library of Congress:

Jefferson Building, East Capitol Street between 1st Street and 2nd Street. Open Mon.–Sat. 10:00 A.M.–5:30 P.M. Closed Sun. and major holidays. Visitor Center on ground level. Free. Call 707-8000 for tour information.

Madison Building, C Street between 1st and 2nd Streets. Open Mon.–Fri. 8:30 A.M.–9:30 P.M., Sat. 8:30 A.M.–6:00 P.M. Free.

Senate Office Buildings: Russell, Dirksen, and Hart, Constitution Avenue from Delaware Avenue to 2nd Street. Open when Congress is in session.

Sewell-Belmont House, 144 Constitution Avenue. Oldest home (1800) on Capitol Hill, now headquarters of the National Woman's Party. Women's Movement Museum. Open Tues.–Fri. 10:00 A.M.–3:00 P.M., Sat. noon–4:00 P.M. Free. Call 546-3989.

Supreme Court, 1st Street and East Capitol Street. Open weekdays 9:00 A.M.–4:30 P.M. Closed weekends and federal holidays. Free. Court convenes first Monday in October and stays in session until all cases have been heard in late June. Two lines for visitors: a quick look through or stay and listen to justices deliberate. If Court is not in session, free lectures given in the main courtroom 9:30 A.M.– 3:30 P.M. every hour on the half hour. Call 479-3000.

Union Station, 50 Massachusetts Avenue. Open daily twenty-four hours. Contains 100 shops on three levels open Mon.–Sat. 10:00 A.M.–9:00 P.M., Sun. noon–6:00 P.M. Free. Metro: Union Station, skylit Main Concourse, a nine-screen movie theater, restaurants, and of course trains to and from D.C.

Restaurants, rest rooms, taxis, Metro, and Washington's Trolley Tours all available here.

United States Botanic Gardens, 100 Maryland Avenue. Charming old-fashioned glass conservatory buildings, with seasonal displays at Christmas, Easter. Open daily 9:00 A.M.–5:00 P.M. Free. Call 225-8333.

Washington Design Center, 300 D Street SW. Art on the seventh floor. The 1996 Show was organized by William Wooby of the Collector. Mon.–Sat. 10:00 A.M.–5:00 P.M. Call 479-2572.

PLACES TO EAT

U.S. Botanic Gardens' Summer Terrace, Independence Avenue and 1st Street. Picnic at outdoor tables in the rose garden.

The Capitol:

Dirksen Senate Office Building's South Buffet Room, 1st and C Streets. All-you-can-eat buffet and do-it-yourself sundaes in an Art Deco setting. Arrive there via the free Capitol subway (ask Capitol Police for directions). Call 224-4249.

House of Representatives Restaurant, Room H118. High ceilings and gilt-framed mirrors. House lunch specialty: Bean Soup. Call 225-6300.

Senate Public Dining Room, first floor on Senate side of Capitol. Serves Senate Bean Soup.

Library of Congress, James Madison Building, 101 Independence Avenue. Sixth-floor cafeteria with a view, adjoining the Montpelier Room Restaurant with midday buffet. Call 707-8300.

Supreme Court, lower-level cafeteria and snack bar popular with D.C. staffers and tourists.

Union Station, Massachusetts Avenue at Columbus Circle.

America, located in the main waiting room of the station.

B. Smith's, located in the Presidential Suite where presidents once greeted visiting VIPs. Call 289-6188.

Food Court, lower-level food vendors of every description operating cafeteria-style. Open twenty-four hours a day seven days a week.

CAPITOL HILL WALK

Begin your walk at the Federal Center Metro Station at 3rd and D Streets. The Washington Design Center is at 300 D Street where William (Bill) Wooby, who ran the Collector Gallery and Restaurant, put on a gallery show called "Art on the Seventh Floor" during 1996. It included artists mentioned in Margaret Truman's *Murder at the National Gallery* (1990). (See Walk 5.)

Take 3rd Street to C Street. In general this is a heavily bureaucratic part of Washington. To your left on 4th Street is the Voice of America and two blocks away at Independence and 6th Street is NASA. You are passing the Department of Health and Human Services.

In Robert Travers's *The Apartment on K Street* (1972), when Education was still part of HEW (Health, Education, and Welfare), Miss Penny, a tenant in the apartment on K Street, worked at HEW. When John Keefer took Miss Penny hostage, then agreed to let her go, she asked him to drop her at her office. She thought Keefer was on drugs when he was actually in charge of an atomic bomb, hidden in the basement of their building.

In P. M. Carlson's *Bad Blood* (1991), Ginny Marshall, an adopted teenager, disappeared to track down her birth mother. Ginny's grandmother told her bridge buddies, one of whom, Marie Deaver, had worked for Lyndon Johnson's War on Poverty at the Department of Health and Human Services. Her revelation led to murder.

Go to Independence Avenue and turn right to cross 2nd Street to the U.S. Botanic Gardens at 1st Street and Maryland Avenue. Built in 1931 it has two old-fashioned domes and a tearoom open Sundays for brunch.

In Charles McCarry's *Shelley's Heart* (1995), the president was threatened with impeachment by WASP extremists. Their plot was foiled by the brilliant Constitutional maneuvering of alcoholic Speaker of the House Tucker Attenborough. Attenborough met secretly with the president's lawyer at the Botanic Gardens, which was the Speaker's favorite place

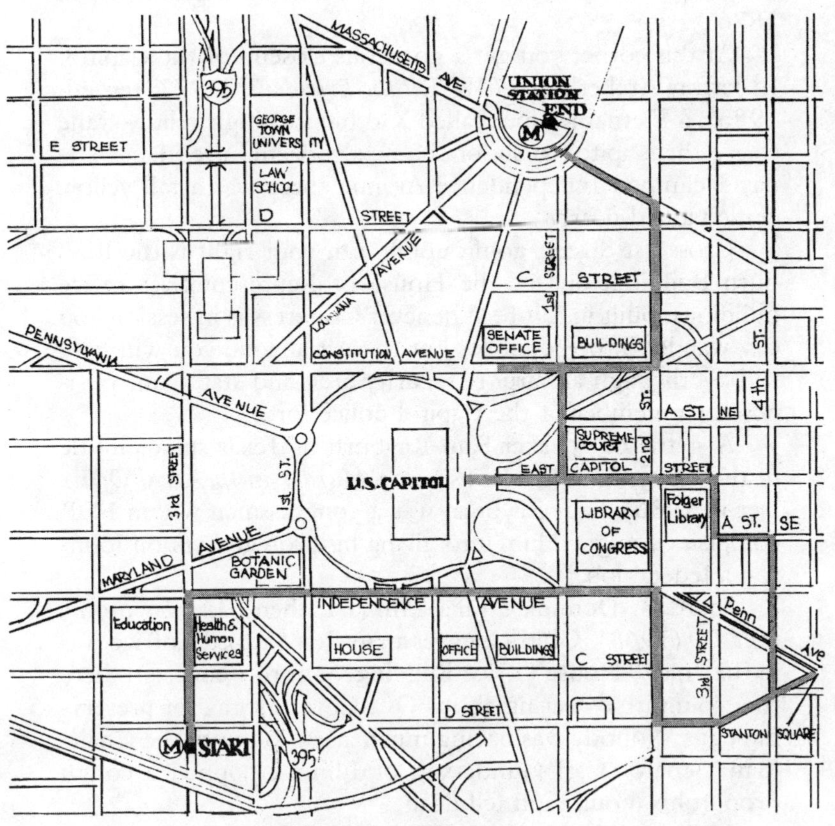

Walk 4: Capitol Hill

to think in private. He had gotten it the money for its elaborate sprinkler system.

Across Independence Drive from the Botanic Gardens is the bronze Bartholdi Fountain, by the same artist who did the Statue of Liberty for the nation's Centennial at Philadelphia in 1876.

At this corner you get a gorgeous closeup of the Capitol. In Jeffrey Archer's *Shall We Tell the President?* (1977; rev. ed. 1985), a Vietnam sniper called Xan hid in a high yellow crane above the Capitol to shoot the newly elected president. The day I climbed Independence Avenue there was a tall yellow crane parked nearby.

Cross 1st Street, going uphill. On your right is the Rayburn Building, one of the House of Representatives office buildings, built in 1965. Whenever Congress is in session you can wander into the lobby, but to visit anyone you will have to pass through an airport security arch and state your business to a member of the Capitol police force.

A statue of Speaker Sam Rayburn of Texas stands inside in the lobby. In Elliot Roosevelt's *Murder in the Oval Office* (set in 1936), Sam Rayburn was a congressman whom FDR complained bugged him into giving his protégé Lyndon Johnson a federal job.

In R. B. Dominic's (aka Emma Lathen) *Murder Sunny Side Up* (1968), Ohio Congressman Ben Safford's office was in the "new" House Office Building. Safford went from there to a committee hearing about Ova-Cote, a spray for preserving eggs. Nobody was paying much attention until the Chairman, Senator Carl Gunderson of Illinois, popped a cough drop in his mouth and fell dead.

In Dominic's *Murder in High Place* (1970), Congressman Safford returned to his office after an afternoon spent on the floor of the House to find his secretary listening outside the door of his administrative assistant Doug Travers. Travers was being yelled at by Karen Kimball Jenkins. Jenkins, a Sears Scholar, single mother, and veteran of Chicago (demonstrations), had been booted out of Nuevador for appearing at the basilica in a bikini. Jenkins had tried to get redress from the

State Department and the Sears foundation. Now she was trying her congressman.

In P. M. Carlson's *Murder in the Dog Days* (1991), a pregnant Maggie Ryan, husband Nick, and daughter Sarah were visiting in Virginia to avoid New York's dog days of August when they got mixed up in the murder of reporter Dale Colby. Colby had been checking into the crash of a small plane that carried some of Ohio Congressman Knox's staff and that Knox himself had meant to take. Typically, Maggie followed up leads in person, even jumping the gun on the police, and went to talk with Representative Knox in his office on the Hill.

In Carey Roberts's *Pray God to Die* (1994), Caroline McKelvey was an aide to Congressman Jim Woodward, who was about to be appointed to an environmental Cabinet post. Caroline had been spying on Woodward for ABC-TV reporter Simone Gray. After her murder Metropolitan Police Department homicide detectives Anne Fitzhugh and Don Dakota came to the Rayburn Building to interview Woodward's staff in his corner office with its thick carpets and signed VIP photos. Fitzhugh and Dakota also went to the Longworth Building where Congressman Woodward was holding a press conference and overheard Gray tell Woodward he was a bastard and she would pull him down. The detectives caught up with Simone Gray on Capitol Hill doing a "live report" under the "TV tree" with her crew.

In Gar Anthony Haywood's *Bad News Travels Fast* (1995), the man who broke into Joe and Dottie Loudermilk's trailer turned out to be Harris Murphy of the Capitol Police. Murphy had been tailing them all over D.C. to protect Senator Graham Wildman from blackmail.

In Margaret Truman's *Murder in the House* (1997), President Joe Scott had just nominated Congressman Paul Latham to be secretary of state. Latham had a suite on the north side of the Rayburn Building overlooking the Capitol. It was painted a dull tan, like all the offices on that side; those on the other side were all robin's egg blue. But before he was confirmed, Latham was shot to death in a tiny Capitol Hill park, then two Russian mafia hit men burst into his office, shot his Chief of Staff Bob Mondrian, and kidnaped Latham's daughter Molly, a House page.

Come out of the Rayburn Building and cross Capitol Street to the Longworth House Office Building, built in 1933. Speaker Nicholas Longworth served in the House from 1909 and was Speaker from 1925 to 1931. He was married to one of D.C.'s Grande Dames, Alice Roosevelt, daughter of President Teddy Roosevelt. Known for her tart tongue, she "ruled" Washington for many years, greatly enjoying her public feuds with Cissy Patterson, a scion of Chicago's Medill-McCormick-Patterson newspaper family and publisher of the *Washington Times-Herald*.

Come out of the Longworth Building and cross New Jersey Avenue to Cannon, the oldest House office building. It was built in 1908 and is a "twin" to the Russell Building, the first Senate Office Building, on the other side of the Hill.

In mysteries written before 1965 you can't always tell if the author meant the Longworth or the Cannon Building. In Mary Plum's *Death of a Redhaired Man* (c. 1945), for example, Jerry Vale was a congressman's secretary who was sent down to Florida by Congressman Meriden to pick up some information about Russ Odden, whom Meriden's daughter Kate was determined to marry.

Nor is it obvious in Barbara D'Amato's short story "Freedom of the Press" in *Danger in D.C.* (1993), where Chicago reporter Cat Marsala interviewed new Chicago Representative Peggy Nicklis. Marsala found Nicklis in a shabby old office with noisy pipes, a small window, a plush blue cat bed and litter box, and a cat called Mugum (MGM). Peggy told Cat that the office was all about how important you are and this one was definitely a starter office because the nearest bathroom for women was seven flights of stairs away!

Come out of the Cannon House Office Building on Independence Avenue and cross 1st Street to walk past the James Madison Memorial Building of the Library of Congress to 2nd Street where you join Pennsylvania Avenue. Go right on

2nd Street past Le Bon Cafe, which has a lot in common with the Capitol Hill Deli, where Gar Anthony Hayward's Loudermilks picked up vital clues in *Bad News Travels Fast* (1995).

You are in the Capitol Hill Historic District with its brick sidewalks and wrought-iron fences. You pass old Federal row houses and a church or two as you walk down 2nd Street. Cross C Street and keep going to D Street and Folger Square. Then turn left at the north side of Folger Square to walk along D Street to 4th Street. Many of the houses have been cut up into apartments in which many Congressional staffers live.

In Jon L. Breen's "Rachel and the Bookstore Cat" in *Danger in D.C.* (1993), L.A. bookstore owner Rachel Hennings went to D.C. to check out a collection of modern first editions. She stayed with Gus and Emma Ordway, who operated Ordway's Bookshop on D Street near the Capitol and Congressional office buildings. The Ordways were an "odd couple." Emma was not yet thirty and looked like a Vogue model, but Gus was fifty and dressed like a beatnik. They once reversed their styles for a Malice Domestic banquet to show that they could. (See Walk 5.)

Gus and Emma had a fat feline called Oswald who had the run of the bookstore. One regular customer from the CIA and another from the House Intelligence Committee both wanted a $2,000 book that Oswald the cat peed on, but it turned out that the cat had been framed.

Straight ahead of you at D and 7th Street is Eastern Market, worth a side trip if you have the time. In Carolyn Banks's *The Girls on the Row* (1983), there was a little stand of houses known as "the Row" across from a playground and about four blocks from Eastern Market. All around the Row old houses were being gentrified, but this group stayed derelict because of the much-publicized murder of young Faye Arensburg at the mansion on the corner. Faye's neighbors like Jessie Wood Trotter preferred not to think about it, but Senator Aubrey Denton persuaded wealthy Claire Albritten to buy the house and move in. Then Claire, too, was murdered.

In George P. Pelecanos's *Down by the River Where the Dead Men Go* (1995), PI-cum-bartender Nick Stefanos worked part-time at the Spot, a neighborhood bar at 8th and G Streets, two blocks south of Eastern Market.

Still farther south on 4th Street is the birthplace of J. Edgar Hoover, the man who put the FBI on the map. According to the Gordons in *Power Play* (1965), before Hoover's appointment in 1924 American kids wanted to grow up to be gangsters, but after Hoover they wanted to be G-Men. Gordon Gordon was an ex-FBI agent, and the most famous mystery he and his wife wrote became a movie called *That Darned Cat*, which Disney Productions redid in 1997.

J. Edgar Hoover often appeared in Elliott Roosevelt's mysteries about First Lady Eleanor Roosevelt, where Hoover was a publicity-hunting, self-important clown whom FDR liked to call "John Edgar." In *Murder and the First Lady* (set in 1939), Eleanor asked FDR how much longer he had to tolerate that man. FDR replied that if he fired him it would mean a fight with Congress.

In Robert Ludlum's *The Chancellor Manuscript* (1977), a secret group known as Inver Brass conspired to murder J. Edgar Hoover because of his unethical use of his private files. But when he was dead they discovered that files M through Z were missing!

In Ross Thomas's *If You Can't Be Good* (1973), syndicated D.C. columnist Frank Size exposed the fact that Senator Robert F. Ames accepted a $50,000 bribe to make a speech on Senate floor favoring a business merger. When Ames resigned, Size hired Decatur Lucas to find out why Ames blew his own career. Lucas, who was working on his Ph.D. at the Library of Congress, lived near the Navy Yard on 4th Street in a narrow eighty-year-old redbrick house close to where J. Edgar Hoover was born.

In Thomas's *Ah, Treachery!* (1994), when "rainmaker" Millicent Altford was robbed of over a million dollars of campaign money, she hired cashiered ex-Major Edd "Twodees" Partain. One of the bad guys after her was Emory Kite, a dwarfish killer for hire who lived in a tiny two-story house in the 400 block of 4th Street, a pleasant stroll from both the Library of Congress and the birthplace of J. Edgar Hoover.

Much of Capitol South has been a slum for a long time. In Louisa Revell's *The Men with Three Eyes* (1955), murders took place near a settlement house run by young Ruth Gibson. In James Patterson's *Along Came a Spider* (1992), MPD's African-American Deputy Chief of Detectives Alex Cross lived on 5th Street with his two kids and his grandmother "Nana Mama," who had raised him. Cross was sent to cover the kidnaping of two VIP children, Maggie Rose Dunne and Michael Goldberg, from a very select Georgetown school.

Farther south you come to the Washington Navy Yard on the Anacostia River, which with Fort McNair was established to guard the junction of the Anacostia and Potomac Rivers. Much of the actual riverside now boasts a number of upscale housing complexes and restaurants.

In G. J. A. O'Toole's *The Cosgrove Report* (set in 1867), Pinkerton agent Nicholas Cosgrove was hired by Secretary of War Stanton to make sure John Wilkes Booth was really dead and buried at the Washington Navy Yard. Cosgrove had the coffin dug up, only to discover that there was no body in the unmarked grave.

In Margaret Truman's *Murder at the National Cathedral* (1990), a British spy named Brett Leighton was secretly flown into the Navy Yard to resolve Anglo-American problems related to the murder of Canon Paul Singletary of the National Cathedral. Singletary's murder was part of an Asian financial manipulation of a worldwide peace mission.

In Pelecanos's *Down by the River Where the Dead Men Go* (1995), drunken Nick Stefanos drove his vintage Dodge past the Washington Navy Yard to the area near the 11th Street Bridge off the road down by the riverside. Before he passed out, Nick heard another car, a scream, a shot, and a splash. In the morning he found a young black man in the water, shot dead.

Unless you want to hike to the rivers, take D Street to 3rd Street, then take North Carolina Avenue, which runs on a diagonal, to Pennsylvania Avenue. (Both North Carolina and

Pennsylvania Avenue bisect Seward Square.) Cross Pennsylvania Avenue to 4th Street and continue to walk north back to Independence Avenue.

Stay on 4th Street, crossing Seward Avenue, then Independence Avenue where there is a church on the corner. Keep going until you reach 4th and A Street SE. This is home turf for James Grady who lived on A Street SE and walked this way each day on his way to work. It was also the way he sent his CIA agent Ronald Malcolm.

Later in 1990 Grady explained that in 1972 he was in D.C. from the hinterlands as a Sears Congressional Journalism Intern, working for a congressional staff and being taught at night by a new breed of "investigative reporters"—perhaps Woodward and Bernstein?

Cross 4th Street and keep going east to 3rd Street, passing by St. Mark's Church. In Grady's time the American Historical Association was located across from St. Mark's between 3rd and 4th Streets, but he never saw anyone go in or out. Grady thought it would be great if that building were a CIA front; then he wondered what he would do if he came back from lunch and found everybody in his office murdered!

As a result, in *Six Days of the Condor* (1974), this obscure building housed the CIA's Department 17 whose job was to keep track of all acts of espionage recorded in literature. Department 17 read spy thrillers and murder mysteries, creating files that went back as far as James Fenimore Cooper. The department also received brief descriptions from Langley (CIA headquarters) of actual events and compared fact and fiction. If there were major correlations, they made a more detailed report about the author and whether he knew more than he should! In addition their files contained lists of helpful tips for agents looking for new tricks. The job sounds like a mystery buff's dream of heaven.

Ronald Malcolm, whose CIA code name was Condor, was sent to get the departmental lunches and when he came back he found everyone else murdered. He called the CIA panic line from a public phone, then hid by joining a line of Iowa

City Jaycees touring the Capitol until it was time to meet other agents waiting for him in Georgetown. In *Condor*, Grady helped destroy the CIA myth that all its agents were heroic boy scouts, but he kept alive the American Dream of the ordinary guy who beats the bad guys at their own game.

Only two blocks to your right (north) there is another A Street. At 316 A Street NE you would find the house of African-American Frederick Douglass before he moved to Cedar Hill. It was also the original home of the Smithsonian's Museum of African Art, which moved to the Smithsonian Quad in 1987. (See Walk 2.)

Then turn left to walk along A Street to 3rd Street. You pass by the Romanesque St. Mark's Episcopal Church which has some Tiffany windows. On your left across 3rd Street is the John Adams Building, part of the Library of Congress.

Turn right at 3rd Street and go to East Capitol Street to the front entrance of the Folger Shakespeare Library. The Folger was privately endowed by Amherst College graduate Henry Clay Folger, who was CEO of Standard Oil of New York. Built to encourage research and public appreciation of Shakespeare, the Folger contains the world's largest collection of Shakespeare's works. It also has a 190-foot-long Elizabethan Great Hall and a reproduction of an Elizabethan theater in which both concerts and plays are performed. There is also an Elizabethan garden.

Recent excavations at Jamestown have discovered a real link to Elizabethan England and Will Shakespeare's play *The Tempest*. The archaeologists have dug up the brass signet ring of William Strachey, whose 1609 account of a Bermuda shipwreck is generally considered to be Shakespeare's source for his play. (See also Walk 8.)

In James M. Cain's *The Institute* (1976), scholar-cum-football star Dr. Lloyd Palmer, who taught at the University of Maryland, wrote his dissertation on Shakespeare and the Dark Lady of the Sonnets and probably did his research at the Folger. Now Palmer wanted twenty-two million dollars to establish a national institute of biography with himself as director.

In Carolyn Banks's *The Girls on the Row* (1983), the first murder victim on the Row was Faye Arensberg, an attractive set designer at the Folger. Her murder even made *Time.*

There have been several panels and discussions about King Richard III of England at Malice Domestic mystery conventions. Malice Ghost of Honor in 1996 was Josephine Tey, whose *The Daughter of Time* (1952) was the topic of a panel chaired by Dean James, coauthor with Jean Swanson of Agatha Award–winning *By a Woman's Hand* (1994), with Folger's acting Director Barbara Mowat, who had just edited a new edition of Shakespeare's *Richard III*, English Professor Douglas G. Greene, biographer of John Dickson Carr in *The Man Who Explained Miracles* (1995), and me. The panel decided that the case for or against Richard III as a murderer is still not proved. In Charles Goodrum's *Carnage of the Realm* (1979), the murders of D.C. coin collectors investigated by the Werner-Bok Library trio: Betty Crighton Jones, Edward George, and Steve Carson, turned out to hinge on a Ricardian coin known as a boar's head groat.

Explore the Folger. Then come outside and turn left on East Capitol Street to go one more block to the huge and magnificent Thomas Jefferson Building of the Library of Congress. Built from 1886 to 1892 in a magnificently ornate Beaux Arts style, it was based on the old Paris Opera House. It is now called the Thomas Jefferson Building, in memory of Jefferson's statement that "there is no subject to which a Member of Congress may not have occasion to refer. . . ." and the fact that when the British burned the first library in 1814 Jefferson sold his own private library to the government as a replacement.

It is now the largest library in the world and since 1864 has been open to the public. It receives (but does not always keep) a copy of every book published in the United States. The post of Librarian of Congress has been held by distinguished scholars, while the Library's resident string quartet, the Juilliard, regularly performs in the great hall. The title of Poet Laureate, conferred once a year, was instituted in 1985 with Robert Penn Warren, but beginning in 1937 there were official Consultants in Poetry who included most of America's best-known poets.

The Library owns a Gutenberg Bible, Jefferson's first draft of the Declaration of Independence, Lincoln's notes scribbled on an envelope for the Gettysburg Address, and other less familiar treasures like a *Bay Psalm Book* (the first book printed in America), part of the eclectic Batchelder Bequest given the Library by my world-traveling great-uncle, John Davis Batchelder.

In addition to the exhibits on display in the Great Hall, or hearing a concert there, look at the Main Reading Room because the Library of Congress is the first place anyone in a mystery goes when they need facts. It was greatly admired by Henry James, who appeared in Sarah Booth Conroy's historical mystery *Refinements of Love* (1993) and is known for his own mystery ghost story, *The Turn of the Screw*.

In Francis Bonnamy's *Dead Reckoning* (1943), spinster Miss Fly, an avid mystery reader of John Dickson Carr, went to the Library of Congress's stacks on an errand. When she reached the bottom of the steep circular stairs, she found the body of Hugh Matteson, who drew maps at the Bureau of Census. Although the murder smelled of buried treasure, Orson McCullough, head of the MPD's Homicide Department, and Francis Bonnamy had a hard time getting criminologist Peter Shane to help with the murder investigation.

In Aaron Marc Stern's *Death Takes a Paying Guest* (1947), Elsie Mae Hunt and Tim Mulligan were in D.C. to read some pre-Columbian manuscripts at the Library of Congress. After Elsie Mae found a roomer with a knife in his back at her rooming house on 19th Street, they had very little time for research.

In R. B. Dominic's *Murder Sunny Side Up* (1968), everyone present at the murder of Committee Chairman Carl Gunderson of Illinois during his committee's hearing on the safety of Ova-Cote headed for the Library of Congress. They all wanted to read the original technical report on this egg-preserving method.

In Jeffrey Archer's *Shall We Tell the President?* (1977; rev.

ed. 1985), FBI Special Agent Marc Andrews was secretly researching the schedules of the senators to find out which one was planning the assassination of the newly elected president. From the Main Reading Room Andrews was sent to Room 244, the Law Library Reading Room, to get the current *Congressional Record.*

In Charles Goodrum's *Dewey Decimated* (1977), the mythical Werner-Bok Library was on the Mall between the National History Museum and the National Gallery, but the Werner-Bok is a dead ringer for the Library of Congress. During a concert by the Kreutzer String Ensemble one staffer stabbed another in the stacks below over a scam which brought letters saying their Gutenberg Bible, Dead Sea Scrolls, etc., were fakes. One of the books questioned was Edgar Allan Poe's first work, *Tamerlane.* A professor from Baltimore who taught Poe had wanted to feel a real copy which he thought gave off special vibes, but the original was in surprisingly poor shape.

In Goodrum's *The Best Cellar* (1987), the original collection of the Library of Congress was hastily moved out of D.C. when the British burned it in 1814. Now the three sleuths, Betty Crighton Jones, Edward George, and Steve Carson, investigated the possibility that the original books were not lost but hidden in some Tidewater plantation basement so that Congress could pay poor Mr. Jefferson an enormous sum for his library. They became involved when a snoopy grad student discovered the secret but came to a sticky end.

In Barbara Michaels's (1989) mystery *Smoke and Mirrors,* she described both the fascination and squalor of politics and gave an excellent account of the daily life of a political campaign. Erin Hartsock, the daughter of a friend of Congresswoman Rosemary White Marshall who was running for Senate, got a job as all around gofer. Another staffer, Nick McDermott, and Erin hitched a ride with campaign manager Joe Esler into D.C. to see the sights. Joe dropped them at the Capitol, then they walked past the Jefferson and Adams buildings to the Madison, where they went into the Newspaper Room hoping to find references to an old fire.

In Michael Bowen's *Washington Deceased* (1990), the murder occurred in the basement of a minimum-security federal prison where former Senator Desmond Gardner was serving time for bribery. Another inmate, Sweet Tony Martinelli, was a Mob enforcer whom Gardner feared was out to murder him so he called his college daughter Wendy and asked her to enlist former Foreign Office diplomat Richard Michaelson's help. Michaelson sent Wendy to the Library of Congress where Wendy discovered Randy Cox, her dad's former chief of staff, had probably used the senator as a fall guy. In Bowen's *Corruptly Procured* (1994), an explosion at a Library of Congress reception gave a group of German nationalists time to steal the Gutenberg Bible.

In Richard Timothy Conroy's *The India Exhibition* (1992), former Foreign Officer Henry Scruggs, now at the Smithsonian, set up the India exhibition on K. V. Chandra—supposedly as important as Gandhi—with the aid of Violet Strauss. When Scruggs finally went to the Library to check up on K. V. Chandra, he found out that there were no references to Chandra in the card catalog!

In Charles McCarry's *Shelley's Heart* (1995), VIP reporter/columnist Ross Macalaster had been recruited by Franklin Mallory to cover the story of the stolen election. On Inauguration Day, Macalaster ducked into the Library of Congress. He sat in the Main Reading Room transcribing his secret interview with Mallory on a miniature computer; then he followed an older reporter, Montague Love, into the men's room, where he found Love mugged and his press badge gone. Macalaster raced toward the Capitol to warn the authorities but slipped on ice.

Come out of the Library of Congress. This is a good time to try the Madison Building's popular sixth-floor cafeteria with its great view down the Mall. Then take East Capitol Street to the Capitol to end the first part of the walk.

Begin the second part of the Capitol Hill Walk by going along East Capitol Street to the Capitol's East Terrace. Before you go inside look up at the dome above you with its bronze statue of Freedom. She is almost twenty feet high and was meant to wear the Roman slave's Cap of Freedom, but Senator Jefferson Davis objected so she got her feathered helmet with stars, which makes her look more like Pocahontas. In spite of some discussion, it was left unchanged when Freedom was renovated.

In Keats Patrick's *Death Is a Tory* (1935), the reporters covering the murders of Marshall Rich's wife and her lover were taken out to dinner by Congressman Gil Lightfoot. As they passed the floodlit Capitol, "Tom" Collins said the dome was actually too big for the building—a metaphor for Congress itself.

In Tom Clancy's *Executive Orders* (1996), a Japanese pilot in a 747 dive-bombed the Capitol, destroying the building and killing the president, Cabinet, and Congress, not to mention the Supreme Court justices. After hastily taking the Oath of Office, new President Jack Ryan went to view the disaster.

In Sam Greenlee's *The Spook Who Sat by the Door* (1969), black CIA agent Dan Freeman commented that within walking distance of the immaculate white center of D.C. lay some of the worst slums in the United States and that by controlling the capital like a colonial fiefdom the bigots made sure it would not change.

In James Grady's *Hard Bargains* (1984), PI John Rankin went to the Capitol and saw TV crews and tourists waiting to see the solar eclipse, but it was too muggy to see it (another metaphor for the times).

Although the public is always allowed free access to the building, what you see depends on whether or not Congress is in session. Security on the Hill has been taken very seriously since a group of Puerto Rican nationalists shot up the House of Representatives in 1950. All Capitol staffers, lobbyists, and others with business on Capitol Hill must wear IDs, there are metal detectors at all the entrances, and the chairs on the floor of the House have bulletproof steel plates in their backs.

In Marilyn Quayle and Nancy Northcott's *The Campaign* (1996), Senator Bob Grant of Georgia had to break into the Capitol to find evidence to clear his name of murder. He took the tunnel from the Russell Building and followed some tourists, with a fat file obscuring the ID he had borrowed from a member of his staff.

The East Terrace is the traditional site of outdoor presidential inaugurations, which began in 1817 when President Monroe was sworn in there so that neither the Senate nor the House could claim superiority. Elderly President William Henry Harrison caught cold there in 1841 and died within a month. There was an assassination threat against President Abraham Lincoln at his second inaugural and, as Pinkerton agent Nicholas Cosgrove reported in *The Cosgrove Report*, there is a photograph that shows all the plotters: John Wilkes Booth, Lewis Paine, George Atzerodt, David Herold, Edward Spangler, and John Surratt near Lincoln as he spoke! Ronald Reagan moved to the West Terrace in 1981, and his second inaugural was indoors in the Great Rotunda.

In Jeffrey Archer's *Shall We Tell the President?* (1977), President Ted Kennedy had just been inaugurated on January 20, 1981, when the FBI learned about a conspiracy to assassinate him on March 10 when he arrived to promote gun-control legislation. In Archer's 1985 edition, the president was a woman, Florentyne Kane.

In Charles McCarry's *Shelley's Heart* (1995), there were to be two ceremonies at the Capitol. One was the formal inauguration of "Frosty" Lockwood who had stolen the election; the other a press conference by ex-President Franklin Mallory. But a gunman in a white caftan shot Mallory's chief aide Susan Grant.

Walk inside the Great Rotunda with its famous allegorical fresco of George Washington and paintings of American history. You are on the main floor. The next (third) floor gives access to the galleries of the Senate and House chambers. The ground floor below has the crypt built for Washington and his wife, rest rooms, the Senate Chapel, offices, dining rooms, and the famous tunnels and underground subways. Each level is accessible by stair, escalator, or elevator.

The Rotunda is the place where the bodies of important members of Congress, Supreme Court justices, and presidents lie in state. For example, in Robert Ludlum's *The Chancellor*

Manuscript (1977), the body of murdered J. Edgar Hoover lay there. In Elliott Roosevelt's *Murder in the West Wing* (set in 1936), Untouchables' Eliot Ness told Eleanor Roosevelt that John Edgar wanted to be the nation's one and only cop, but he wasn't as smart as Capone. Since the Capitol was destroyed in Clancy's *Executive Orders* (1996), President Durling's body lay in state at the White House.

Tony Hillerman's fans all reminded me about *The Fly on the Wall* (1971), in which political reporter John Cotton became a crusader when his best friend jumped off the balcony of the Capitol Rotunda, but Hillerman was writing about state politics. He had been a political reporter, and at the 1995 Nottingham Bouchercon banquet I heard him compare notes with another ex-political reporter, Ed Gilbreth, the *Chicago Sun-Times* mystery reviewer.

In Stephen Coonts's *Under Siege* (1990), hired assassin Henry Charon shot down President Bush's helicopter, then killed the Senate majority leader just before a band of men armed with Uzis came into the Rotunda and shot the security guards, then anyone else they saw. When told, Vice President Quayle insisted on going to the Capitol where he viewed the dead and ordered out the National Guard to protect the city.

In Warren Adler's *Immaculate Deception* (1991), Congresswoman Frances (Frankie) McGuire, an antiabortion activist, was found poisoned—and six weeks pregnant. Her state funeral was held in the Capitol Rotunda, where the Speaker of the House spoke, followed by the Secretary of Health and Human Resources, the two senators from Massachusetts, and her old pro-choice opponent, Congressman Charles Rome. MPD homicide detective Fiona FitzGerald was also there with her African-American partner Randolph Winston Cates III, and their boss, Captain Luther (the Eggplant) Greene.

In 1997 a massive statue of three women suffragists, Susan B. Anthony, Lucretia Mott, and Elizabeth Cady Stanton, was moved from the crypt to a place of honor in the Rotunda. Guided tours begin here every fifteen minutes and last about half an hour. If Congress is not in session, you can only go into the Rotunda, the Statuary Hall, crypt, and present-day chambers of the House and Senate. If you made arrangements ahead of time, you can also meet your representative or senator and lunch with him or her on bean soup. To see a session of Congress you need a pass from one of them, too.

Turn left to walk out of the Rotunda into Statuary Hall. Restored for the 1976 Bicentennial, this hall used to be the House Chamber and its strange acoustics let people on one side hear a whisper on the other. Former president John Quincy Adams, grandfather of the Henry Adams in Sarah Booth Conroy's *Refinements of Love* (set in 1885), had a stroke here and soon died.

In McCarry's *Shelley's Heart* (1995), after the issue of election fraud became public, House Speaker R. Tucker Attenborough met the press here. The media wanted to know if illegally elected President Lockwood were impeached, the Speaker, as next in line of succession because the vice president was dead, would step aside to let someone else preside over the trial in the Senate. Instead of answering, Attenborough, a brilliant but alcoholic Constitutional scholar, was busy hunting legal ways to keep the group who stole the election from taking over the government.

In Truman's *Murder in the House* (1997), the Capitol's tribute to the late Congressman Paul Latham was held in the Statuary Hall, where he once took his three children to hear its strange accoustical trick.

Beyond the Statuary Hall is the House Chamber with the offices of the Speaker and the Ways and Means Committee to your left and the Committee on Appropriations on your right. To enter the House Gallery where you can look down on the chamber you go to the third floor (and you need a pass).

In Elliott Roosevelt's *The White House Pantry Murder* (set in 1941), British Prime Minister Winston Churchill, here on a secret wartime mission, was acutely conscious that he was making history when he addressed a joint session of Congress. He played his audience like a master musician and the Congress stood and cheered as he left.

In McCarry's *Shelley's Heart* (1995), when Speaker Attenborough took his seat as the presiding officer he formed the House into a Committee of the Whole, which elected a Committee of Managers to draft articles of impeachment. The Monday after the House committee had prepared the articles of impeachment against President Lockwood, all the members of the House of Representatives walked in solemn procession from their own chamber across the length of the Capitol and knocked thunderously on the door of the Senate. Admitted by the sergeant at arms, their chairman told the president pro tempore that by order of the House they were ready at the bar of the Senate to present articles of impeachment against the president of the United States. These exact words were spoken on March 4, 1868, when the House voted to impeach Andrew Johnson, and doubtless would have been said again if President Nixon had not resigned in 1974.

In Preston Lerner's *Fools on the Hill* (1995), ex-reporter Jeff Carmichael was hired to do PR for Texas Congressman Frederick Hale Longfellow who was running for the Senate. But Longfellow staffers turned up dead and the Congressman was implicated.

In Truman's *Murder in the House* (1997), House page Molly Latham, the daughter of California Representative Paul Latham, was dragged onto the floor of the House when it was in session by a hired Russian killer seeking a way to escape unharmed.

Although the House Chamber is large and elegant, Congress is really run by committees. In R. B. Dominic's *Epitaph for a Lobbyist* (1974), Ohio Congressman Ben Safford was made chair of the Congressional committee to investigate the murder. During the investigation Safford told his colleagues as they waited to vote on the House floor that he couldn't wait for voting machines so he wouldn't have to be physically present.

In R. B. Dominic's *Murder Out of Commission* (1976), Safford remarked to his Congressional cronies Tony Martinelli of Rhode Island, Elsie Hollenbach of California, and Val

Oakes of South Dakota that the whole point of a democracy was that you can go to your congressman when you want government action. You can throw yourself on his mercy, sweet-talk him, bribe him, or blackmail him, but you still have to talk to the man.

Take the escalator or stairway to the ground floor where there are rest rooms in the House wing. Turn right to walk through the small House Rotunda to the center of the Capitol where you will find the crypt. The catafalque for the caskets for lying in state is stored here and a compass stone in the floor marks zero point, the center from which the city's four quadrants start.

In G. J. A. O'Toole's historical mystery *The Cosgrove Report* (1979; set in the year of the impeachment of President Andrew Johnson), two Pinkerton agents met in the crypt. One was the woman sculptor, Vinnie Ream, working on a statue of Lincoln, the other was Nicholas Cosgrove, who was tracking John Wilkes Booth. The assassination of Lincoln was not listed in the Articles of Impeachment, but everyone believed Johnson was implicated. Later Cosgrove made his final report to Secretary of War Stanton here in front of accused President Johnson and Senator Edmund Ross who had the deciding vote. The next day Senator Ross bravely cast the deciding vote against impeaching President Johnson, an action John F. Kennedy admired and wrote up in *Profiles in Courage*.

In ex-Senator William Cohen and Thomas B. Allen's *Murder in the Senate* (1993), the murder of Senator Julia Bristow in the Senate subway was solved when Chief of Capitol Police Jeff Fitzgerald got a tour of the crypt and saw the Architect of the Capitol's imaging equipment.

In Quayle and Northcott's *The Campaign* (1996), the president, Attorney General Jonathan Hunter, and Chief of Staff Eugene Corforth worked to defeat Senator Bob Grant for reelection because he would challenge the president. They hired an international spy-terrorist called Bonfire to set Grant up for a murder rap. To prove he was innocent, Grant followed instructions from the murdered man to "kneel and pray" by going into the Senate Chapel and feeling under the altar for the letter left there.

Walk past the chapel (open only to members of Congress) to the Old Supreme Court Chamber, its home until 1860, when it moved to the Old Senate Chamber. One of the most infamous decisions handed down here was the Dred Scott Decision of 1857 that led to the carnage of the Civil War.

Then go back upstairs and go right from the Rotunda through the small Senate Rotunda to the Old Senate Chamber. Restored for the Bicentennial of 1976, it is furnished the way it was during the early nineteenth century with a portrait of George Washington by Rembrandt Peale and an elegant gilt shield and eagle over the president pro tem's desk.

Walk into the Senate wing. When it is in session you need a pass for the third-floor gallery. The one hundred senators have mahogany desks, with Democrats on the right and Republicans on the left. There is a great marble podium where the vice president, or when he is absent, the president pro tem—fourth in line for the presidency as many mysteries remind us—presides. One of the most memorable presidents pro tem was actor Charles Laughton, who played South Carolinian Senator Seab Cooley in the movie of Drury's *Advise and Consent* (1959).

In (Representative) Barbara Mikulski and Marylouise Oates's *Capitol Offense* (1996), newly appointed Senator Eleanor (Norie) Gorzack was puzzled when she was sworn in by the vice president in the Senate Chamber, then taken to the Old Senate Chamber for a TV reenactment for her family and friends. The reason was that only senators or their employees can be on the Senate floor at any time.

In Geoffrey Coffin's '30s *Murder in the Senate*, a march on D.C. by disgruntled pension seekers was used by the Pretorians, a Nazi-like militia group, for a coup d'etat. It was thwarted by MPD Inspector Scott Stuart, on loan to the Justice Department, who carried his pet marmoset Monica in his pocket. But Senator Jefferson Pickett was shot dead on the floor of the Senate.

In Mary Plum's *Susanna, Don't You Cry* (1946), the Army's purchase of an old Iowa resort as an "R and R" facility for wounded veterans led to murder. When Iowa Senator Lucius Noel found out his campaign manager Rufus Flannagan was responsible for the dirty deal, the senator, who had lost his only son on Iwo Jima, cleared up the sale and the murder.

In Edgar Box's (Gore Vidal) *Death Before Bedtime* (1953), Peter Cutler Sargeant III was hired to run the presidential campaign of Senator Les Rhodes (a "Senator Claghorn"). Sargeant reported to Senator Rhodes's office on Capitol Hill, where they took the tunnel subway to the cloakroom off the floor of the old Senate Chamber. Then they went to the Senate Dining Room which had a "a pre-Civil War feeling" with its old-fashioned tile floor, cornbread, and bean soup. Sargeant saw Senator Robert Taft and other landmarks, including Senator Paul Douglas and Senator Robert Byrd.

In Allen Drury's *Advise and Consent* (1959), the hearings before the Senate Foreign Relations Committee on the nomination of Robert Leffingwell to be secretary of state dramatized the Congressional committee process. But in today's world, the gay episode which ruined Senator Brigham Anderson of Utah seems very tame.

In Alexandra Roudybush's *A Sybaritic Death* (1972), Senator Driscoll was murdered on D.C.'s mean streets, causing a flood of oratory and letting White House anticrime legislation pass like a breeze. But it turned out that the source of the crime was a major Mafia loan the senator had not repaid.

In Spiro T. Agnew's *The Canfield Decision* (1976), a China agent posing as an Israeli activist persuaded Vice President Canfield to take a hard-line position on nuclear missiles for Israel. Canfield presided over the Senate, his only constitutional duty and very boring until a demonstration by the master spy's recruits made Canfield order the galleries cleared. When the Capitol police moved in, there was a scuffle and a girl fell over the balcony.

In Jeffrey Archer's *Shall We Tell the President?* (1977; rev. ed. 1985), Special Agent Marc Andrews went to the Senate

Gallery to listen to the debate on gun-control legislation. Andrews also went to the Senate Dining Rooms to check up on the suspected senators' lunch schedules for Thursday, February 24.

In Margaret Truman's *Murder on Capitol Hill* (1981), Virginia Senator Cale Caldwell, who was both Majority Leader and chair of the Senate Appropriations Committee, met his younger son Cale, Jr., at the Senate dining room for lunch just before he was murdered with an ice pick.

In James Grady's *Runner in the Street* (1984), PI John Rankin was hired by columnist Ned Johnson to find out why hooker Janet Armstrong, a Harvard University grad, was murdered. During his investigations Rankin ate with Senator Woodson in the private Senate Dining Room where he saw bean-soup celebrities like Senators George McGovern, Frank Church, Scoop Jackson, and Jesse Helms. To Rankin, the whole dining room smelled of Power.

In Cohen and Allen's *Murder in the Senate* (1993), Chief of Capitol Police Jeffrey Fitzgerald was in the Senate gallery because he had gotten word the black Mayor of D.C., Lydell Mitchell, was going to make a surprise visit. Senator Julia Bristow had just risen to speak when a crazy called Preacherman stood up waving a gun. Knocked down, he jumped up with a knife, then flipped over the balcony to land on the floor of the Senate, ending Bristow's speech.

After exploring the Capitol, go out on the West Terrace to admire the view down the Mall to the Lincoln Memorial. Then leave by the east entrance to take East Capitol Street to 1st Street.

In James Grady's *Six Days of the Condor* (1974), the final shoot-out between Malcolm (aka Condor), the young CIA researcher on the lam, and the mobsters took place there when they accidentally ran into the two Mafia hit men who shot both Wendy and a cop. There were screaming tourists and Capitol police all over the Hill, but Malcolm escaped again.

Turn left on 1st Street to the Supreme Court's white marble steps and go inside. When the Court is not in session, lectures on it are held in the Courtroom every half hour. Court sessions are open to the public on a first come, first served basis; for more information consult the *Washington Post*.

In Patrick's *Death Is a Tory* (1935), reporter "Tom" Collins told his wife he heard a swell story he couldn't use. The young architect of the Supreme Court building told him it was meant to be all American marble, but the main courtroom would have to be Italian marble, because the kind of Tennessee marble they planned to use was in all the best public toilets in the country!

In Aaron Marc Stern's *Death Takes a Paying Guest* (1947), archaeologists Elsie Mae Hunt and Tim Mulligan, doing research at the Library of Congress, went to the Supreme Court's basement cafeteria for lunch. They filled their trays and snagged a table only to see immaculate Davie Weaver, their chum from the State Department, with a lovely blond. To their amazement she turned out to be Elsie's slovenly landlady, "Cousin Helen," who was involved in the mysterious murder of a roomer on 19th Street. (See Walk 5.)

In Allen Drury's *Advise and Consent* (1959), Mr. Justice Tommy Davis was pushing hard for the choice of "his boy" Robert Leffingwell for secretary of state. He was a very political animal, not at all rising above the fray.

In R. B. Dominic's *There Is No Justice* (1971), when Supreme Court nominee Coleman Ives's love life became public, instead of withdrawing to save the president embarrassment, Ives fought for the nomination until he was poisoned. Then Congressman Ben Safford found out that two of his Ohio constituents had been Ives's clients—on either side of the same case!

In Margaret Truman's *Murder in the White House* (1980), when Secretary of State Lansard Blaine was caught taking big bribes, then murdered in the White House, President Webster appointed White House assistant Ron Fairbanks as Special Counsel to handle the investigation. Fairbanks consulted his mentor, Supreme Court Justice William G. Friedrich for whom he had once clerked.

In Margaret Truman's *Murder in the Supreme Court* (1982), Chief Clerk Clarence Sutherland was found shot dead in the Chief Justice's Chair. Sutherland turned out to have blackmailed every VIP in D.C., including the Chief Justice and President Randolph Jorgens. All the justices had dark secrets, but eighty-four-year-old Justice Temple Conover, a media-minded liberal with a very young wife, does remind one of the late Justice Douglas.

In John Grisham's *The Pelican Brief* (1992), an even older, feebler, and nastier Justice called Abraham Rosenberg could only function with tubes in his nose and a wheelchair, but he was still a legend on the Bench and would not quit until a Democratic president got elected. In the meantime he enjoyed watching the often violent First Amendment demonstration held opening day.

Look at the scene of the crime, then go to the basement to make a pit stop or to get some lunch at the Supreme Court cafeteria. Or come out and go right on 1st Street NW and cross Maryland Avenue to Constitution Avenue. Cross Constitution Avenue and turn left to walk to the Senate Office Buildings (also connected with the Capitol via the underground subway tunnels).

Mystery writers tend not to name the Senate Office building their characters visit. The oldest, now called the Richard Russell Building, is at Delaware and Constitution Avenues. It is a mirror image of the House of Representatives' Cannon Building and was also built in 1908.

In Van Wyck Mason's *The Washington Legation Murders* (1935), Captain Hugh North of Army G2 intelligence was trying to protect Senator Freeman, the sponsor of a bill promoting intelligence work. North went to his office to urge the senator to leave town until they captured the Guardsman and his confederates, but as they talked North yelled at a janitor with a wastebasket. When the janitor dropped it, a hand grenade fell out.

In Bill Goode's *The Senator's Nude* (1947), Senator Caleb Casper Smudge took a cab from Police Headquarters where he had been questioned about the nude body in his bed to the Senate Office Building. The disheveled senator sneaked in a rear door only to have his secretary, who had read Storey Hawk's story in the *Blade*, look at him pop-eyed!

In Miriam Borgenicht's *Corpse in Diplomacy* (1956), *Mirror* columnist Katherine (Kate) Whipple liked getting anonymous tips for her column, so when architect Tobey Hart found a dead body under Kate's bed, he dashed off to find her. He caught up with her as she interviewed Senator Strang in his office, but when Tobey told Kate about the body, instead of hiding, she called the MPD so she could get an exclusive on the story!

In Fletcher Knebel and Charles W. Bailey's *Seven Days in May* (1962), Marine Colonel Martin (Jiggs) Casey had found out there was a coup planned by the hawkish Chairman of the Joint Chiefs of Staff, "Gentleman Jim" Scott. Since General Scott was testifying at the Armed Services Committee Room in the Old Senate Office Building, Casey's ally Senator Clark tried to find out about Scott's secret communications base in the desert.

In Greenlee's *The Spook Who Sat by the Door* (1969), Senator Gilbert Hennington, who was up for reelection, sat at his desk with the Washington Monument framed in the window behind him as his staff told him his reelection hinged on the Negro vote. They suggested he accuse the CIA of bias because it had no Negro officers, but when Senator Hennington told a senate committee there were no Negro officers in the CIA, other committee members were shocked. They knew Senator Hennington had a close race, but this was hitting below the belt.

In James M. Cain's *The Institute* (1976), scholar-cum-football star Dr. Lloyd Palmer needed twenty-two million collars to establish a national institute of biography. He had gotten Nebraska Senator Hood's son out of a college jam, so the senator introduced Palmer to the CEO of a Delaware company. But after the Institute opened, Palmer was called to testify in the Senate Office Building by Senator Pickens of Georgia, who was looking into tax-exempt foundations.

In Jeffrey Archer's *Shall We Tell the President?* (1977; rev. ed. 1985), at a Foreign Relations Committee hearing Senator Thornton, one of the suspects, surprisingly said he was going to support the president on gun control, and *Washington Post* reporter Sinclair said he must have been bought off.

In Margaret Truman's *Murder on Capitol Hill* (1981), after Senator Cale Caldwell was murdered, his wife insisted that Senator MacLoon, who was in charge of the Senate hearings on the murder, hire family friend Lydia James as Special Counsel. But his administrative assistant, Rick Petrone, spied on her.

In Mary Higgins Clark's *Stillwatch* (1984), glamorous young television producer Pat Traymore went to the Russell Senate Office Building to interview Senator Abigail Jennings. Traymore had been brought to D.C. from New York just to do a TV series on Jennings who was about to be nominated vice president of the United States. Researching this show, Traymore, who had a secret Washington past herself, not only found Jennings hard to deal with, but discovered more about the admired senator than anyone wanted her to know.

Look around the Russell Building, then walk along Constitution Avenue to 1st Street. Cross 1st Street to the Dirksen Building, built in 1956 and named for Illinois' Senator Everett McKinley Dirksen. Its cafeteria and dining room on the lower level are open to the public.

In Elliott Roosevelt's *Murder in the Blue Room* (set in 1942), Illinois Congressman Dirksen was sleeping with White House press office secretary Emily Ryan, who was found murdered in the Blue Room when "Mr. Brown," aka USSR Foreign Minister Vyacheslav Molotov, was there on a secret wartime mission. Dirksen said he had been introduced to Emily by FDR's confidential advisor Harry Hopkins!

In Michael Bowen's *Washington Deceased* (1990), former Senator Desmond Gardner was serving time for bribery in a federal prison with a Mafia enforcer he feared might kill him. Gardner got his college daughter Wendy to go to his office in the Dirksen Building to meet his administrative assistant Randy Cox. To prove Cox was the key, Wendy had to spend the night with him, but she got into his computer.

In William Moore's *The Last Surprise* (1990), PI Russell McGarvey was hired by the widow of Senator Warren Harmon to investigate his murder. Senator Harmon had been checking on the purchase of secret information by friendly foreign governments, an unpopular project because his staff had a tiny office in Dirksen's basement.

In Gar Anthony Haywood's *Bad News Travels Fast* (1995), the senior Loudermilks found the kiss-and-tell diary of Senator Graham Wildman in a Foggy Bottom bookstore and went to his office in the Dirksen Building. Dottie went in alone, taking a page copied from the diary, and told the receptionist she wondered if the book she'd found in the FBI's ladies room belonged to the senator? His staff's reaction made it obvious the diary was in Senator Wildman's handwriting, but when asked who she was, Dottie said she was Mrs. Washington and she and George were staying at the Four Seasons Hotel, and left.

Look over the Dirksen Building, then go left to the modern Hart Building, which is connected to the Dirksen Building. In its atrium there is a mammoth Alexander Calder sculpture named *Mountains and Clouds.*

In Tom Clancy's first thriller about CIA researcher Dr. Jack Ryan, *The Hunt for Red October* (1984), a maverick USSR sub was defecting and the United States wanted to find it first. Senator Donaldson, Chair of the Senate's Select Committee on Intelligence, had his office in Hart. Since Donaldson was given to leaking information, the CIA's Ritter went to swear him to secrecy on orders of the White House. Walking out, Ritter thought that the atrium looked like the local Hyatt.

In Quayle and Northcott's *Embrace the Serpent* (1992), when Fidel Castro died he was succeeded by Valles, a USSR/Iranian stooge who knew all the right people in D.C. The only person in D.C. who disbelieved Valles's PR was African-American Republican Senator Robert Hawkins Grant from Georgia. Grant's office was in Hart, where the Senate's Intelligence Committee also met.

In Joseph Finder's *Extraordinary Powers* (1993), ex-CIA superspy Ben Ellison was re-recruited after the death of his father-in-law, former CIA Director Harrison Sinclair, who was accused of getting rich by selling out the USSR to Germany. At a Senate Select Committee on Intelligence hearing held at the Hart Office Building Ellison, who had discovered the real traitors, got inside in a wheelchair with a hidden gun. The hearing turned into a shoot-out which appeared live on national TV.

Come out of Hart Office Building and go left on Constitution Avenue past the brick Sewell-Belmont House at 144 Constitution Avenue. Built in 1800, it burned and was rebuilt in 1814. Bought in 1929 by Alva Smith, a Southern belle-cum-women's rights militant, for the National Woman's Party headquarters, it is a feminist museum.

Visit the museum if you have time, then cross Maryland Avenue at 2nd Street. If you went one more block east on Constitution Avenue to 3rd Street NE, crossing Maryland Avenue again, you would come to the Capitol Hill Deli where two of Eddie Loudermilk's roommates, Stacy and Angus, worked in Gar Anthony Haywood's *Bad News Travels Fast* (1995).

Turn left to C Street and walk one block to D Street. Cross D Street to go to Massachusetts Avenue, which crosses 2nd Street, then cross Massachusetts Avenue and walk left to the plaza in front of Union Station.

If you had continued west on Massachusetts Avenue to New Jersey Avenue, you would come to the downtown campus of Georgetown University Law School with its shining new Edmund Bennet Williams Law Library. In Patricia Cornwell's *All That Remains* (1992), Chief Medical Examiner Kay Scarpetta talked about going to Georgetown University Law School. She had already gotten her M.D. but still was overwhelmed by the "brilliant and beautiful." One of those socially privileged types Scarpetta met (and fell for) was future Special FBI Agent Mark James, whom she met in the library, but she married someone else. In *Body of Evidence* (1991), James reappeared—for a time—in her life.

Go inside the magnificently renovated Union Station, designed by Daniel Burnham to be a triumphal gateway to our capital city. The waiting room has a lofty, coffered ceiling, redone in gilt, and the 760-foot-long Grand Concourse, based on the Roman baths of Diocletian, is one of the largest spaces ever built in the country. Since its major renovation in 1988,

Union Station has movie theaters, T-shirt and souvenir shops, fast-food restaurants, and rest rooms.

The station has a tourist information desk and the Old Town Trolley tours begin here. You can always find a cab here, too. If you waited until now to eat, try America located in the waiting room, upscale B. Smith's in the old Presidential Suite, or the fast-food court on the lower level.

In Mary Roberts Rinehart's classic *The Man in Lower Ten* (1909), young Washington lawyer Lawrence Blakely was working for an old Pittsburgh millionaire. Blakely went to Pittsburgh on the Pennsylvania Railroad's Washington Flyer, but on his return trip he came back from the dining car to find another man murdered in his Pullman car berth (Lower Ten) and all his clothes and legal papers gone. Blakely not only was accused of the murder, but there was also a train wreck in which he broke his arm and met the millionaire's granddaughter Alison.

In her biography of Mary Roberts Rinehart, *Had She But Known* (1994), mystery writer Charlotte MacLeod reported that Rinehart tried to get a Pullman berth on the Pennsylvania Railroad on her way home. The only one left was Lower Ten and the clerk told Rinehart that some fool woman had written a book in which somebody got murdered in Lower Ten, so no one would sleep in that berth!

In Elliott Roosevelt's *Murder in the Executive Mansion* (set in 1939), President Roosevelt and First Lady Eleanor went to Union Station to welcome Britain's King George VI and Queen Elizabeth on a state visit. FDR was in a cutaway while the king was wearing the dress uniform of an admiral of the fleet. The royal couple were charming, tireless, and so petite the Roosevelts towered over them. As they left the station there was a twenty-one-gun salute and cheering crowds lined Pennsylvania Avenue all the way to the White House.

In Haynes Johnson and Howard Simons's *The Landing* (set in 1942), Nazi spy Gunther Haupt went to Union Station where he went into the USO Servicemen's Lounge (in the Presidential Suite) and set up a rendezvous with his fellow spy Willi at Arlington National Cemetery. (See Walk 8.)

In Edgar Box's (Gore Vidal) *Death Before Bedtime* (1953), Peter Cutler Sargeant III and Senator Rhode's promiscuous daughter Ellen arrived by the same train, having spent the night in bed together. Ellen was not thrilled by daddy's presidential ambitions because poor Margaret Truman was trailed everywhere by detectives.

In Louisa Revell's *The Men with Three Eyes* (1955), retired school teacher "Miss Julia" came to visit her great-niece's friend Ruth Gibson, the director of Neighborhood House on D.C.'s southeast side. When Ruth did not appear, Miss Julia got in a cab but told the villainous-looking driver to wait in front of the station. Miss Julia had not taught Latin for forty years to be bullied by a cab driver, so there they sat. When Ruth appeared, the cabby became all smiles because he knew Neighborhood House.

In Richard Conroy's *Old Ways in the New World* (set in 1976), the Smithsonian's Henry Scruggs went to Union Station on Christmas Eve to meet Phoebe Casey who had been working at a high-paying job in New York City. The station was a mess because the powers that be had dug up the floor of the waiting room to make a pit where tourists could watch slides of D.C. and then—hopefully—go home. Conroy seems to have agreed with James Grady, whose *Runner in the Street* (1984) ended with a sour comment about Congress turning Union Station into a disaster by trying to graft a National Visitors Center on it.

In Jeffrey Archer's *Shall We Tell the President?* (1977; rev. ed. 1985), the head of the Secret Service and the Director of the FBI met secretly by going to the cab rack in front of Union Station. They both got into the seventh cab, driven by an agent, and the Director briefed the Secret Service on the plot and their plan to protect the president.

In David Baldacci's *Absolute Power* (1996), lawyer Jack Graham was on the run because all the president's men knew that he had evidence linking them and POTUS to the murders of Christy and Walter Sullivan and burglar Luther Whitman. Graham called the Virginia detective Seth Frank who was handling the case on a public phone at Union Station and they planned to meet at the Farragut West Metro Station so Jack could give Frank his evidence. Graham got some burgers and fries at the Food Court and took the Metro from Union Station to Farragut West where he and Frank walked into a trap.

In Quayle and Northcott's *The Campaign* (1996), Senator Bob Grant issued an ultimatum to the attorney general to be at Union Station a day before the election or he would tell the media that the president and his inner circle had hired an international spy to frame him. The attorney general's Nazi-like organization, the NIIA, staked out the station, but the attorney general missed the rendezvous because he was dead.

End your walk at the Union Station Metro Station on 1st Street, which can be reached on the west side of Union Station. If you prefer to drive, you can park a car here and do this walk in reverse, or return here to try some of the possible side trips.

Possible Side Trips

These mystery sites may be reached by train from Union Station or by car.

Annapolis/Maryland's Eastern Shore/Chesapeake Bay: thirty miles by car on Route 50, an extension of D.C.'s New York Avenue.

Annapolis is a historic town founded in 1649. The Treaty of Paris ending the Revolutionary War was signed there and it served as the nation's first peacetime capital. Filled with eighteenth-century buildings, it is also home to the U.S. Naval Academy and St. John's College, where the only textbooks are the great books. They do not include mysteries yet, but there are a number of Annapolis mysteries which give you a perfect excuse to spend the day there.

For mystery fans it is the home of Mystery's Grand Mistress Leslie Ford (aka David Frome) who was related to Maryland's founding family, the Calverts, and set several mysteries in Annapolis.

In Leslie Ford's *Date with Death* (1959), Jonas Smith was a new doctor who became mixed up with the Darrells, an old

Annapolis family, when he rented part of their house. When two Baltimoreans, Gordon Darcy Grymes and his identical twin Franklin, had a row over their inheritance from their grandfather, murder followed. Many scenes take place in Annapolis, giving you a wonderful feel for the prewar town. Visit St. John's College on King George Street and its neighbor across the street, the United States Naval Academy where Midshipman Tom Darrell was about to graduate but went AWOL instead. Among the many eighteenth-century houses worth seeing are the Ogle House at College Avenue and King George Street, the Chase-Lloyd House and Hammond-Harwood House facing each other on Maryland Avenue, and the William Paca House at Prince George Street, which was the probable model for Ford's Blanton-Darrell House. At State Circle you can see the Maryland State House and Governor's Mansion, together with the Market Space, then go to Church Circle to see historic St. Anne's Church and the Reynolds Tavern. The Visitors Center, where you can get a map and information about tours, is just past the Reynolds Tavern on West Street.

In Eleanor Pierson's *Murder Without Clues* (1942), "wild" D.C. socialite Lila Donnelly was tried for murder, only to be murdered herself. Investigating the murder, law partners John Hadley and Ross Allen took the ferry to the Eastern Shore because during Lila's funeral in D.C. the body of another socialite, Flo Davis, was found at the Donnelly summer home near Annapolis in the trunk of her old retainer's car.

In Barbara Lee's *Death in Still Waters* (1995), a Malice Domestic Best First Novel Winner, Eve Elliott, in retreat from her big-time ad job, came to visit her aunt in Pines on Magothy. Her aunt had a real-estate business she wanted Eve to take over, so along with back-country murders both ancient and modern, Eve found herself having to deal with the competition, Mitch Gavlin. Gavlin took Eve to dinner at Annapolis, which was swamped by tourists but being abandoned by the natives whose ancestors went back to colonial days. Mitch fed Eve at his home on the waterfront; then they toured the town, seeing the City Docks, the Naval College, St. John's

College, and the Maryland State House, ending at a garden bar favored by politicians.

Baltimore, Maryland: about forty miles by car taking New York Avenue (U.S. 50) to I-95. A forty-minute ride from D.C.'s Union Station to Baltimore Washington International Airport (BWI) by train on Amtrak or, on weekdays only, on Maryland Rail Commuter Service (MARC).

Baltimore has been a mystery town ever since Edgar Allan Poe, who invented the detective story (and the detective) in "Murders in the Rue Morgue" (1842), died there in 1849. He was reported to have died of drink, but recent medical investigation suggests he died of rabies, making his end more mysterious! Poe was buried in the Poe family lot in the Presbyterian Cemetery, so a visit to his grave in the Westminster Church graveyard on Green Street and a pilgrimage to the Edgar Allan Poe House and Museum seem appropriate.

Recent mysteries have focused on Poe's last days and give you a feel for the Baltimore of 150 years ago. Stephen Marlowe's *The Lighthouse at the End of the World* (1995), is a retrospective autobiography narrated by a dying Poe which tries to explain where he was during the last week of his life. Mysteriously, this search for Poe is assisted by his own creation, Poe's fictional detective C. Auguste Dupin.

In George Egon Hatvary's *The Murder of Edgar Allan Poe* (1997), the same fictional character Dupin received a letter in Paris about the untimely death of Poe. Dupin went to America to pay his respects to the Poe family and make sure Poe had not been murdered. Dupin arrived by boat and upon landing took a hackney to the Presbyterian Cemetery on Fayette and Greene to lay a wreath. He later had Poe's body exhumed and found arsenic, then discovered that Poe's lawyer was convinced Poe had stolen his material.

Baltimore has other illustrious mystery writers, most of whom were suggested to me by Kathy Harig who has led her own Baltimore Mystery Tour and compiled a list titled *Baltimore Mysteries.* Wherever else you go in Baltimore, you must go visit Kathy Harig and Paige Rose's bookstore called Mystery Loves Company at 1730 Fleet Street across the harbor at

Fells Point. Named the best specialty store in the city by *City Paper*, Kathy and Paige have set up mystery seminars at the Smithsonian and run a mystery seminar at Baltimore's Johns Hopkins University. Both featured present-day practitioners of the art like Annette and Marty Meyers (who write New York historicals as Mann Meyers).

Leslie Ford set *The Girl from the Mimosa Club* (1957), starring one of the earliest women PIs, in Baltimore. In *Trial by Ambush* (1961), when a serial rapist stalked and caught Mary Melissa Seaton just before she married the scion of an old Baltimore family, she bravely decided to testify against him. Ford set the courtroom scenes at the Baltimore City Courthouse, located between Fayette and Marion Streets across Calvert Street from Battle Monument (1812).

Mean-streets writer Dashiell Hammett grew up on Stricker Street and set scenes in Baltimore in *The Continental Op* and *The Glass Key*, which were partly based on his experiences there as a Pinkerton agent. According to Harig, Baltimore even has a building trimmed with stone falcons! Martha Grimes, better known for her cosy British locales, is another Baltimore mystery writer, who used its locations for *The Horse You Came in On* (1993).

In Kelsey Roberts's *Legal Tender* (1993), lawyer Caitlin Jeffrey was working late at her law office in downtown Baltimore when a masked intruder broke in. He escaped but when the police came they found Jeffrey's boss murdered in the next office. Accused of the murder, Jeffrey tried to find the intruder and unexpectedly ran into him at Baltimore Harbor on the veranda of the American Cafe. They sparred with each other, but eventually teamed up to find the real killer.

In Louise Titchener's mysteries Baltimore is also the setting. In *Homebody* (1993), Antoinette Credella had been living at Mount Vernon Square, but moved into a Charles Village corner row house where the rent was lower. After moving in, Credella found out that Rebecca Kelso, a Johns Hopkins grad student, had been knifed to death in the living room, and had to solve the case to save herself from a similar fate.

In Titchener's *Mantrap* (1994), Sally Dunphy was a tough cop who had just moved into a Federal Hill townhouse in Baltimore when she had to scare away burglars. Then she learned that her ex-fiance had committed suicide and people were saying it was her fault. She did not believe it, but discovered there was a connection between Joe's death and the burglary.

In F. Paul Wilson's medical mystery *The Select* (1994), arrogant malpractice was being carried out at the select Ingraham Medical School, located in the country less than an hour from Baltimore. The medical school was underwritten by Kleederman Medical Industries, the family company of a former senator who often visited. Tim Brown, a maverick student, liked to sneak off campus now and then to go gambling in Baltimore. But he also figured out that students were being programmed by ex-CIA operatives to make use of derelict people as guinea pigs.

5

DUPONT CIRCLE/ EMBASSY ROW WALK

BACKGROUND

This walk combines one of D.C.'s trendiest locations with the pomp and circumstance of great mansions now turned into embassies, clubs, and lawyers' offices. Originally a swamp, the development of Dupont Circle was a major effort by post–Civil War Public Works "Boss" Shepherd, who owned real estate nearby, and his developer friends, the "California Syndicate," who bought up land and built themselves mansions near "Pacific Circle." In 1882 Pacific Circle was renamed Dupont Circle in honor of Civil War Admiral Samuel Francis duPont. In the 1920s the duPont family moved his statue to a Wilmington park and replaced it with a fountain designed by Daniel Chester French.

By the 1980s housing around Dupont Circle had become a habitat for young professionals and a hangout for the gay and trendy. North of Dupont Circle Embassy Row institutionalized its upper-class international flavor, while south and east near Scott Circle there is still an architectural melting pot of old brownstones, embassies, and modern high-rise offices in "new" Downtown. Dupont Circle's up-and-down social history is well documented in mysteries set there.

During the twentieth century the mansions along Massachusetts Avenue became "Embassy Row," the two-mile stretch of Massachusetts Avenue from Scott Circle to the Naval Observatory where the vice president lives. Its hilly, parklike neighborhood was developed in the early twentieth century by wealthy movers and shakers who then fell victim to income tax and the Great Depression. In 1931 the British and Japanese embassies moved north, beginning the creation of this diplomatic enclave famous for its Beaux Arts buildings.

Still farther north at Mount St. Albans where Massachusetts and Wisconsin Avenues intersect is Washington Cathedral, colloquially called the National Cathedral, and officially known as the Cathedral Church of St. Peter and St. Paul. It was proposed by D.C. planner Pierre L'Enfant, but it was only in 1893 that Congress granted a charter to the Episcopal Church to build it. President Theodore Roosevelt laid the cornerstone in 1907, but the building was not completed until 1990. It is the scene of the crime (and of many VIP funerals) in D.C. mysteries.

Directly east up Connecticut Avenue from Dupont Circle is another Washington treasure: the National Zoological Park with our only remaining giant panda. Originally the zoo was a collection of native American animals like bison housed on the Mall, but in 1889 Congress funded a new zoo to be run by the Smithsonian Institution. A huge tract of land above Rock Creek Park was bought and architect Frederick Law Olmstead drew up the original plans. In D.C. mysteries a surprising number of stakeouts or chases occur there.

LENGTH OF WALK: About 2 miles up- and downhill

This walk is divided into two parts, which can be done on separate days. Part One begins at Dupont Circle, goes halfway up Embassy Row, and back again. Part Two begins two Metro stops up the Red Line at Cleveland Park and takes you to the

National Cathedral, along the upper part of Embassy Row, and through Rock Creek Park to the Zoo.

See the map on page 133 for the boundaries of this walk and page 274 for a list of the books and detectives mentioned.

SPECIAL TOURS

Embassy Row: each May there is an embassy tour to benefit Goodwill Industries, which includes a free shuttle bus to the participating embassies. Embassies are normally open only to official visitors. Fee. Call 636-4225* for more information.

Dupont-Kalorama Museum Walk Day: first Saturday in June. Open to the public free of charge. Call 667-0441.

PLACES OF INTEREST

Barney Studio House, 2306 Massachusetts Avenue. Studio-home of artist Alice Pike Barney, donated to the Smithsonian Institution by her daughters. Not open to the public.

B'nai B'rith Klutznick Museum, 1640 Rhode Island Avenue. Donation. Open Mon.–Fri. 10:00 A.M.–5:00 P.M. Closed Sat., federal and Jewish holidays. Call 857-6583.

Cosmos Club, 2121 Massachusetts Avenue. 1901. Prestigious private club. Not open to the public.

Cathedral of St. Matthew (Roman Catholic), 1725 Rhode Island Avenue. Seat of the Catholic Archbishop of Washington.

Dupont Circle Plaza Hotel, 1500 New Hampshire Avenue.

Embassy Row:

British Embassy, 3100 Massachusetts Avenue. Embassy complex built in 1931.

Brazilian Embassy, 3000 Massachusetts Avenue. (McCormick House built in 1931 for reaper/newspaper McCormick family of Chicago.)

*The telephone area code is 202 unless otherwise indicated.

Indonesian Embassy, 2020 Massachusetts Avenue. Formerly the Walsh mansion, home of Evalyn Walsh McLean, owner of the Hope Diamond and the *Washington Post*. Tours by appointment. Call 775-5306.

Japanese Embassy, 2516 Massachusetts Avenue. Built in 1932.

Historical Society of Washington, D.C. (Heurich Mansion), 1307 New Hampshire Avenue. Fee. Guided tours Wed.–Sat. at noon. Call 785-2068.

Hotel Tabard, 1739 N Street. Three Victorian townhouses with Old World charm including an open fire on the hearth. Call 785-1277.

Kramerbooks, next door to Afterwords Cafe, 1517 Connecticut Avenue. Call 387-1400.

MysteryBooks, 1715 Connecticut Avenue. Call 483-1600.

Mystery Bookshop: Bethesda, 7700 Old Georgetown Road, Bethesda, Maryland. Call (301) 657-2655. (See Possible Side Trips.)

National Trust for Historic Preservation (Patterson apartments), 1785 Massachusetts Avenue. Lobby open Mon.–Fri. 9:00 A.M.–5:00 P.M.

National Zoological Park, 3000 Connecticut Avenue. Open daily April 15–October 15; grounds 8:00 A.M.–8:00 P.M., October 16–April 14 8:00 A.M.–6:00 P.M. Animal buildings open year-round 9:00 A.M.–4:30 P.M. Free. Call 673-4800.

Omni-Shoreham Hotel, 2500 Calvert Street. Call 234-0700.

Phillips Collection of Modern Art, 1600 21st Street. Private collection that became the first museum of modern art in America. Tues., Wed., Fri., and Sat. 10:00 A.M.–5:00 P.M., Thurs. 10:00 A.M.–8:30 P.M., Sun. noon–7:00 P.M. Fee. Call 387-2151.

Ritz-Carlton Hotel (now the Luxury Collection Hotel), 2100 Massachusetts Avenue. Call 293-2100.

Second Story Books, 2000 P Street. Specializes in mystery, detective, and espionage fiction. Also rare and used books. Call 659-8884.

Society of the Cincinnati (Anderson House built in 1902), 2118 Massachusetts Avenue. Headquarters of Revolutionary War society. Open Tues.–Sat. 1:00 p.m.–4:00 p.m. Closed Sun., Mon., and federal holidays. Free. Call 785-2040.

Sulgrave Club (Wadsworth House), 1801 Massachusetts Avenue. Not open to the public. Donated to Red Cross in 1918. Sold to group of Washington ladies for private club in 1932.

Textile Museum, 2320 S Street. Mon.–Sat. 10:00 a.m.–5:00 p.m., Sun. 1:00 p.m.–5:00 p.m. Closed major holidays. Donation. Call 667-0441.

U.S. Naval Observatory, 3450 Massachusetts Avenue. Free. Go to Visitors' Gate. Call 653-1507. Also site of vice president's official home, not open to the public.

Washington Club (Patterson House), 15 Dupont Circle. Not open to the public. Home of Cissy Patterson, publisher of the *Washington Times-Herald*.

Washington National Cathedral, Massachusetts and Wisconsin Avenues at Mount St. Albans. Donation. Open May 1–Labor Day Mon.–Fri. 10:00 a.m.–9:00 p.m., Sat. 10:00 a.m.–4:30 p.m., Sun. 7:30 a.m.–4:30 p.m.; rest of the year Mon.–Sat. 10:00 a.m.–4:30 p.m., Sun. 7:30 a.m.–4:30 p.m. Tours Mon.–Sat. 10:00 a.m.–3:15 p.m., Sun. 12:30 p.m.–2:45 p.m. Tues. & Thurs. afternoon tours followed by tea. Fee. Call 537-6200.

Woodrow Wilson House, 2340 S Street. Wilson was the only president to stay in D.C. after leaving the White House. Open Tues.–Sun. 10:00 a.m.–4:00 p.m. Closed major holidays. Fee. Call 387-4062.

Places to Eat

Afterwords Cafe, next door to ***Kramerbooks***, 1517 Q Street. In-store cafe with weekend folk music. No reservations. Call 387-1462.

C. F. Folks, 1225 19th Street. Call 293-0162.

Cafe Luna, 1633 P Street. Popular inexpensive Italian. Recommended by Richard Klein, an inveterate D.C. tourist who checked out this guide.

Jockey Club, the Luxury Collection Hotel, 2100 Massachusetts Avenue. A restaurant with English ambience. Call 293-2100.

National Zoological Park, 3000 Connecticut Avenue. Several fast-food outlets within the grounds.

Omni-Shoreham Hotel, 2500 Calvert Street. Restaurant and bar, snack bar, lounge. Call 234-0700.

Phillips Collection of Modern Art, 1600 21st Street. Use 21st Street and Q Street entrance. Small basement cafe which keeps museum hours. Call 387-2151.

Tabard Inn, 1739 N Street. Very cosy British ambience even in the bar! Named for the Southwark, London, starting point for Chaucer's *Canterbury Tales.* Call 833-2668.

DUPONT CIRCLE/ EMBASSY ROW WALK

Begin your walk at the Dupont Circle Metro Station. Come out of the 19th Street exit at the south side of Dupont Circle. Walk around the Circle to your right, admiring the fountain and appreciating its eclectic ambience, crowded with young people and tourists.

In Sarah Booth Conroy's historical mystery *Refinements of Love* (set in 1885), Henry Adams's wife Clover wrote that Dupont Circle—the new name for Pacific Circle—had added a statue of Admiral duPont, but she still felt Lafayette Square was the true heart of Washington.

In mysteries, however, Dupont Circle is a very popular rendezvous. In Janice Law's *The Big Payoff* (1976), Anna Peters worked for T. William (T. Bill) Harrison at New World Oil. Anna had made a career of blackmailing her bosses, so when she discovered that T. Bill was being paid to control North Sea oil, she tried to get a piece of the action. She contacted the British Embassy, then met embassy spy Austin Lloyd at Dupont Circle, sitting on a rough concrete bench, feeding peanuts to the pigeons.

In R. B. Dominic's *Murder in High Place* (1970), former '60s activist and Sears Scholar Karen Kimball Jenkins was booted out of Nuevador because she danced in front of the

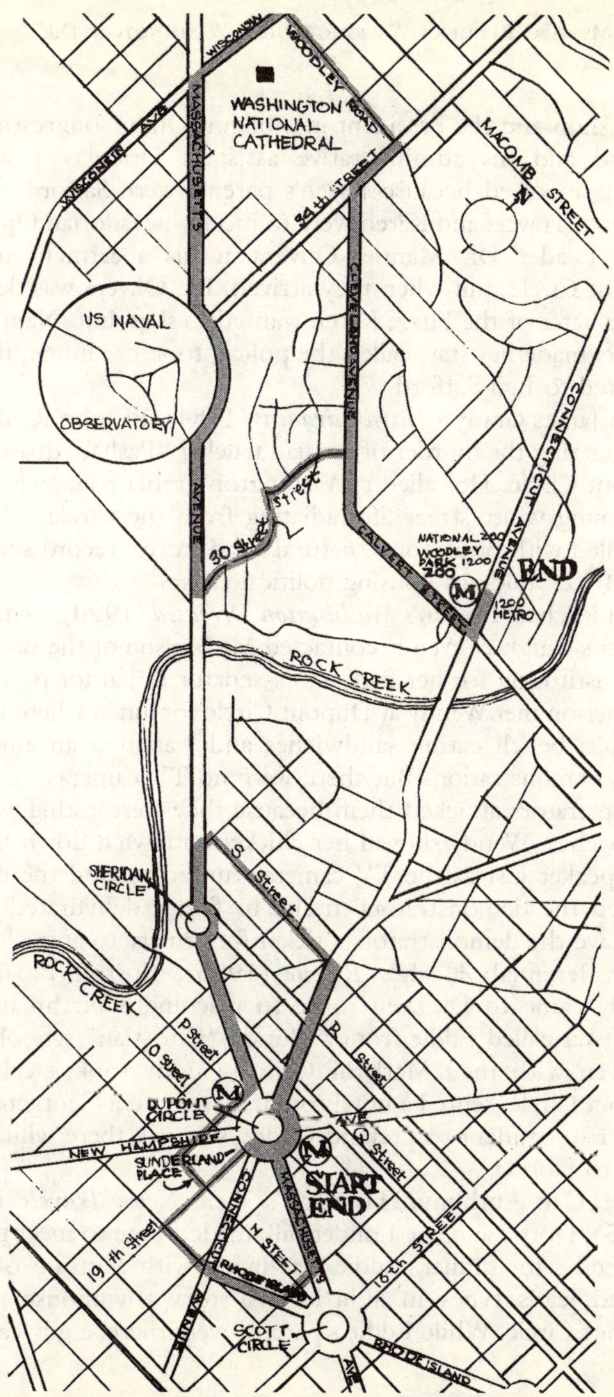

Walk 5: Dupont Circle and Embassy Row

archbishop and the president in a bikini. Ohio Congressman Safford and his administrative assistant Douglas Travers became involved because Karen's parents were Safford constituents. Travers and Karen were to meet Nuevadorian Opposition Leader Dr. Manuel Olivera at his apartment near Dupont Circle, but when they arrived, Dr. Olivera was dead. A true hater of the Fuzz, Karen wanted to skip, but 'Nam vet Travers made her stay, called the police, took her home, then reported to Ben Safford.

In James Grady's *Hard Bargains* (1984), PI John Rankin, investigating the murder of Iranian trucker "Pasha," drove by Dupont Circle. He called it Washington's rebel zone, with its gay young white street life radiating from the Circle, which was filled with bookstores, natural food stores, record shops, and office buildings housing political causes.

In Michael Bowen's *Washington Deceased* (1990), Senator Garner's daughter Wendy contacted Michaelson of the Brookings Institution for her dad, an ex-senator in jail for payoffs. Michaelson met Wendy at Dupont Circle for lunch where they sat on a bench eating sandwiches and watching an animal rights demonstration. But there were no TV cameras, so the demonstrators attacked them because they were eating *meat* sandwiches. Wendy shoved her chicken sandwich down their loudspeaker just as the TV cameras turned up and the cops opened the demonstrators' trailer to find a dehydrated calf and gave the demonstrators a ticket for cruelty to animals.

In Jeremiah Healy's *Rescue* (1995), Boston PI John Cuddy came to D.C. en route to rescuing a birthmarked youngster called Eddie from a Florida "Christian" school for children with the "Mark of Cain." Cuddy took a cab to Dupont Circle, rented a hotel room, then hired a Georgetown University student to pretend Cuddy was still there while he went to Florida.

In Gar Anthony Haywood's *Bad News Travels Fast* (1995), Dottie and Joe Loudermilk made a date to meet their son Eddie for dinner. Eddie was living with a group of T-shirted jeans types in a little two-story townhouse near Dupont Circle. While Eddie's parents were there, a guy called

Emmett came by, got into a row with Eddie over a girl, and pulled a gun. Next morning Emmett was found dead, and Eddie was jailed for murder.

Go around Dupont Circle to your left to New Hampshire Avenue and take New Hampshire Avenue left (south) to tiny Sunderland Place. On the left side of New Hampshire just before Sunderland Place you come to the Historical Society of Washington, D.C., in the Heurich mansion. Built for a wealthy brewer, it is a brownstone Richardsonian mansion with a tower trimmed with gargoyles. Inside it is a magnificently preserved house museum and a center for D.C. history.

In James Grady's *Runner in the Street* (1984), Rankin went to see lawyer Art Dillon, whose offices were near the D.C. Historical Society. Dillon hired Rankin to find out about any legacies left from the Reverend James Jones's Kool-aid massacre in Guyana. Most of the buildings you pass sport shiny brass law firm nameplates.

Cross New Hampshire Avenue to 20th Street and turn right to O Street.

In Paul Valentine's *Crime Scene at "O" Street* (1989), D.C. civil servant Frank Kadinsky was found dead by his roommate Florian Boldt in their classy old apartment on O Street. Kadinsky had been strangled and MPD Detectives Magnus Johnson and Dewey Hudlow assumed the murder was gay-bashing, but it turned out to be caused by family "skeletons in the closet" that led the MPD detectives to deep Alabama caves.

Cross O Street and walk up 20th Street to P Street. At the southwest corner of P and 20th you see Second Story Books & Antiques at 2000 P Street. They specialize in used and rare mystery, detective, and espionage fiction, so take time out to browse if you can. This might be Bowen's Cavalier Books, run by Michaelson's old friend Marjorie Randolph, or The Whodunit in Quayle and Northcott's *Embrace the Serpent* (1992). Both of those fictional bookstores could also be Mystery-Books or Kramerbooks on the other side of Dupont Circle, too.

To your right there is a CVS Drugstore, once a Peoples Drugstore. In Patricia Cornwell's *All That Remains* (1992), a serial killer near Richmond, Virginia, was targeting young lovers and hiding their bodies. The fifth couple included the daughter of Patricia Harvey, the National Drug Czar. *Washington Post* reporter Abby Turnbull, an old friend of Richmond's Medical Examiner Kay Scarpetta, was investigating the murders and called Scarpetta while waiting for a source outside Dupont Circle's Peoples Drugstore. Abby was sure she was being tailed, her phone tapped, and her mail read. She told Scarpetta she suspected it was the law enforcement agencies, scared one of their own was the serial killer.

To your left on P Street between Dupont Circle and the P Street Bridge in George Pelecanos's *Down by the River Where the Dead Men Go* (1995), there was an upscale gay bar known as the Fire House. PI Nick Stefanos went there because African-American Calvin Jeter had a box of Fire House matches in his pocket when Nick found his body. Stefanos showed the bartender photographs of Jeter and his missing pal Randall, but he said the boys were not habitues but probably street hustlers.

Cross P Street to walk one block up to Massachusetts Avenue. You are at the southern end of Embassy Row which stretches all the way to the National Cathedral.

In Mary Plum's *Death of a Redhaired Man* (1950), Congressman Meridian's secretary Jerry Vale had been sent to Florida to pick up some information about Russ Odden, whom Meriden's daughter Kate was determined to marry. As he came through the Everglades Jerry stopped a murder attempt on Deborah Todd and decided Deborah would be safer in Washington. But violence and murder still followed her to the embassies of Washington.

Turn left and walk up Massachusetts Avenue. You pass two stately mansions: the Blaine Mansion and its neighbor, the Beale House. The Blaine Mansion was built for James G. Blaine, a cofounder of the Republican Party who ran for president but lost to Grover Cleveland. It is now an office building. In Conroy's *Refinements of Love* (1993), President Grover Cleveland invited the Henry Adamses to dinner at the White

House. The Beale House next door is now the headquarters of the National Federation of Business and Professional Women's Clubs.

The third house, at 2020 Massachusetts Avenue, is now the Indonesian Embassy. Built by Thomas Walsh who struck it rich in the Gold Rush, it was the most expensive house in D.C., with a gold bar in the pediment. Walsh's daughter Evalyn, who married *Washington Post* heir Edward Beale McLean, inherited the sixty-room mansion but only lived there until 1916. During World War II it was used by the Red Cross and could have been the place where Leslie Ford's Georgetown widow Grace Latham went to roll bandages in *All for the Love of a Lady* (1943). In 1951 Evalyn Walsh sold it to the Indonesian government.

Evalyn was the owner of the cursed Hope Diamond once owned by Queen Marie Antoinette of France. It now belongs to the Smithsonian where you can see its new display case if Henry's cat Carnegie has not swallowed it, as he was taught to do in Dan Brawner's "A Taste for the Good Life" in *Danger in D.C.* (1993).

In Max Allan Collins's *Stolen Away* (set in 1932), Chicagoan Nate Heller was sent east to work on the Lindbergh kidnaping case because one theory was that Al Capone, in jail for income-tax evasion, had the Lindberghs' son snatched as a bargaining chip. Nate became Evalyn Walsh McLean's chauffeur and drove her in her powder-blue Lincoln Continental to her deserted country place to meet with a gangster who pretended he had a hot tip.

Any of these Massachusetts Avenue mansions could be the home of Senator Les Rhodes in Edgar Box's (aka Gore Vidal) *Death Before Bedtime* (1953). Peter Cutler Sargeant III had been hired to run the senator's presidential campaign, but the very night Sargeant arrived to stay at the senator's home with a very mixed bag of guests, Senator Rhodes was blown up in his study.

In Margaret Truman's *Murder in the Smithsonian* (1983), the curators at the Natural History Museum remeasured the

Hope Diamond with new equipment the morning after the dramatic murder of British historian Dr. Lewis Tunney and the theft of the Order of Harsa.

Across 21st Street is the former Ritz-Carlton Hotel at 2100 Massachusetts Avenue. Now an ITT Sheraton Hotel, its small lobby would be hard to lurk in, but any number of mystery characters lived there. It also is the home of the Jockey Club, a wood-paneled restaurant hung with racing prints.

In R. B. Dominic's (aka Emma Lathen) mysteries about D.C., bachelor Ohio Congressman Ben Safford lived at the Ritz-Carlton. In *Epitaph for a Lobbyist* (1974), when lobbyist Shirley Knapp was murdered after bribing a congressman, who also lived at the Ritz-Carlton, Safford told his cronies that there's no such thing as a free lunch.

Cross Massachusetts Avenue at 21st Street to the Phillips Collection (Gallery), located in an old brownstone mansion with a modern wing. Originally the Phillips family home, the house was opened to the public in 1923, eight years before New York's Museum of Modern Art. A lovely gallery reminiscent, as travel agent Richard Klein reminded me, of London's Courtauld Institute, it has a small basement cafe where you can get snacks and make a pit stop.

In Janice Law's *The Big Payoff* (1976), Anna Peters found her British contact Austen Lloyd dead in a green Chevrolet parked on Massachusetts Avenue. Anna decided to "go it alone," so she and her boyfriend Harry used Harry's van and his graphic art supplies as a cover. While Harry dropped off his latest job at the Phillips Gallery, Anna went to look at the museum's famous Renoir, *The Luncheon of the Boating Party*. She saw a covered Chinese vase and impulsively dropped the secret roll of film into it.

Recross Massachusetts Avenue at 21st Street and Q Street to look at the imposing Larz Anderson House, which is now the headquarters of the Society of the Cincinnati. This opulent museum, reminiscent of Newport mansions like the Breakers, has a collection of Revolutionary War artifacts open to the public. Named for fifth-century General Lucius Quinctius Cincinnatus, a famous Roman hero who left the plow to lead a victorious army, then returned to farm, the Society was founded in 1783 by former Revolutionary War officers. George Washington was its first president-general. Membership in the Society descends from eldest son to eldest son. Larz Anderson, the diplomat who built the mansion, was a member of the Society; his widow gave the house to the Society.

In Margaret Truman's *Murder in the Smithsonian* (1983), there was considerable discussion between Tunney's fiancee Heather McBean and MPD Captain Mac Hanrahan about the relative merits of the Society of the Cincinnati and its democratic "competitor," Truman's mythical "Legion of Harsa."

Across Massachusetts Avenue at number 2121 you can see the elegant limestone Townsend House. Built in 1900 by the CEO of the Erie & Pittsburgh Railroad on the site of an earlier mansion of one of the California Syndicate, it incorporated the foundations of the earlier house because a soothsayer said if it did not, evil (murder?) would happen! Since 1950 it has been the home of the very private Cosmos Club, and you can only go inside if you are or know a member.

The Cosmos Club is undoubtedly the Minerva Club in Charles Goodrum's mysteries. In *Carnage of the Realm* (1979), Yale librarian Edward George, on a D.C. visit, became involved in the search for the killer of some coin collectors and invited his fellow sleuths, Werner-Bok Library PR person Betty Crighton Jones and historian Steve Carson to breakfast at the Minerva Club. Later, in *The Best Cellar* (1987), while George, Crighton Jones, and Carson were hunting for a missing grad student who had discovered the original Library of Congress books lost when the British burned D.C. in 1814, they met at the Minerva Club for breakfast in the Garden Room. (According to mystery bookseller Barbara Gauntt, at that time the Cosmos Club allowed females only in the Garden Room, which certainly establishes the Minerva Club's identity! It also explains why my Great-Uncle John Batchelder entertained the family elsewhere.)

Walk up Massachusetts Avenue to the intersection of Florida Avenue and 22nd Street and cross both streets to

Sheridan Circle. In the area between the Cosmos Club and Sheridan Circle are located the Moroccan Embassy, the Luxembourg Ambassador's residence, the Irish Embassy, the United Arab Military Attaché Office, the Greek Embassy, the Rumanian Embassy, and the Turkish Ambassador's residence—to name a few! Nearly all once were private mansions.

Sheridan Circle was originally called Decatur Circle for Naval hero Stephen Decatur, then renamed for Civil War General Philip Sheridan who helped make Robert E. Lee surrender at Appomattox. The bronze equestrian statue of Sheridan was done by Gutzon Borglum, who carved the presidents on Mount Rushmore. In 1976 a former Chilean ambassador to the United States was blown up there by a car bomb.

Walk around Sheridan Circle to your left. You pass the Barney Studio House, which was an artists' salon during the life of its owner, Alice Pike Barney, who had studied with James Whistler in Paris and once had a one-woman show at the Corcoran Gallery. She has been called D.C.'s Gertrude Stein but Richard Klein suggested to me that she also resembled New York's doyenne of the arts, Gertrude Vanderbilt. Barney's studio was given to the Smithsonian by her daughters, but is not open to the public.

The area north of Sheridan Circle known as Kalorama is a very exclusive residential area which has become an extension of Embassy Row. Look for the many signs and flags as you walk past. Perhaps as a sign of diplomatic delicacy few of them appear in mysteries; the one big exception is the British Embassy, no doubt because the classic mystery is an Anglo-American invention!

In Van Wyck Mason's *The Washington Legation Murders* (1935), Captain Hugh North of G2, the Army's General Staff Intelligence, decided to walk to his apartment on California Street from the Swedish Legation near Sheridan Circle. Upset at the sudden murder of Swedish Count Oxenstahl by an international spy known as the Guardsman, Captain North hiked home up Massachusetts Avenue in the snow, but stopped in Rock Creek Park to sit on a bench and think! A bedraggled young woman suddenly sat on the bench opposite him and waved a knife as if about to kill herself, so the gallant Captain took her home to his apartment to dry off.

Continue up Massachusetts Avenue from Sheridan Circle to R Street. Cross R Street and walk to Decatur Place, cross Decatur Place, and walk to S Street. If you kept going north to California Street, you would come to the 1931 Japanese Embassy in a Georgian Revival mansion with a cobblestoned courtyard. In its garden is an authentic Japanese teahouse brought over in 1960 and next door a starkly modern chancery building was added in 1986.

None of these buildings existed when Prince Hojo, cousin of the Emperor of Japan, was murdered at the old Japanese Embassy east of Dupont Circle at 16th and Massachusetts in Diplomat's *Murder in the Embassy* (1930). It took Dennis Tyler, Chief of the State Department's CPI (Current Political Intelligence) to solve Prince Hojo's murder without international repercussions.

When you come to the intersection of Massachusetts Avenue and 24th Street, cross Massachusetts to 24th Street where you go by the Cameroon Embassy, a limestone chateau built in 1907 by Christian Hauge, Norway's first ambassador to the United States. In 1927 it became the Czechoslovakian foreign mission until the Cameroon government bought it in 1972. A huge palace, it is now for sale. This was the embassy where would-be defector Czech Jan Brovic had to report to his bosses in Helen MacInnes's *I and My True Love* (1952).

Turn right on S Street and crossing 24th Street, keep walking east on the south side of S Street. Across the street, Number 2419 Massachusetts Avenue was the D.C. home of mystery writer Mary Roberts Rinehart before she moved to New York. Rinehart wrote over twenty mysteries set in D.C., but her most famous was *The Man in Lower Ten* (1909). (See Walk 4.) One of Mystery's Grande Dames, Rinehart is the subject of a biography by fellow mystery writer Charlotte MacLeod called *Had She But Known* (1994) and British Diamond Dagger winner H. R. F. Keating included *The Circular Staircase* (1908) in *Crime & Mystery: The 100 Best Books* (1987). The Rinehart residence is now the Zambian Embassy.

Walk along S Street to the Woodrow Wilson House at 2340 S Street where President Wilson lived after he had served his second term. It is a museum showing how upper-middle-class families lived before the Great Depression. Next door to the Wilson House in two townhouses at 2320 S Street is the Textile Museum. It has a collection of handmade carpets and textiles, including a pre-Columbian collection from Peru. Both places have excellent gift shops, too.

Continue on S Street to 23rd Street, cross it and walk to the set of stairs called the Spanish Steps. They take the place of 22nd Street and connect S Street with Decatur Place to the south. Look down the steps, but stay on S Street to go past Kalorama Square to Phelps Place.

Cross Phelps Place and Florida Avenue (originally Boundary Avenue because it was the northern boundary of D.C.) to Connecticut Avenue. Turn right to walk down Connecticut Avenue back to Dupont Plaza.

Be sure to stop at MysteryBooks at 1715 Connecticut Avenue. A bookstore devoted to mysteries, it has been a strong supporter of the annual mystery convention Malice Domestic held every April in the Washington D.C. area. I first met Barbara Gauntt, who read this book in manuscript, at the bookstore. Without her eagle eye, especially in this walk, I would be using "street" for "avenue" and "avenue" for "street" and sending you in circles! MysteryBooks now has two new enthusiastic proprietors, Tina McGill and Martha Pennigar, who looked at this guide for me, too.

After visiting MysteryBooks, continue walking down Connecticut Avenue to R Street. Cross R Street and continue walking to Hillyer Place. Between Hillyer Place and Q Street at 1517 Connecticut you will find the Anchorage Building. It was once a swank apartment building that housed celebrities like Charles Lindbergh, whose son was kidnaped in Collins's *Stolen Away* (1991), actress Tallulah Bankhead, daughter of a senator, who reminds one of murdered D.C. hostess Vivian Taliafero in Elliott Roosevelt's *Murder in the Rose Garden* (1989), and Speaker of the House Sam Rayburn of Texas, who pushed his protégé Lyndon Johnson on FDR in Roosevelt's *Murder in the Oval Office* (1989).

Now in the Anchorage you will find two neighborhood fixtures: Kramerbooks and the Afterwords Cafe.

In Michael Bowen's *Washington Deceased* (1990), Richard Michaelson met ex-Senator Gardner's daughter Wendy at Cavalier Books, a bookstore on Connecticut Avenue with a coffee bar, run by his old friend Marjorie Randolph who knew everybody. When Michaelson had to meet some VIP, Marjorie called a secretary to tell her that she had a new shipment of English mysteries. In return, the secretary put Marjorie in touch with another secretary who arranged for Marjorie and Michaelson to be invited to a party the VIP attended.

In Marilyn Quayle and Nancy Northcott's *Embrace the Serpent* (1992), international superspy Edmund Miller (aka Bonfire) used The Whodunit, a bookshop on Dupont Circle, as a drop. Miller was known on the Hill as a collector of mysteries who made frequent lunchtime visits to the bookshop. Before buying anything, Bonfire would roam about, but he always opened the last volume on the second from the top row of the books of literary criticism where his contact placed messages for him. If Bonfire had a message he would put it in the same book.

In Leslie Ford's World War II mystery, *All for the Love of a Lady* (1943), a Garfield Hotel at Connecticut Avenue and Dupont Circle had an air-conditioned cocktail lounge, where, after doing her Red Cross stint, Grace Latham was meeting friends for lunch. But she met her perennial admirer Colonel John Primrose and ended up lunching with him instead. They were in the midst of a scandal over war supplies that made Grace say she'd like to apply to the Ration Board for enough gas to drive herself to St. Elizabeth's! (St. Elizabeth's is the D.C. mental hospital where poet Ezra Pound was locked up after the Allies freed him from an Italian cage.)

Turn left to walk around Dupont Circle to 19th Street, which bisects it north and south. Originally, it had old houses with slave shacks in back, but by World War II, many were rooming houses down on their luck. In Aaron Marc Stern's *Death Takes a Paying Guest* (1947), Elsie Mae Hunt had rented a room on 19th Street in a narrow redbrick house owned by Mrs. Lee Beauregard Purnell, a Gentlewoman in Reduced Circumstances and a Colonel's Relict. Elsie Mae and Timothy Francis Mulligan were in D.C. to read about pre-Columbian sites at the Library of Congress. Tim was at another house whose landlady would not take women. Elsie found another roomer with a knife in his back but by the time she had wakened her landlady and called the police, the body had vanished. Elsie Mae then moved to another derelict house owned by Mrs. Purnell's cousin Helen.

In Alexandra Roudybush's *A Sybaritic Death* (1972), VIP lawyer Evander Thorpe and his Russian emigre wife Xenia, whom he had picked up on the streets of Constantinople, lived in a little house on 19th Street just off Dupont Circle where Xenia celebrated Christmas and Easter twice. Evander Thorpe invited his young client Vanessa Prestwick there for breakfast before Vanessa went to Istanbul to hunt for her missing stepmother Claire. Like Senator Driscoll, another Thorpe client, Claire was heavily in debt to the D.C. Mob.

Cross 19th Street to the Dupont Plaza Hotel, built just after World War II on the site of Levy Leiter's mansion. Until early 1997 the Collector, a combination art gallery and restaurant managed by Bill Wooby, was located on the ground floor. The Collector appeared in Margaret Truman's *Murder at the National Gallery* (1996), and in September 1996 I met Bill and two of the artists who helped make D.C.'s artistic atmosphere "real" for Miss Truman: Judy Jashinsky and Virginia Daley there. Bill Wooby gave me a special copy of the mystery autographed by all the artists who had contributed to the book, and told me that the Truman mystery was to end at the Collector, but the movie contract called for a chase through the National Gallery.

Murder at the National Gallery (1996) is the first mystery in which Truman used real people or places apart from public buildings. In the mystery Annabel Reed-Smith; her spouse, law professor Mac Smith; and Steve Jordan, head of the MPD's art squad, met at the Collector after Jordan persuaded Annabel to help with a sting operation to get back some pre-Columbian art objects stolen from Dumbarton Oaks.

Visit the Dupont Plaza Hotel to make use of its rest rooms, then continue left around the Circle to New Hampshire Avenue. Cross New Hampshire and walk past the Washington Club at number 15. This ornate palazzo was built for Robert Patterson of Chicago's Medill-Patterson-McCormick newspaper family, who was the father of flamboyant Washington hostess Eleanor (Cissy) Patterson. Cissy, who was a social archrival of Theodore Roosevelt's daughter Alice Longworth, was publisher of the *Washington Times-Herald*. Cissy's mansion later was used as the headquarters of the Red Cross, then sold to the elite private club, the feminine equivalent of the Cosmos Club.

Cross P Street to Massachusetts Avenue and turn left on Massachusetts to pass the yellow brick Sulgrave Club, a mansion built by the Wadsworths, who donated it to the Red Cross in 1918. The Red Cross sold the mansion in 1932 to the Sulgrave Club, another private ladies' club. With so many Dupont Circle mansions used for Red Cross activities, feel free to imagine Leslie Ford's widowed Grace Latham playing bridge or rolling Red Cross bandages in any of them.

Walk along Massachusetts Avenue to 18th Street. Cross 18th Street to the National Trust for Historic Preservation Building. Originally known as the McCormick Apartments, it was D.C.'s most luxurious apartment building with a single apartment on each floor. Among other illustrious tenants were Secretary of the Treasury Andrew Mellon and Perle Mesta, a latter-day "hostess with the mostest." Next door is part of the Carnegie Institute for International Peace. This part of Massachusetts Avenue was another millionaires' row and a historic district as well as "old" Embassy Row.

At 1770 Massachusetts Avenue there used to be a mansion owned by the writer Frances Hodgson Burnett. Known to her intimates as "Dearest," the creator of *Little Lord Fauntleroy* was very much a part of the social scene in D.C. Thanks to the multimedia, there are still very few people who haven't heard, read, or seen her *Little Princess* or the more mysterious *The Secret Garden*.

Past the site of the Burnett house you come to the Brookings Institution at 1775 Massachusetts Avenue, housed in a big utilitarian building. In Michael Bowen's *Washington Deceased* (1990), diplomat Richard Michaelson had retired to work at the Brookings Institution while trying to get a job as head of the CIA. Michaelson wrote *Bright Lines and Slippery Slopes: Nine Fallacies in Current Foreign Policy Discourse*, which jailed Senator Gardner's daughter Wendy bought at Cavalier Books. Wendy also went to hear Michaelson lecture at the Brookings Institution.

Keep going on Massachusetts Avenue past a Johns Hopkins University building. This stretch of Massachusetts is no longer residential, so mystery references to old brownstones and boarding houses show their age.

In Helen MacInnes's *I and My True Love* (1952), set during the Cold War, socialite Sylvia Pleydel, was married to cold, correct State Department bureaucrat Payton Pleydel but in love with Czech Jan Brovic, secretly trying to defect. Anne and Martin Clark, who were old friends of Sylvia Pleydel, lived between Scott Circle and Connecticut Avenue in an old Victorian mansion converted into small apartments and Sylvia fled there after a fight with her husband.

Cross 17th Street to tiny Bataan Street which runs north and south between Massachusetts and Rhode Island Avenues at the edge of Scott Circle. Scott Circle was named for Mexican War hero General Winfield Scott. In Diplomat's *Murder in the Embassy* (1930), the Japanese Embassy was near Scott Circle at 16th and Massachusetts Avenue. Prince Hojo, the Emperor's nephew, was incognito so the blinds were down and windows shuttered. While the Prince talked with Lord Robert Murray, His Britannic Majesty's Chargé d'Affaires, in the upstairs library, the Japanese Ambassador Viscount Kondo and Mr. James B. Acorn, assistant secretary of state, waited below. When the Prince's valet gave the alarm they all entered the library to find the British Chargé unconscious and the Emperor's cousin dead.

In Leslie Charteris's *The Saint Steps In* (1943), the Saint (aka Simon Templar), was asked for help by Madeleine Gray who was in D.C. to help her chemist dad. She had been warned not to talk to top government official Frank Imberline who lived in a mansion near Scott Circle. When the Saint found a note in his pocket saying "MIND YOUR OWN BUSINESS," he followed Gray from the Shoreham Hotel and rescued her from two toughs who claimed to be FBI.

Turn right on Bataan Street to Rhode Island Avenue and turn right again to walk along Rhode Island Avenue to 17th Street. You pass the B'nai B'rith Klutznick Museum just before you cross 17th Street. On its ground floor there is a large collection of Jewish ceremonial fine art and folk art.

Then continue to St. Matthew's Roman Catholic Cathedral, a huge redbrick Romanesque 1899 building with a green dome and a gorgeous gold and red mosaic of St. Matthew over the front entrance. St. Matthew is the patron saint of civil servants, and once a year the "Red Mass" is said here, attended by Supreme Court justices, members of Congress, Cabinet and diplomatic corps, and other government departments. But as Episcopal Bishop George St. James of Washington's National Cathedral commented in Margaret Truman's *Murder at the National Cathedral* (1990), churches are not a big item on the D.C. tourist circuit, and it took President Kennedy's assassination to put St. Matthew's "on the map." This is where President Jack Kennedy attended mass and where his funeral was held on November 25, 1963, after his body had lain in state at the White House and the Capitol. Go inside to admire the gorgeous mosaics and look for the tablet in front of the High Altar that shows where his coffin rested before the funeral cortege took it to Arlington National Cemetery (See Walk 8).

In Walter J. Sheldon's *Rites of Murder* (1984), Bishop Paul Burdock of D.C.'s Roman Catholic archdiocese had a visit from call girl Laureen Triplett who wanted his help getting her daughter into St. Ursula's School. When Triplett was found murdered, the bishop not only investigated her murder with the help of his ex-jailbird chauffeur Marty Feist, but also made certain her daughter Alicia continued at St. Ursula's.

In David Baldacci's *Absolute Power* (1996), the funeral of multimillionaire international tycoon Walter Sullivan, a long-time booster of President Alan Richmond, was held here with a moving eulogy by President Richmond.

Take the alley called Matthew's Court on the far side of the cathedral and turn right to N Street and then turn right to take N Street to a D.C. "tradition" called the Tabard Inn at 1739 N Street. Both a cozy old-fashioned hotel and a power lunch restaurant, the building combines three townhouses and is famous for its real British atmosphere with an open hearth and good food.

In Jerome Doolittle's *Head Lock* (1993), Boston PI Tom Bethany got a call from his lover Hope Edwards in D.C. telling him she was pregnant. Bethany flew to D.C. to be with her at the Arlington abortion clinic, staying as usual at the Tabard Inn. Unfortunately, the Reverend Howard Orrin's Life Force group demonstrated against the clinic the day they went, so they were on TV for Hope's husband and sons to see.

According to syndicated columnist Jeff Greenfield in *The People's Choice* (1995), [as well as "Anonymous" Joe Klein of *Newsweek* in *Primary Colors* (1996)], the media run the world. In Greenfield's mystery, President-Elect MacArthur Foyle died before the Electoral College could formally elect him, so when the College elected Vice President–Elect Ted Block as president, Al DeRossa, the main man for polls, and Sharon Kramer, one of Ted Block's staffers, met at the Tabard Inn to compare notes and plan strategy for what they expected to be the administration of a boob.

Check out the Tabard Inn, then continue on N Street to 18th Street. Cross 18th Street and go to Connecticut Avenue. You can either turn right on Connecticut Avenue to return to Dupont Circle or cross Connecticut Avenue on N Street to go to 19th Street. Turn right on 19th Street and walk back towards Dupont Circle past C. F. Folks at 1225 19th Street, another little restaurant you might like to try.

In Margaret Truman's *Murder at the National Gallery* (1996), Annabel Reed-Smith met her husband Mac Smith there for lunch after her first meeting with the Caravaggio exhibition committee at the National Gallery. Reed-Smith, a college roommate of the vice president's wife, Carole, was representing her on the committee. At C. F. Folks, Annabel told Mac that there were some pretty big brains and bigger egos in that committee room that would have put some politicians to shame! Try out C. F. Folks, then continue up 19th Street to the entrance to the Dupont Circle Metro Station to end the first part of this walk.

Part Two begins at the Cleveland Park Metro Station two stops north of Dupont Circle. In Mark Olshaker's *The Edge* (1994) with a vicious neurosurgeon-cum-serial killer on the loose, homicide detective Sandy Mansfield took the Metro at Farragut North after dark. After the train left the Dupont Station en route to Woodley Park, three young dudes got up, gave the other passengers the eye, then accosted Sandy. She kept her hand on her gun inside her purse as she told them very slowly and deliberately that if they f***ed with her, they'd be very very sorry. Miraculously, the other passengers began staring, too, and the three guys gave up and got off the train at Woodley Park.

There is a very high escalator at Cleveland Park where you are climbing up St. Alban's Mount to the National Cathedral. Take the east side exit for Connecticut Avenue. Turn left (heading south) on Connecticut Avenue to Ordway Street. This is a strip-mall area with small ethnic restaurants. Cross Ordway and stay on Connecticut. You will pass a Starbucks Coffee at 3420 Connecticut Avenue. Open by 9 A.M. seven days a week, this makes a very hospitable place for coffee and a pit stop, since none of the D.C. Metro stations have public rest rooms. Across Connecticut, there is also a McDonald's next to a Crown Books.

Keep walking to Newark Street, which dead ends at Connecticut Avenue. Cross Newark and go one more block to Macomb Street. Turn right on Macomb to walk uphill through a pleasant residential neighborhood of well-kept houses, built close together, with old trees and very narrow sidewalks.

In Judith Viorst's *Murdering Mr. Monti* (1994), Brenda Kovner who wrote a syndicated column called "In Control of Our Lives" lived in an old Victorian in Cleveland Heights with her husband Jake, a pediatric surgeon. Brenda was feeding Jake and their younger son Wally on their front porch one August evening when Mr. Monti appeared to threaten them all if Wally didn't leave his daughter Jo alone. The Kovner family were Jewish, while Mr. Monti was Roman Catholic. There was a row and some hitting, after which Brenda decided the only sensible solution to the problem was murder.

On the left before you reach 33rd Place you pass the wooded grounds of Washington's International School. Cross 33rd Place and walk to 34th Street. Turn left at 34th Street past an elementary school to Lowell Street and the Cleveland Park Congregational Church.

Turn right to take Lowell Street to 35th Street, where you turn left on Woodley Road, which borders one side of the cathedral close. You are now at the cathedral close (grounds) and you have walked one mile (uphill).

In Leslie Ford's *Washington Whispers Murder* (1953), Grace Latham went to a cocktail party given by wealthy divorcee Sybil Thorn for her new protégé Congressman Hamilton ("call me Ham") Vair at her Woodley Road mansion. Vair came from the same state as industrialist Rufus Brent, who had been chosen to head a new Industrial Techniques Commission but was being vilified by a whispering campaign until Grace involved her perpetual suitor Colonel Primrose.

Turn right on Woodley Road and walk past the playing fields of the Episcopal Church Schools: St. Alban's School for Boys and the National Cathedral School for Girls. The girls' school is straight ahead of you at the corner of Woodley Road and Wisconsin Avenue. St. Alban's originally was the National Cathedral School, intended to educate young cathedral choirboys, but now it is the school of choice for the sons of presidents and vice presidents, who may or may not sing.

Stay on Woodley Road until you reach the second road to your left leading into the Close. Take it past the College of Preachers, the library, and the Deanery. All lovers of English cozies know that Church of England cathedrals are run by their deans, while the cathedra, or chair, is the seat of the bishop, who sits in it when present but often has a palace elsewhere. A canon is a priest who is a member of the cathedral staff, real or honorary.

Note the Bishop's Garden down a flight of steps across from the cathedral to your left. In Carey Roberts's *Pray God to Die* (1994), a photograph of murdered Caroline McKelvey was taken in the Bishop's Garden and MPD homicide detectives Anne Fitzhugh and Don Dakota interviewed Canon Jesse Clore there.

Walk to the cathedral's south transept. The Visitors Entrance, with a gift shop where you can get a map of the cathedral, is in the crypt. Capital architect Pierre L'Enfant had planned a church for national prayer, but construction did not begin until 1907 when President Theodore Roosevelt laid the cornerstone. The Bethlehem Chapel in the crypt below the High Altar was the first part, opened in 1912. The cathedral was not completed until St. Michael's Day (September 29), 1990.

The seat of both Washington's Episcopal bishop and the presiding bishop of the Protestant Episcopal Church of the United States of America (PECUSA), its official name is the Cathedral Church of St. Peter and St. Paul. It towers 676 feet above sea level; lit up at night, it can be seen far and wide. Unlike official D.C. which closes down for the weekend, the cathedral hums on a Sunday.

Still, in Louisa Revell's *The Men with Three Eyes* (1955), settlement director Ruth Gibson told her guest "Miss Julia" that she had wiggled in church because they went to the cathedral. Ruth insisted the cathedral had a bad effect on her because it was so big and cold and you were so far away from the choir you were afraid to sing. The next Sunday they went to St. John's. (See Walk 1.)

The cathedral is a popular site for VIP funerals in mysteries. In Edgar Box's (aka Gore Vidal) *Death Before Bedtime* (1953), after Senator Les Rhodes was blown up in his Massachusetts Avenue mansion, his funeral was held at the cathedral in a chapel filled with official Washington. The senator was then buried at Arlington National Cemetery.

In Allen Drury's *Advise and Consent* (1959), a memorial service was held at the cathedral for young Senator Brigham M. Anderson who had committed suicide. Senator Orrin Knox of Illinois noted grimly that the media was giving him hell for using Anderson's death to beat the nomination of Robert Leffingwell for secretary of state.

In ex-Senator William Cohen and Thomas B. Allen's *Murder in the Senate* (1993), Capitol Police Lieutenant Alexandra Phelan was on duty at the National Cathedral funeral of murdered Senator Julia Bristow. All ninety-two senators were present as well as the president and the governors of Louisiana, Texas, and South Carolina. Phelan stood in the nave when she noticed two men strolling behind the High Altar. One was the governor of Louisiana, the other Congressman Michael Royal who was soon appointed to fill the vacant Senate seat.

In Carey Roberts's *Pray God to Die* (1994), when Caroline McKelvey was found murdered, she turned out to have been spying on Congressman Woodward for ABC-TV's investigative reporter Simone Gray, the sister of Canon Jesse Clore. Canon Clore had Caroline's funeral at Washington Cathedral and afterward MPD detectives Anne Fitzhugh and Don Dakota interviewed both Canon Clore and the young Italian stonecutter Caroline had been tutoring in English. Later the funeral of Gertrude Woodward, the Congressman's wife, was held in the Bethlehem Chapel.

Charles McCarry's *Shelley's Heart* (1995), opened at the National Cathedral with the state funeral of the chief justice the day before the president's inauguration. His death complicated the fact that the election had been stolen electronically from former President Franklin Mallory, who lay in wait at the funeral for President-Elect Lockwood and told him they must meet before he took the oath of office. The funeral of Vice President Williston Graves was also held here on the second day of President Lockwood's impeachment trial.

In Ron Nessen and Johanna Neuman's *Knight and Day* (1995), environmentalist Curtis Davies Davenport's funeral was attended by VIPs including talk-show celebrity Jerry Knight. Davenport had been murdered just after he appeared on Knight's show.

In Tom Clancy's *Executive Orders* (1996), the state funeral of President and Mrs. Durling was held at the National Cathedral. Despite incredible security problems, the Durlings' and the new President Jack Ryans' children were there, with dignitaries from around the globe, led by Britain's Prince of Wales who knew President Ryan personally.

Go into the Visitors Entrance which leads to the Gift Shop (all cathedrals here and abroad are poor as the proverbial church mice). Get a map of the cathedral, buy yourself a nice gargoyle or other souvenir, and find out about the tours and services. The main public rest rooms are just inside the twin towers but there are also rest rooms nearby.

Coming in the Visitors Entrance you entered the crypt, or basement, with its many chapels. If you don't want to shop, turn right toward the apse. Go past the Chapel of St. Joseph of Arimathea and turn right to the Visitors Lounge for the rest rooms. Then go to the Bethlehem Chapel, located directly under the High Altar. The Bethlehem Chapel was built in the Norman style with thick pillars and round arches.

In Truman's *Murder at the National Cathedral* (1990), law professor Mackensie Smith was married here to Annabel Reed by Canon Paul Singletary. Mac Smith knew the bishop of Washington, George St. James, but not only was St. James out of town, but Smith felt that asking the bishop to officiate smacked of "overkill." (He could have asked the dean, but there is no dean in this mystery.)

Walk across the back of the Bethlehem Chapel to the corridor which leads to the flight of stairs in the north transept. You pass the wooden partition of the choirboys' dressing room. Then take the north transept steps to the Chapel of the Good Shepherd which is always open for private prayer.

In addition to his position at the cathedral Canon Singletary was a leader of an interdenominational movement called Word of Peace, which turned out to be corrupted by Asian contributors. Later that fall choirboy soloist Joey Kelsch was in the choir room when he overheard two people quarreling in the Bethlehem Chapel. Then Joey heard someone dragging something heavy along the corridor to the stairs to the north transept up to the Chapel of the Good Shepherd. The next day as Bishop George St. James held the funeral of former Attorney General Adam Vikery, Singletary's body was discovered in the chapel, and the bishop promptly called Mac Smith.

From the north transept stairs you can leave the cathedral by the transept door or go past the Chapel of the Holy Spirit to walk down the long nave and leave by the twin towers entrance which opens on Wisconsin Avenue.

Take the North Road that leads to Wisconsin Avenue, then turn left along Wisconsin Avenue past the South Road exit and St. Alban's parish church to Massachusetts Avenue, which crosses Wisconsin Avenue at the northwest corner of the Cathedral Close.

Stand there to look north into what is a high-rent district. A block north is Cathedral Avenue (which reappears on the other side of the Cathedral Close). Republican Senator Bob Grant's administrative assistant Cynthia Novitsky, a widow with a degree from Georgetown University Law School, lived at 3604 Cathedral Avenue in Marilyn T. Quayle and Nancy T. Northcott's *Embrace the Serpent* (1992). In *The Campaign* (1996), when the African-American senator was accused of murder in the middle of a reelection campaign, Novitsky hid the senator's children there from the attorney general.

In Roberts's *Pray God to Die* (1994), murder victim Caroline MacKelvey lived at the Alhambra two blocks northeast on Wisconsin Avenue. It had a doorman twenty-four hours a day, but he left the front door unlocked long enough for the murderer to get in.

In Warren Adler's *Immaculate Deception* (1991), the scene of the crime was at 4000 Massachusetts Avenue where antiabortionist Congresswoman Frankie McGuire was found poisoned (and pregnant) in her bedroom. The crime scene was examined by MPD homicide detective Fiona FitzGerald, her black partner, and their publicity-hungry boss Captain Luther Greene, known as the Eggplant.

In Jerome Doolittle's *Head Lock* (1993), Boston PI Tom Bethany's mistress Hope Edwards, head of the Washington ACLU, lived in a white brick house on a winding road north of Massachusetts Avenue with her lawyer husband, Martin Edwards, and their two sons. Like Chelsea Clinton, the Edwards children went to Sidwell Friends School, a very exclusive private school not far away at 3825 Wisconsin Avenue. The exclusive nature and location of Sidwell Friends makes it something of a prime suspect, too, for the unnamed school "in Georgetown" attended by the two kidnaped VIP children in James Patterson's *Along Came a Spider* (1992).

Farther up Massachusetts Avenue at the edge of the District is American University, founded in 1893 by Methodist Bishop John Fletcher Hurst. In Richard Conroy's *Old Ways in the New World* (set in 1976), Henry Scruggs of the Smithsonian asked American University to house the K'ng-Gui whom he had brought over as part of the folklore exhibit on the Mall. The K'ng-Gui had been in jail for roasting a dog to celebrate the birth of a baby Hereditary Moote-apparent on the Fourth of July. When the general public caught on that the red and black bugs the K'ng-Gui had brought from their Indian Ocean island were eating everything made of cloth in D.C., Scruggs made a deal that American University's grad students hide the K'ng-Gui in return for an account of their legends about the second coming of the Baga-ag. (See Walk 3.)

Turn left on Massachusetts Avenue and walk past the Pilgrim Road which leads to St. Alban's School for Boys. Cross 36th Place and continue south on Massachusetts Avenue to 36th Street. You are now going downhill. At 36th Street you pass St. Sophia Greek Orthodox Cathedral, whose cornerstone was laid by President Dwight Eisenhower in 1956. Next cross Fulton Street and keep going past St. Nicholas Cathedral, a Russian Orthodox church at 34th Street, then a Mormon church, to the beginnings of Embassy Row with the Cape Verde Embassy at 3415 Massachusetts Avenue. There are embassies all about here.

At 34th Street you reach the grounds of the Naval Observatory. The Observatory was moved here in 1893 to keep it away from the noise and vibration of downtown D.C. You may tour the Observatory, but not the white Victorian Admiral's house taken over in 1975 as the residence of the vice president. Nelson Rockefeller was the first vice president to move in. He also appeared in Elliott Roosevelt's *Murder in the Blue Room* (1990), set in 1942 during a secret visit by USSR Foreign Secretary Molotov. During the First Lady's investigation into the murder of Press Office secretary Emily Ryan in the Blue Room, it turned out that Rockefeller had been monkeying around with Mayflower Hotel waitress Peggy Shearson, who was also murdered.

In Spiro Agnew's *The Canfield Decision* (1976), the Observatory had just become the official home of the vice president, but Vice President Canfield refused to live there. He bought a Federal house in Georgetown for his rich Main Line wife, who was seldom there (see Walk 7).

In Barbara D'Amato's *Killer.app* (1996), computer genius Dean Utley, head of SJR Systems, had stayed connected to every computer system his company installed, including Chicago hospitals and the Chicago Police headquarters at 11th and State. Since the vice president was already under his thumb, he planned to use these connections to murder the president. Utley called the Veep at home to discuss where the presidential party would have dinner in Chicago.

In Margaret Truman's *Murder at the National Gallery* (1996), vice president's wife Carole Aprile asked her college roommate, Annabel Reed-Smith, to come to the Admiral's House, where they talked in the kitchen about the Caravaggio exhibition at the National Gallery. Aprile had done her master's thesis on Caravaggio and wanted the exhibition to go well, so she asked Annabel to act as her liaison on the exhibition committee.

In recent times, the vice-presidential residents of the Admiral's House have been the Bushes, the Quayles, and the Gores. In *A Memoir* (1994), Barbara Bush mentioned enjoying Margaret Truman's mysteries. Marilyn Quayle and her sister Nancy Northcott write mysteries, while President Clinton, another big fan, invites mystery authors like Edgar-winning African-American Walter Mosley to the White House. This mysterious tradition has a venerable past, for both FDR and Harry Truman liked to read detective stories, and JFK was a great admirer of Ian Fleming's tales about Secret Agent James Bond.

As you walk down to 31st Street you pass still more embassies and glimpse the dome of the Naval Observatory through the trees to your right. At 31st Street you come to the British Embassy, which is the most popular embassy for scenes of the crime. It is a major complex of buildings and has the distinction of being one of the few embassies built for the purpose. Until the USSR built its gigantic embassy in the 1960s, this was D.C.'s largest (and most socially acceptable) diplomatic enclave. The British also dubbed D.C. a hardship post and built "way out here" to escape Washington's foggy bottom climate.

The first building you come to is the annex to the Chancery (offices), a modern, nondescript office building whose cornerstone was laid by a young Queen Elizabeth II, using George Washington's trowel (a form of burying the hatchet, no doubt).

Next, you come to the Chancery proper with elegant wrought-iron gates, and behind it, hardly visible, the gardens and residence of the ambassador, deliberately designed in elegant eighteenth-century style by Sir Edward Luytens in 1931. Built of Indiana limestone and Pennsylvania brick, his buildings look just like Colonial Williamsburg.

Guests who get inside describe the cavernous two-story foyer with red carpeted twin staircases rising to the main (upper) floor, lined with full-length portraits of the British kings and queens. The upper floor has a wide corridor the full length of the mansion and an elegant ballroom. But most of us will visit the embassy by reading mysteries set there.

In Van Wyck Mason's *The Washington Legation Murders* (1935), Captain Hugh North of Army's G2 Intelligence had an old crony at the British Embassy named Major Bruce Kilgour. Together they were pursuing the elusive international spy known as the Guardsman, who was selling intelligence secrets to the highest bidder. After the Guardsman's spies murdered

Swedish Count Erich Oxenstahl at the Swedish Legation, Kilgour had to tell Captain North that his best investigator, Sergeant Baker, had been killed and his body dumped inside the Chancery Gate of the British Embassy. The ambassador wanted to cooperate but with no publicity!

In Elliott Roosevelt's *Murder and the First Lady* (set in the summer of 1939), Eleanor Roosevelt had hired an English girl named Pamela Rush-Hodgebourne to work on her column "My Day." But Pamela was jailed for poisoning her lover, Phil Garber, the son of a New Jersey congressman. Pamela was also implicated in a British jewel theft, but the First Lady rode to the rescue, even making an unofficial visit to the embassy where she showed second secretary Sir Rodney Harcourt how to open their old safe.

In Jocelyn Davey's *A Capitol Offense* (1956), Oxford don-cum-Secret Agent Ambrose Usher was sent back to the D.C. Embassy, where he had served during World War II. On his arrival Usher mused that the British Embassy stood at the center of the D.C. world because there was no place where Britain was more respected or despised than at the Court of George Washington! He also noted that the massive portraits of English monarchs included George III.

The wacky ambassador, Admiral Junius Throttle, V.C., appointed by Prime Minister Winston Churchill by mistake, had a pet hobby: fireworks. He decided to celebrate Guy Fawkes Day (November 5). During the extravaganza the ambassador's aide was found shot in the grounds so Secret Agent Ambrose had to handle the jurisdictional mess. During his sleuthing at an embassy cocktail party Ambrose said that MWA Grand Master Mickey Spillane was the writer everyone at Oxford was reading and compared Spillane's *This Gun for Hire* to Euripedes' *Medea*.

In Evelyn Anthony's *The Avenue of the Dead* (1982), British secret agent Davina Graham was in charge when Elizabeth Fleming, wife of British-born Edward Fleming with a top-level job in the United States, demanded sanctuary at the British Embassy because her husband was a Soviet spy. Davina's partner was ex-Major Colin Lomax, supposedly working there on visas.

In Margaret Truman's *Murder on Embassy Row* (1984), Ambassador Geoffrey James, who had served as ambassador to Iran, was poisoned in his study the night of an embassy gala. Since embassies are legally foreign soil, the American authorities, even the White House, were told to "forget it." MPD detective Captain Sal Morizio and Officer Constance Lake investigated anyhow and were suspended. But they discovered that Ambassador James not only had done illicit smuggling, but had known ahead of time that the Iranians were going to take Americans hostage!

In Tom Clancy's *Patriot Games* (1987), when the Prince of Wales came over to help the CIA's Jack Ryan capture the IRA terrorist who had tried to assassinate him and his family, he stayed at the Embassy. Later in Clancy's *Executive Orders* (1996) His Royal Highness returned to attend the funeral of President Durling and pick up where he had left off with his old chum, the new president, Jack Ryan.

On your left across Massachusetts Avenue just beyond the British Embassy is the Kahlil Gibran Memorial Garden. South of the embassy with one foot on American soil and the other firmly planted on British embassy land, is a statue of Winston Churchill, making the V for Victory sign. The statue was unveiled by Secretary of State Dean Rusk in 1966, on the third anniversary of Churchill's honorary American citizenship. Churchill starred in both Elliott Roosevelt's *The White House Pantry Murder*, set in 1941 just after Pearl Harbor when Churchill made a secret visit to D.C., and in Haynes Johnson and Howard Simons's *The Landing* (1986; set in 1942). (See Walks 1 and 4.)

South of Churchill's statue there is a modern dark glass box on stilts which is the chancery of the Brazilian Embassy, built in 1971. Next door is the Brazilian ambassador's residence in the 1908 McCormick Villa, built like a Roman palace with a red-tiled roof.

In Miriam Borgenicht's *Corpse in Diplomacy* (1956) intrepid columnist Katherine (Kate) Whipple who wrote "The Nation's Capital and How It Stays That Way" for the *Mirror* had a terrible alibi for the murder of Martin Langsdorph, whose body was found under her bed. Kate had gotten a tip that something exciting would happen at the Brazilian Embassy that night and sat on a bench, watching, from 8 P.M. to midnight. Needless to say, no one saw her there.

Also across Massachusetts Avenue from the Brazilian Embassy at number 3005 with a blue dome is the boarded-up Iranian embassy. In Truman's *Murder on Embassy Row* (1984), after the murder of the British ambassador, his Iranian valet-chauffeur Nuri Hafez, who was suspected of his employer's murder, took refuge there and attacked an Embassy Row security guard who saw his light. Hafez then fled to Copenhagen, followed by detectives Morizio and Lake. They brought him back and hid out in the deserted embassy, only to be found and shot by another British embassy official who, like most embassy employees, doubled as a spy.

Keep walking to 30th Street. About a block farther south on Massachusetts Avenue you would come to Rock Creek Drive and the Charles Glower Bridge across Rock Creek, which flows down the middle of the long winding Rock Creek Park.

In Margaret Truman's *Murder at the National Gallery* (1996), Italian cultural attaché Carlo Giliberti was "importing" art on the side, using the diplomatic pouch. The night the Caravaggio Exhibition opened two Mafioso from the staff of the Italian Embassy dumped Giliberti's body in Rock Creek Park. It is a popular place for that.

Ramble in Rock Creek Park if you have time, but beware: the streets around the park are very hard to follow. We met a young woman who thought she was in Georgetown! There are few sidewalks and street signs were conspicuously lacking. To be on the safe side, turn left at 30th Street. You will have enough trouble following 30th Street as it winds its way eastward past Benton Place, crosses Normanstone Drive, and goes right (easterly) again!

The whole park area is charming, but there were no restaurants to be seen. But in Ross Thomas's *If You Can't Be Good* (1973), there was a restaurant on Normanstone Drive (just to your right) "near" the Shoreham Hotel. Decatur Lucas, hired by syndicated D.C. columnist Frank Size to find out why Senator Robert F. Ames accepted a $50,000 bribe to make a speech on the Senate floor that favored a business merger, then resigned, made a date to meet Senator Ames's daughter Carolyn there. But as Carolyn walked toward Lucas, her attaché case blew up, killing her.

Try to stay on 30th Street until you reach Cleveland Avenue. Turn right on Cleveland and follow it to a four-way intersection of Normanstone Lane, Woodland Drive, McGill and Calvert Streets. This neighborhood is a "cave-dweller" (i.e., old pre–New Deal Washington society) haunt, full of handsome mansions.

In Eleanor Pierson's *Murder Without Clues* (1942), she described Washington as in transition from a sleepy Southern town to the Corridors of Power. "Wild" D.C. socialite Lila Donnelly had shot (and killed) man-about-town George Adams but defended by John Hadley, the attorney for her father's company, she was acquitted. Hadley's wife Sue threw a party to celebrate at their mansion at 2445 Woodland Drive, during which Lila Donnelly was stabbed to death on the balcony overlooking Rock Creek Park.

Turn right on Calvert Street and take it to 24th Street (all one long block). At 24th Street just before Connecticut Avenue you come to the spacious yellow brick '20s hotel now called the Omni-Shoreham but known in mysteries simply as the Shoreham Hotel. Around its long driveway there are cars and many cabs. Turn right to go to the front entrance and go inside the handsome Art Deco lobby and lounge. There is a bar, music being played, and many clusters of chairs and palms. There are also rest rooms at the end of the lobby, near the terrace which looks out over Rock Creek Park.

In Keats Patrick's *Death Is a Tory* (1935), reporter "Tom" Collins told a story about the Shoreham Hotel. A dapper senator arrived and while looking for his party, was taken for a waiter by a British Embassy wife who told him to find her a table. He did, but then left to join his own party, insulting the lady who then demanded he be fired. Told who he was, she stalked out, but the next day the British Embassy demanded that the senator commit suicide—because he had insulted the empire!

In Leslie Ford's *The Murder of a Fifth Columnist* (1940),

the murder victim was the fifth best-known syndicated D.C. columnist, a pompous know-it-all named J. Corliss Marshall, who wrote "Marshalling the Facts." Marshall got his nickname from competitor Pete Hamilton who wrote "The Capital Calling." Pete Hamilton was accused not only of publishing another reactionary newsletter spilling vital secrets but of murdering the fifth columnist at a party to which Georgetown's widowed Grace Latham was invited. Both Grace and Colonel Primrose, her perennial suitor, were involved in solving the murder.

According to Mignon Eberhart's *The Man Next Door* (1942), D.C. had very few nightclubs and guests were entertained in one's home, but if one was in the mood there was always dancing somewhere like the Shoreham Terrace. That's where wartime bureaucrat Steve Blake took his secretary, murder suspect Maida Lovell, dancing to celebrate a great naval victory (the Battle of Midway). He proposed marriage after they solved the murder of the man next door.

In Leslie Charteris's *The Saint Steps In* (1943), Simon Templar (aka the Saint) was approached in the Shoreham's cocktail room by Madeleine Gray, who had an appointment with a VIP official called Imberline about her father's formula for synthetic rubber. She had received threatening notes telling her not to go. The Saint urbanely gave her lunch, but Madeleine then took off without him.

In Helen MacInnes's *I and My True Love* (1952), set during the Cold War, Sylvia Pleydel, married to a stuffy State Department VIP, was due at the Shoreham for a Red Cross lunch to promote Pleydel's career. She was secretly in love with Czech Jan Brovic who wanted to defect.

In Jocelyn Davey's *A Capitol Offense* (1956), British secret agent Ambrose Usher was assigned to the British Embassy but he lived at the Shoreham Hotel. Arriving there after a cocktail party at which he had flaunted a small briefcase, Usher took out a bottle marked "headache powder," sprinkled it on the briefcase and brought up fingerprints. Later when Usher had solved the murders, he went swimming at the hotel and for the first time in his life, dived in. The sensation was terrific, if scary, and convinced him not to return to Oxford but to take the assignment he'd been offered in Peru.

In R. B. Dominic's (aka Emma Lathen) *Murder Out of Commission* (1976), Ohio Congressman Ben Safford flew into Murren, Ohio, on the order of his sister Janet, for a meeting about building an atomic energy plant there. The meeting quickly became a confrontation between the representative of the Atomic Energy Commission, the local utility magnate, and PEP—Pure Environment for Posterity. In D.C. when the Murren, Ohio utility company threw a big party at the Shoreham, inviting Congressman Safford and his sister and brother-in-law in hopes of promoting the deal, the result was murder.

In Robert A. Carter's *Final Edit* (1994), publisher Nicholas Barlow and his editor-in-chief Sidney Leopold checked in at the Shoreham for the American Booksellers Association convention. Barlow continued to stay there, although he knew the Shoreham was a trifle shabby-genteel, because of nostalgia; as a boy when he came to ABA conventions with his dad they stayed there. Then the ABA was always held in D.C. and the exhibits were set up in the basement garage of the hotel. Barlow remembered wandering the hotel's halls looking for parties, and there was always at least one democratic poker game where publishers faced their own sales reps.

Come out of the Shoreham Hotel and turn right on Calvert Street to 25th Street. Cross 25th Street to Connecticut Avenue and go two blocks north to the entrance to the zoo at 3001 Connecticut Avenue.

Like other city zoos, the National Zoo is a popular tourist attraction that is fun to visit at 11 A.M. or 3 P.M. when the pandas are fed. When the zoo was founded in 1889, this area was uninhabited—its original settlers were Native American Algonquin Indians. Administered by the Smithsonian, the zoo is home to over two thousand animals and occupies 163 acres along Rock Creek; like Rock Creek Park, it is quite hilly. There are two major trails, the Olmstead Walk, which goes past the panda habitat and the Valley Trail, which goes past the water animals.

Go inside the gate and stop at the Educational Building

where you can get a map or buy a souvenir. There is also a cafeteria called the Mane House (pun intended) where you can get something to eat.

In Haynes Johnson and Howard Simons's *The Landing* (1986; set in 1942), Nazi spy Gunther Haupt had been murdering blacks in D.C. to start a race riot. He also pretended to be a Jewish refugee named Rosenweig to assassinate FDR, but he was recognized by a Secret Service agent as the murderer on wanted posters. Escaping, Gunther dashed into the zoo grounds where he was confronted by Naval Intelligence Lieutenant Henry Eaton.

In Richard Timothy Conroy's *Mr. Smithson's Bones* (1993), a Smithsonian staffer who had murdered several department heads was also murdered and her body cut up and sent to be fed to the lions at the zoo.

In R. B. Dominic's (aka Emma Lathen) *Epitaph for a Lobbyist* (1974), Congressman Ben Safford was made chairman of the congressional committee investigating Shirley Knapp, a lobbyist accused of bribing three congressmen for votes on Section C of the Industrial Pollution Act. (She was fingered by her teenage daughter who slipped the memo to the *Washington Post.*) When Knapp was murdered her husband Charlie from Safford's Ohio district arrived in town to protect his daughter, setting up a meeting at the zoo with a potential murderer. Knapp made the rendezvous himself just before closing time (not too many tourists) and chose the Bear Pit.

In British author Susan Moody's *Penny Black* (1984), Penny Wannawake, a gorgeous tall black whose parents were British Lady Helena Hurley and Senangaland's U.N. ambassador Dr. Wannawake, came to Washington to investigate the murder of her school chum, Senator George Lund's daughter Marfa (Martha), who was a top model. Senator Lund, a senator from the Deep South, was not fond of Penny, so she did not see Marfa's younger sister Susie until the funeral when they agreed to meet at the zoo. Penny was escorted to the rendezvous by Aaron Kimbell, a black PI originally hired by Senator Lund. They met Susie by the pandas Hsing-Hsing and Ling-Ling, who were sitting in the sun looking bored. Susie told them both she thought her father might have killed Marfa himself to keep her from talking about his new black mistress!

In Dorothy Sucher's *Dead Men Don't Marry* (1989), PI Vic Newman did the legwork for Sabina Swift, a shrink who owned a detective agency and was married to Professor Bruno Herschel, a theoretical physicist. Sabina had her own private cloister where she painted and drank tea. She sent Newman to the zoo in the early morning to stake out the area because a number of animals like a lemur and some tropical birds had been killed and the Smithsonian didn't think the police were doing a good job. Vic never found anyone, so he was just as glad to be pulled off the surveillance to work on finding a murderous psychotic male.

In Judith Viorst's *Murdering Mr. Monti* (1994), Brenda Kovner's plan to murder her son Wally's future father-in-law, Mr. Monti, was complicated by her twenty-four-hour extramarital binge with three men. One of them was superstar TV commentator Philip Eastlake, who insisted on a rerun. Brenda finally met him at the zoo (a handy walk from her Cleveland Park Victorian house), only to run into an old friend with his daughter.

In syndicated columnist Jeff Greenfield's *The People's Choice* (1995), TV news producer Steve Baer promised his daughter Hillary to take her to the zoo because he had missed every important occasion in her life. They went to look at the pandas eating straw but when his media itch took over, he called the Desk and found out he was supposed to take off at once for China. Soon afterward he was put on the story of the president-elect who was thrown from a horse and died before the Electoral College had met to elect him president.

Enjoy the zoo—especially the Giant Panda—and then end your walk by going back outside the entrance and turning left to walk down Connecticut Avenue to the Woodley Park-Zoo Metro Station.

Possible Side Trips

These mystery sites may be reached by Metro or by car.

Chevy Chase, Maryland, just over the D.C. boundary. Take the Metro Red Line north from Woodley Park or Cleveland Park to Friendship Heights Station.

In Patricia Moyes's *Black Widower* (1975), Mavis, the wife of Ambassador Sir Eddie Ironmonger from newly independent Tampica, was murdered at an embassy party, causing incredible diplomatic problems and bringing Scotland Yard's Chief Superintendent Henry Tibbett and wife Emily to D.C. The best help turned out to be retired Tampican Bishop Matthew Barrington and his wife Prudence, who lived in Chevy Chase and had known all the principal suspects since childhood, but when Prudence Barrington took the Chevy Chase Episcopal Women's Club to the annual Georgetown Garden Tour, murder followed (see Walk 7).

In R. B. Dominic's (aka Emma Lathen) *Murder Out of Commission* (1976), during the confrontation between PEP (Pure Environment for Posterity) and the Atomic Energy Commission, Congressman Ben Safford found himself in the middle. One of his congressional cronies Elsie Hollenbach of Marin County, California, stamped everything she touched. There was a Hollenbach way to question a witness, a response to horsetrading bids, a style for badgering agencies. She drank martinis and served sherry, lunched on cottage cheese and kept a stock of fresh corsages in her office refrigerator. Representative Hollenbach's nondescript house in Maryland also had spectacular gardens where each spring she threw an open house. It was at Elsie's annual garden party that Ben Safford planned how to smoke out the murderer.

Bethesda, Maryland. Take the Metro Red Line to the Bethesda Metro Station. When you come out of the station you will find yourself just around the corner from the Hyatt Hotel.

The Hyatt Hotel, One Bethesda Metro Center, is where the international cozy mystery convention called Malice Domestic took place from 1988 to 1997. (It will be in D.C. beginning in 1998.) Go into the hotel atrium lobby, where mystery greats hobnobbed with their fellows and fans, go to the lower level to peek into the ballroom where the banquets were held when the Ghosts of Honor were recognized, the Guests of Honor spoke, and the Agatha Awards were announced and their famous teapots with the skull and crossbones given out.

In Jon L. Breen's story "Rachel and the Bookstore Cat" in *Danger in D.C.* (1993), Gus and Emma Ordway of Ordway's Bookshop were an odd couple: Gus was a tall, lean, and bearded poet with beatnik clothes and Emma, considerably his junior, dressed like a Vogue model. But they attended a Malice Domestic banquet in Bethesda with Gus dressed like Sayers's Lord Peter Wimsey in white tie, tails, and monocle and Emma in an Elmore Leonard T-shirt.

Come out of the Hyatt Hotel and turn left to Old Georgetown Road where you will find the Mystery Bookshop: Bethesda at 7700 Old Georgetown Road [call (301) 657-2665]. Proprietors Jean and Ron McMillan have been prime movers and shakers of Malice Domestic.

In Edgar-winner Benjamin M. Schutz's *Embrace the Wolf* (1985), a Mrs. Saunders, the mother of twin five-year-old girls who had been kidnaped and never found, lived in Bethesda in a typical Bethesda house with a quarter acre for a quarter of a million dollars, built in the early '60s when the Beltway was finished. She hired black PI Leo Haggerty when her husband disappeared, afraid he had gotten some kind of a clue about the girls. Haggerty followed Saunders to North Carolina where he caught up with a serial killer, too.

P. M. Carlson's *Bad Blood* (1991), was set in Bethesda where Pat herself grew up. Ginny Marshall, an adopted teenager, ran away to hunt for her real mother who turned out to be statistician-cum-amateur sleuth Maggie Ryan. But when John Spencer, one of Ginny's adoptive grandmother's bridge group, was found murdered near the public library, runaway Ginny was a suspect.

Camp David. This top-secret presidential retreat is located near Detour, Maryland. FDR called it Shangri-La after James Hilton's story about a secret kingdom in the Himalayas, but Ike renamed it for his grandson David. Tourists are not invited but in reading mysteries it helps to "locate" it geographically.

In Elliott Roosevelt's *The White House Pantry Murder* (set in 1942), when spies were found to have infiltrated the White House and tapped its phones while Churchill was there on a secret visit, FDR angrily demanded to know if he had to move the government to Shangri-La.

In Margaret Truman's *Murder in the White House* (1980), special assistant Ron Fairbanks spent a weekend there with the First Family. Unlike some presidents, Webster brought lots of company, including Secretary of State Blaine, a compulsive womanizer who made a play for a woman professor. Blaine was later found murdered in the Lincoln Bedroom and Fairbanks was put in charge of the delicate murder investigation.

In Lawrence Sanders's *Capital Crimes* (1989), the president and his wife invited charismatic faith healer-cum-con artist Brother Kristos to visit them and their hemophiliac son George at Camp David. When Brother Kristos stopped a hemorrhage George suffered, they became true believers, ready to let Brother Kristos run the country.

In Stephen Coonts's *Under Siege* (1990), hired hit man Henry Charon brought down President Bush's helicopter as it landed at Camp David, making Vice President Quayle acting president.

6

FOGGY BOTTOM WALK

BACKGROUND

Foggy Bottom today is a mixture of university, institutional, and residential neighborhoods, with culture at the Kennedy Center and politics at the Watergate Complex. Historically, its graphic nickname did not come from the behavior of State Department diplomats, but from the malarial mists and smelly smokestacks of the Potomac riverfront. Squeezed into a swampy area between D.C. proper and "independent" Georgetown, Foggy Bottom was laid out in 1765 by Jacob Funk, and its original settlers were German immigrants who worked in the breweries and factories in what was known as Hamburg (or Funktown). There were wharves along the river as well as the Tiber Creek which ran from the C&O Canal east to what became Constitution Avenue.

K Street was the main thoroughfare to and from Georgetown, and from Washington Circle east to the White House. Mansions like the Octagon House were built as early as 1799. But most of Foggy Bottom's residents were workers who lived in brick tenements, while on higher ground there was a fort lookout called Camp Hill where the original Naval Observatory was located in the 1840s (see Walk 5).

During the Civil War Foggy Bottom was used as a Union camp. Afterward Southern blacks who had migrated to the city for jobs settled there. They overwhelmed the local churches, like St. John's on Lafayette Square, where African-Americans were only allowed to sit in the balconies and take communion after the whites. Instead of integrating their congregations, the Church of the Epiphany and St. John's paid to build Foggy Bottom's Victorian Gothic St. Mary's Episcopal Church for blacks only. Today St. Mary's is integrated, but in spite of the valiant efforts of Eleanor Roosevelt and others, "Jim Crow" remained alive and well in Washington, D.C., until the '60s.

By the 1880s the Army Corps of Engineers had dredged the Potomac River and filled in the Tiber Creek and low land west of the Washington Monument, making development possible in the southern half of Foggy Bottom. But the biggest change occurred in 1912 when George Washington University moved there, gradually becoming the major landlord. In 1947 the State Department moved out of the Old Executive Building into its large utilitarian-looking complex at 23rd and D Streets, then in 1971 both the John F. Kennedy Center for the Performing Arts and the Watergate Complex opened, creating the area's contemporary aura of culture crossed with corruption.

LENGTH OF WALK: About 2½ miles

See the map on page 175 for the boundaries of this walk and page 278 for a list of the books and detectives mentioned.

PLACES OF INTEREST

American Red Cross, 430 17th Street. The 1917 Neoclassic building is a memorial to the heroic women of the Civil War. Three Tiffany windows in Board of Governors hall. Open weekdays 8:30 A.M.–4:45 P.M. Free. Call 737-8300.*

Camp Hill, Navy Bureau of Medicine and Surgery, 23rd Street across from State Department. Not open to the public.

*The telephone area code is 202 unless otherwise indicated.

Constitution Hall, 1776 D Street. Daughters of the American Revolution built it for public concerts, but its most famous one never took place: Marian Anderson in 1939. Behind it is ***Continental Hall***, which houses DAR headquarters and the American Revolution Museum. Open weekdays 8:30 A.M.–4:00 P.M., Sun. 1:00 P.M.–5:00 P.M. Free. Call 879-3240.

Department of State (nicknamed "Foggy Bottom"), 2201 C Street. Not open to the public except for the ***Diplomatic Reception Rooms***, 23rd Street between C and D Streets. Free. Guided tours (reservations required). Call 647-3241.

Department of the Interior, C Street between 18th and 19th Streets. The "Mother" of Agriculture, Labor, Education, and Energy Departments. ***Museum*** open weekdays 8:00 A.M.–5:00 P.M., closed federal holidays. Free (adults show photo ID). Indian (Native American) Craft Shop. Call 208-4743.

Federal Reserve Building, 21st Street and Constitution Avenue. Board hearings held Wed. at 10:00 A.M., usually open to public. Tours of galleries given Thurs. afternoons. Free. Call 452-3000.

George Washington University, extends from Washington Circle to G Street, from 19th Street to 24th Street. Endowed by George Washington, it was the Baptist Columbian College until 1904. In 1912 it moved to Foggy Bottom and became George Washington University. You can get a map of the campus in the University Bookstore in the basement of the Marvin Center on 21st and I Streets.

Howard Johnson's Premier Hotel, 2601 Virginia Avenue at New Hampshire Avenue. Watergate headquarters of G. Gordon Liddy in 1972. Call 965-2700.

John F. Kennedy Center for the Performing Arts, New Hampshire Avenue at Rock Creek Parkway. First suggested by President Eisenhower, it was finally built as a memorial to JFK and opened in 1971. Free. For tour information call 416-8341. Open daily 10:00 A.M.–9:00 P.M. or until last show lets out. Box office open Mon.–Sat. 10:00 A.M.–9:00 P.M., Sun. and holidays noon–9:00 P.M. Call 467-4600.

Octagon House, 1799 New York Avenue. Built in 1801. When the British burned the White House in 1814, the Madisons stayed here. Later Madison signed the Treaty of Ghent, ending the war here, too. Now the headquarters of the American Institute of Architects (AIA). Open Tues.–Fri. 10:00 A.M.–4:00 P.M., weekends noon–4:00 P.M., closed December 25 and January 1. Donation. Call 638-1538.

Organization of American States (OAS) Building, 17th and Constitution Avenue. Next door to Pan-American Union and built on site of the historic Van Ness mansion. Open weekdays 9:00 A.M.–5:30 P.M. Free. Call 458-3000.

St. Mary's Episcopal Church, 728–730 23rd Street. Gothic church built for African-American congregation in 1887.

Watergate Complex (apartments/commercial), 2650 Virginia Avenue. Complex named for the statuesque flight of steps from the Lincoln Memorial to the Potomac River. Opened in 1962. "Watergate" break-in occurred June 17, 1972. Call 965-2300.

World Bank, 1818 H Street.

Places to Eat

America's Best, diner in Howard Johnson's Premier Hotel, 2601 Virginia Avenue. Call 965-6869.

Foggy Bottom Cafe, in River Inn, 924 25th Street. Restaurant and carry-out. Call 337-7600.

Galileo's, 1110 21st Street. Jacket-and-tie haunt of VIPS. Call 293-7191.

Kennedy Center, New Hampshire Avenue at Rock Creek. ***Cuppa, Cuppa*** (indoor-outdoor cafe), ***Encore Cafe***, and ***Roof Terrace Restaurant***. Call 416-8560.

2000 Pennsylvania Avenue Complex, corner of Pennsylvania Avenue and 22nd Street. Vertical mall at edge of George Washington University campus with fast-food places and rest rooms.

Maison Blanche, 1725 F Street. Elegant French cuisine and ambience. Call 842-0070.

Marvin Center, George Washington University, 800 21st Street. Student Center.

Watergate Complex: Watergate Hotel, 2650 Virginia Avenue. ***The Aquarelle***, opened in late 1996. Call 965-2300.

FOGGY BOTTOM WALK

Begin your walk at the Foggy Bottom/George Washington University Metro Station at 23rd Street just south of Washington Circle. Bisected by K Street (the home of lawyers and lobbyists, according to General Colin Powell) and by major avenues like Pennsylvania and New Hampshire Avenues, Washington Circle is a big traffic hub. In the center of the circle a mounted statue of George Washington faces east toward the Capitol.

Outside the 23rd Street Metro entrance you see a large bronze bust of George Washington. There are identical busts at each corner of George Washington University's campus, which occupies most of Foggy Bottom from K Street on the north to F Street on the south, and east along Pennsylvania Avenue to 19th Street (see map).

In Robert Travers's *The Apartment on K Street* (1972), John Keefer walked through the George Washington University campus past the Student Center and took I (Eye) Street past the George Washington University Hospital, then went left around the Circle on his way to his apartment on K Street. A foreign agent, Keefer was the janitor of an old building on K Street. He was in charge of an atomic bomb hidden in the basement. He was on his way to a meeting with his superior, but was hit by a car at Washington Circle. He made it back to his building, doctored his leg, met with his control, then collapsed in front of one of his tenants, Miss Penny, who hauled him off to Columbia Hospital on L Street.

In Gar Anthony Haywood's *Bad News Travels Fast* (1995), Dottie and Joe Loudermilk, trying to save their son Eddie from a murder rap, went to a storefront bookstore called Get It in Writing located near Washington Circle. They found *The Power of Modern Litigation*, but inside the book turned out to be a handwritten diary by Senator Graham Wildman who was facing charges of sexual harassment.

Across 23rd Street is the George Washington University Hospital where President Ronald Reagan was rushed on March 30, 1981, when John Hinckley, Jr., shot him outside the Washington Hilton Hotel.

In *Runner in the Street* (1984) by James Grady, PI John Rankin was taken to the George Washington University Hospital emergency room after a mugging. He was trying to get the facts on the street murder of Janet Anderson, a hooker from Seattle who had gone to Harvard University.

In David Baldacci's *Absolute Power* (1996), President Alan Richmond was a kinky womanizer whose Secret Service procurers had to kill the young wife of a powerful industrialist when she attacked him. Her murder was seen by hidden burglar Luther Whitney, but only Middleton detective Seth Frank and lawyer Jack Graham believed Whitney's story. When Detective Frank met Graham secretly at Farragut West Metro Station he was mugged by Secret Service agents, who took him to George Washington University Hospital.

Take 23rd Street to I (Eye) Street. Two blocks farther south at H Street is the Victorian Gothic St. Mary's Episcopal Church, designed by James Renwick for an African-American congregation. The church was paid for by the white congregations of St. John's and Epiphany who did not want blacks in their pews.

Turn right on I Street and walk two blocks, crossing New Hampshire Avenue, to 25th Street. You are in the heart of the Foggy Bottom Historical District which is filled with Federal houses handsomely kept up and has brick sidewalks like Georgetown and Alexandria.

Keep an eye out for a narrow two-story brick house with shutters and a blue door, where George Washington University's law professor Mackensie Smith lived. In Margaret Truman's *Murder at the Kennedy Center* (1989), Mac Smith, a widower, was living there with his Great Dane Rufus while his significant other, Annabel Reed, lived nearby in a Watergate condo. By the time of Truman's *Murder at the National Cathedral* (1990), they were married and both lived in the small house with Rufus.

Turn right on 25th Street. As you walk along the eastern side toward K Street the buildings become bigger and more modern. Continue until you are across the street from the River Inn with its Foggy Bottom Cafe where Mac Smith went to get takeout food or have an occasional meal.

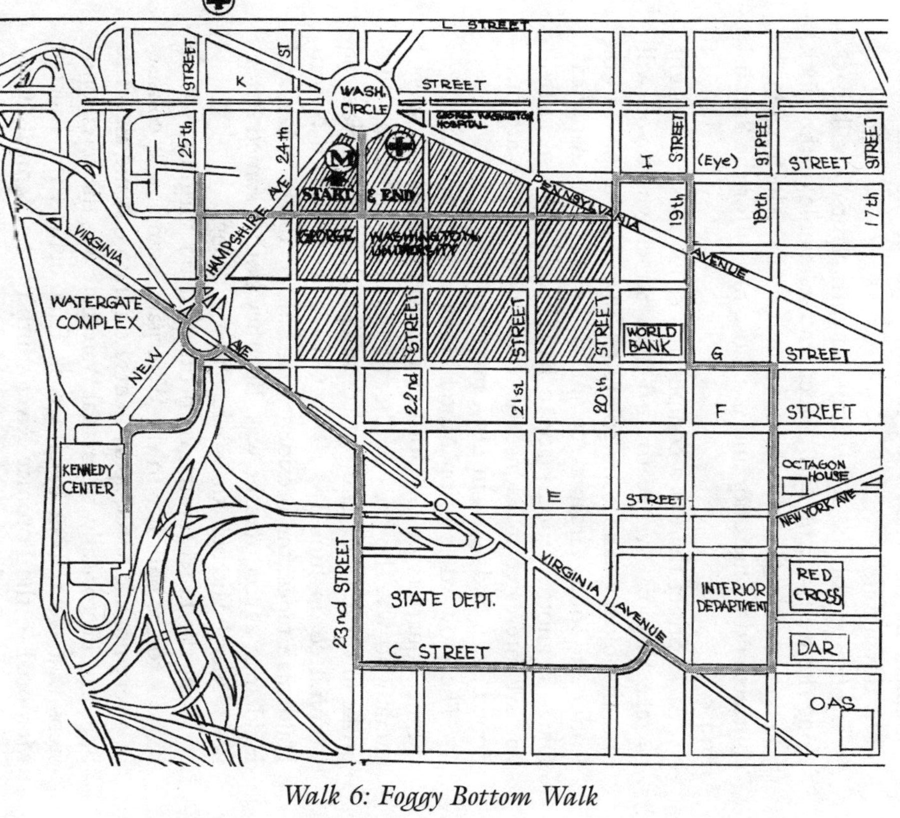

Walk 6: Foggy Bottom Walk

Cross 25th Street to go into the River Inn's small lobby. The Foggy Bottom Cafe is to your left. It serves breakfast, lunch, and dinner seven days a week and it's a good place to take a break before you hike around Foggy Bottom's public buildings. Its rest rooms are to your right at the end of the lobby downstairs.

Come out of the River Inn and turn right to walk back along the west side of 25th Street. In the middle of the block you come to the Carrow House (number 914) which has both shutters and a blue door and is a close match for the Smiths' house.

At H Street there is a complicated crossroads. Turn right to take Virginia Avenue toward 27th Street where you will find the blocky sandstone-colored Howard Johnson Motor Lodge at 2605 Virginia Avenue. Its restaurant, America's Diner, is another good place to have breakfast—especially if you are interested in its historic associations, which are mentioned again and again in D.C. mysteries.

The Howard Johnson Motel became instantly famous as the headquarters of G. Gordon Liddy, a former FBI special agent who was the boss of the "Plumbers," the group who broke into the Watergate Offices of the Democratic National Committee on June 17, 1972. On recently released Nixon-Haldeman tapes, the president said Liddy must be crazy, and Haldeman agreed that he was. But they both assumed Attorney General Mitchell knew what he was doing.

Visit the hotel/motel, then turn left on Virginia Avenue to walk to the entrance to the Watergate Complex. It consists of a very upscale hotel, apartments housing VIPs, and an office building. Historically, the actual Watergate was the ceremonial steps that went from Rock Creek Park behind the Lincoln Memorial to the Potomac River south of the Kennedy Center. Important visitors once arrived there by ship.

There was a very famous restaurant here on the river called the Water Gate Inn which served spectacular popovers and chicken salad. In Bill Goode's humorous *The Senator's Nude* (1947), Senator Caleb Casper Smudge had a rendezvous at the River Gate Inn with his blackmailer, Daisy Dane, who was later found dead in his bed.

But the term "Watergate" now stands for corruption and scandal in high places because it was here at 2:00 A.M. on June 17, 1972, that a security guard noticed tape over the lock of the door to the Democratic National Committee's campaign headquarters. He investigated and found the "Plumbers," who had been hired by Attorney General John Mitchell, head of CREEP (Committee to Reelect the President) to wiretap McGovern's headquarters and photograph sensitive documents. The Plumbers were arrested and a White House insider known as "Deep Throat" then gave *Washington Post* reporters Carl Bernstein and Bob Woodward information which led to President Nixon's resignation. "Deep Throat" supposedly met the reporters in the Kennedy Center's underground parking garage next door.

Twenty-five members of President Nixon's staff went to jail for lying in a Congressional hearing presided over by jovial "good ole boy" Sam Ervin, and *Time* magazine named Watergate Judge John Sirica "Man of the Year." The president resigned on August 9, 1974, rather than face impeachment, but subsequent leaks and tapes from FDR's administration onward make it obvious other presidents have played similar games, but not all were caught at it when it counted.

D.C. mystery writers love to comment on "Watergate." In Jeffrey Archer's *Shall We Tell the President?* (1977; rev. ed. 1985), FBI agent Marc Andrews commented that since 80 percent of D.C.'s citizens and 90 percent of those arrested on criminal charges were black, the break-in at the Watergate had been suspicious from the beginning. He also recalled that at the Watergate hearings a retired NYPD detective told Sam Ervin's committee there was no reason to bug the place because politicians and officials will tell you anything you want over the phone or mail it to you.

In Zach Adams's *Pursuit* (1986), an FBI procedural set outside D.C., FBI Special Agent Martin Walsh said it was really an FBI leak that led reporters Woodward and Bernstein to investigate Richard Nixon's administration. He added that an FBI investigation had been going on for a year before a single line appeared in the *Washington Post.*

In Truman's *Murder at the National Gallery* (1996),

National Gallery curator Luther Mason invited his straitlaced mother from Indiana to come to the Caravaggio exhibition opening. Luther told her he would put her up at the Watergate Hotel "where Richard Nixon . . ." and his mother tartly told him that she remembered! Truman's Annabel Reed-Smith said she'd help Steve Jordan of the MPD art squad on a sting as long as she didn't end up like the fools who'd broken into Watergate because they'd been duped into thinking *their* cause was worthwhile.

At the Watergate complex the first building you come to is the Watergate Office building where the Plumbers broke into an office on the sixth floor. Go up and look if you like, then return outside and go right at 25th and Virginia, following the hotel driveway past an old-fashioned red London phone booth to the canopied entrance. On its ground floor are an upscale shopping arcade and marble floors with oriental rugs and expensive chairs to sit and watch the VIPs go by.

The hotel restaurant is at the end of the lobby (down the stairs to your right there are rest rooms and a passageway to the Kennedy Center, which is not always open). Until 1996 this restaurant was called Jean Louis, now it is the Aquarelle. It is very like the extremely posh French restaurant described in Phyllis Richman's *The Butter Did It* (1997). Her amateur sleuth, Chas (Charlotte Sue) Wheatley, ate there to write it up for her *Washington Post* restaurant column (just like Richman). It could even be the site of Richman's mythical Chez Laurence, run by murdered French chef Laurence Levain.

In Ross Thomas's *If You Can't Be Good* (1973), Decatur Lucas was hired by Frank Size, syndicated D.C. columnist, to find out why Senator Robert F. Ames had accepted a $50,000 bribe to make a speech that favored a business merger, then resigned. The ex-senator had holed up with call girl Connie Mizelle in a Watergate penthouse. When Lucas went there to interview the ex-senator and Connie, he met a chum, PI Dain, who took him to interview Mrs. Ames near Annapolis. Lucas also knew a deputy assistant secretary of agriculture who lived at Watergate and "owed" him, so Lucas got into the Ames apartment again and found a gun hidden in a Bible.

In Nick Carter's *Death of the Falcon* (1974), Nick Carter, aka Agent N3 of AXE, had the job of keeping Sherima (the Silver Falcon), ex-wife of Shah Hassan of Adabi, safe on a D.C. trip. The Silver Scimitar planned to kidnap her and make it look like the CIA had done it. Carter's boss Hawk booked him a suite at the Watergate next door to the queen. Carter lurked in the lobby's shopping arcade to meet the queen and her friend Candy Knight and took them to the Terrace Room for breakfast, then sightseeing.

Case the Watergate Hotel, then come out and walk past the condo complex with its VIP apartments. In mysteries, many of them are love nests.

In James Cain's *The Institute* (1976), scholar-cum-football star Dr. Lloyd Palmer got the twenty-two million dollars he needed to establish a National Institute of Biography from wealthy Richard Garrett, head of ARMALCO. Garrett and his gorgeous young wife Hortense lived in Wilmington, Delaware, but maintained a pad in East Watergate.

In Truman's first mystery, *Murder in the White House* (1980), Secretary of State Lansard Blaine turned out to be taking bribes and President Webster told him to resign. But Blaine decided to blackmail the First Family instead, which led to his murder. Blaine had lived lavishly at the Watergate Apartments with expensive art objects and a succession of young women. Ron Fairbanks, appointed by the president to look into his murder, got to view the apartment.

In Truman's *Murder on Capitol Hill* (1981), Senate Majority Leader Cale Caldwell was murdered at a party given in his honor by his wife, Veronica. Quentin Hughes, a celebrity interviewer for WCAP-TV had a tape showing him fighting with the murdered man. In Hughes's Watergate apartment he entertained young women, including his assistant Christa Jones, but when he fired Christa, she stole the tape and took it to Special Prosecutor Lydia James.

In Tom Clancy's *The Hunt for Red October* (1984), suspecting that Senator Donaldson's administrative assistant Peter Henderson was leaking top-secret information, Special Agent Hazel Loomis, pretending to be a George Washington University student, moved in next door to Henderson's one-bedroom condo at the Watergate and bugged his phone.

In Mary Higgins Clark's *Stillwatch* (1984), recently widowed Congressman Sam Kingsley now lived in the Watergate where glamorous television producer Pat Traymore visited him. One of the reasons Pat had agreed to leave New York and come work in D.C. was Sam. She was still in love with him, but he insisted he was too old for her.

In Truman's *Murder in Georgetown* (1986), New Jersey Senator John Froelich maintained a secret apartment at the Watergate Hotel where he entertained Elsa Jenkins. She was the wife of his best friend, millionaire developer Marshall Jenkins. After Senator Froelich's daughter Valerie was found murdered in the C&O Canal, their assignations were discovered by *Washington Post* crime reporter Joe Potamos.

In Lawrence Sanders's *Capital Crimes* (1989), because President Abner Hawkins's son George was hemophiliac, the president and his wife fell under the spell of a charismatic faith healer called Brother Kristos, whom they listened to on policy matters. President Hawkins's Chief of Staff Henry Folsom held open house in his Watergate apartment that Christmas and took his executive assistant John Tollinger into the bathroom. Locking the door, he told Tollinger that they must get rid of Brother Kristos.

In Marilyn Quayle and Nancy Northcott's *Embrace the Serpent* (1992), Fidel Castro died, and USSR stooge Valles took over. The only person who mistrusted Valles was black Republican Senator Robert Hawkins Grant of Georgia, while Valles's biggest dupe was *Washington Herald*'s VIP reporter Peter Evans, who had a love nest at the Watergate.

Come out in front of the Watergate Complex to face Juarez Circle. Across Juarez Circle is the huge contemporary Saudi Arabian Embassy with its green flag. Take New Hampshire Avenue to your right to the Kennedy Center. You pass a little outdoor/indoor cafe called Cuppa Cuppa, open seven days a week, where you can also stop for coffee or use the rest rooms.

Cross New Hampshire at F Street and go inside the

Kennedy Center for the Performing Arts. The Kennedy Center was built on the site of the Christian Heurich Brewery, makers of Senate Beer. Architect Edward Durrell Stone was hired in 1959 to design a National Cultural Center, but funding languished until President John F. Kennedy was killed in 1963. The project was renamed for him and the whole world contributed to it as his memorial. At the official groundbreaking in 1964 President Lyndon Johnson used the gold-plated shovel that had been used for the Lincoln and Jefferson Memorials. The Center opened in 1971.

Known today as the Ken Cen, it contains an Opera House, Concert Hall, Eisenhower Theater, Terrace Theater, Theater Lab, and the American Film Institute, and is the focal point for the performing arts in Washington. Coming from the north you enter the Hall of States, lined with their fifty flags, then walk back to the red-carpeted Grand Foyer lined with Belgian mirrors, with a huge, rough-hewn bronze bust of JFK by Robert Berks. Everywhere are donated art objects and imperial splendor. At the other end of the Grand Foyer is the Hall of Nations, flying the flags of all countries diplomatically accredited to the United States.

In Anne Morice's *Murder in Mimicry* (1977), Tessa Crichton, the actress wife of Chief Inspector Robin Crichton of Scotland Yard, came to Washington with a play called *Host of Pleasures* which was opening in the Eisenhower Theater. Tessa went to the Center by cab from the airport to "case the joint" in all its slab-cake glory. The Eisenhower Theater was much bigger than most London theaters, which gave the British cast problems with voice projection, lighting, and staging.

Later, although Tessa knew that no one was safe from street crime in D.C., she became suspicious of the supposedly "perfectly natural" death of a cast member who was mugged outside the theater. After her snooping was noticed, Tessa got a phony telegram telling her to meet her American hostess in the Grand Foyer bar. Tessa was nearly stabbed to death in the crowd but then was rescued by undercover agents of MPD Detective Meek who knew her husband.

In John Ehrlichman's *The Company* (1977), when President Esker Scott Anderson announced he would not seek reelection, William Martin, the head of the CIA, had to move fast to protect his job. Anderson had taken office after the plane-crash death of President William Arthur Curry, but earlier Martin had obeyed the personal order of President Curry to have Father Julio Benitimes, leader of a South American invasion force, killed, so the invasion failed. That order and the report on the failed invasion were recorded in the top-secret Primula Report, which would not only destroy the "Camelot" image of President Curry (aka Kennedy), but get Martin fired. Maneuvering to get hold of the Primula Report to destroy it, Martin met his mistress Sally Atherton in front of the Concert Hall at the Kennedy Center to talk her into acting as a courier for him.

Ehrlichman's *The Company* (1977), inevitably reminds one of the Kennedy "Bay of Pigs" fiasco, which in turn reminds you of William F. Buckley's *Mongoose R.I.P.* (1987; set in 1963). In it superagent Blackford Oakes was involved in the effort to retrieve JFK's reputation with "Operation Mongoose" by invading Cuba in 1963, but the assassination of Kennedy ended the plan.

In Truman's *Murder in Georgetown* (1986), Elsa Jenkins, the wife of developer Marshall Jenkins, went to the Kennedy Center, followed by *Washington Post* crime reporter John Potamos. He saw Elsa go into the Grand Foyer, take a program from an usher, then walk outside and take a cab to the Watergate Hotel, leading him to Senator Froelich's love nest.

In Truman's *Murder at the Kennedy Center* (1989), a benefit gala for presidential hopeful Senator Kenneth Ewald was held at the Center, starring Sarah Vaughan, Sammy Davis, Jr., and opera diva Roseanna Gateaux. During the gala Andrea Feldman, a young woman who worked for Ewald's election committee, was murdered and the main suspect was Ewald's son Paul. Senator Ewald quickly called in his old friend Mackensie Smith, who had been the one to find her body.

Look out the windows of the Grand Foyer at the Potomac River. In Marcy Heidish's *The Torching* (1992), on a cold November day a group of customers from the burned Georgetown bookstore ran by Alice Grey sang "Amazing Grace" as they threw the ashes of murdered street person Dinah Lasko into the wind behind the Kennedy Center's white slab form. Lasko had liked to go to the great marble terrace on summer evenings and watch the concert-goers at intermission.

Go back outside in front of the Center. Look across the sidewalk to a huge cast sculpture presented to us by Germany called *America* (perhaps it should be called *Kafka's Amerika*). It was behind *America* that Mac Smith and his dog Rufus had found the body of presidential candidate Ewald's aide. Check out the space yourself, then turn left and walk past Spain's gift, a statue of Don Quixote (or perhaps Cervantes) on a Guernica-like horse.

Keep walking until you reach the traffic light at Juarez Circle. Cross the street behind Saudi Arabia's marble embassy to reach Virginia Avenue.

In Noel Hynd's *Truman's Spy* (set in 1950), Allen Dulles, World War II master spy (and brother of future Secretary of State John Foster Dulles) had just been made head of the embryonic CIA. It was housed about here at 2430 E Street, just south of Virginia Avenue and east of the Kennedy Center, next door to an abandoned brewery. (It may have occupied the prefab quarters of the OSS, housed there during World War II according to a retired OSS officer who attended one of my mystery seminars at Chicago's Newberry Library.) FBI Director Hoover had assigned Special Agent Tom Buchanan to trace missing Pennsylvania banker John Taylor Garrett, suspected of being a soviet agent, because Buchanan had once been engaged to Garrett's younger daughter Ann. But Alger Hiss was being tried for perjury on Whitaker Chambers's testimony and the Rosenbergs were near execution, so a worried President Truman wanted his own spy and secretly recruited Buchanan.

Turn right on Virginia Avenue and go past the Western Presbyterian Church to cross Virginia Avenue at 23rd Street and F Street. You are now in the high-rise, high-rent residential part of Foggy Bottom. Turn right on 23rd Street and walk toward the State Department (aka Foggy Bottom) located between E and C Streets. Across 23rd Street high above you on Camp Hill is the Navy Bureau of Medicine and Surgery where the old Naval Observatory used to be. It is closed to visitors. (See Walk 5.)

The Department of State's building looks as if it, too, were a temporary government annex thrown up during World War II.

In Ian Fleming's *Diamonds Are Forever* (1956), British secret agent James Bond (007) got himself hired to smuggle diamonds into America. He also wanted to get out of America in one piece, so his buddy at the CIA made sure he and his girlfriend were met at New York's La Guardia airport by a State Department flunky with passports and tickets.

Go past State's main entrance on 23rd Street between C and D Streets; this is the place you would go for the tour of the magnificently decorated Diplomatic Reception Rooms on the eighth floor, filled with historical artifacts such as the desk on which President Jefferson wrote the Declaration of Independence. To see them you have to make reservations several months in advance.

In William H. Hallahan's Edgar-winning *Catch Me, Kill Me* (1977), a defected Russian poet Boris Kotlikoff was kidnaped by the USSR in New York because he was involved in an underground railroad operation for other Russian Jews. To try to rescue him federal agents from State, FBI, Immigration, and the CIA had a top-level meeting in the seventh-floor conference room at State, a windowless room furnished with leftovers from Woodrow Wilson's administration known as "the Mad Hatters Tea Room." The poor poet's rescue turned into a fight to the death between a CIA operative called Gus Geller and an Immigration official called Leary.

In Michael Bowen's *Worst Case Scenario* (1996), (described on its jacket flap as a *Primary Colors* written by Agatha Christie) Foreign Office retiree Richard Michaelson remarked that to get inside information it was always better to talk to the secretary of state's secretaries than to talk to the top. But when a wannabe State Department staffer turned up dead, Michaelson and his friend Marjorie Randolph of Cavalier Books investigated. They discovered the top-level secret involved was information about a coup d'etat planned during Iran-gate. When they had solved the crime, pompous State Department cop Pilkington entertained Michaelson and Marjorie Randolph with a top White House official at a formal dinner in the State Department Diplomatic Rooms. He even offered them after-dinner Havana cigars.

When his thriller *Death Duty* (1996) came out Stephen Kimball read from it in the multilevel State Department library. The plot grew out of the bizarre experiences his family had with a State Department official known as a "death officer" when his brother died in China. Kimball described a conspiracy of government bad guys known as "the Circle" and had a shoot-out in State's eighth-floor Benjamin Franklin Dining Room with its Savonnerie rug and Franklin's portrait.

If you have no reservation to see the Diplomatic Reception Rooms, go around the corner on C Street to the regular State Department lobby. It is heavily guarded but you can walk in and look about.

In Truman's *Murder in the White House* (1980), after the murder of Secretary of State Lansard Blaine, Ron Fairbanks also went to State to check out Secretary Blaine's office. He found that Blaine owned some very expensive art, including a Louise Nevelson wood sculpture, and had a secretary who was a prim and proper fifty—an odd choice for a man known for his womanizing.

In James Grady's *Runner in the Street* (1984), PI John Rankin went to Foggy Bottom (the State Department), a concrete maze of interconnected tan blockhouses with metal detectors and WPA-like murals to do research. But he reported to lawyer Art Dillon that he had found no "leftover legacies" from the James Jones Kool-aid massacre in South America.

In Ann Ripley's *Mulch* (1994), State Department official (and CIA spook) Bill Eldridge worked at Foggy Bottom. Eldridge got a call from Tom Paschen, the President's Chief of Staff, who wanted him to do an illegal check on his suburban neighbor Peter Hoffman. (It's strictly illegal for the CIA to work inside the United States.) Hoffman, a freelance gunrunner, had been nominated for deputy secretary of defense by the president, who wanted a hawk in the job!

Come out of State and go left along C Street to 22nd Street. Along C Street you pass several government institutions that "front" one block south on Constitution Avenue. You pass the National Academy of Sciences with a statue of Albert Einstein done by Robert Berks, who also did the huge JFK bust in the Kennedy Center. Cross 22nd Street and walk to 21st Street, passing the Federal Reserve Building, whose annex is on your side of the street. At 20th Street take C Street as it curves left to Virginia Avenue past a park filled with prairie grass, passing Interior Department South. Then turn right on Virginia Avenue and cross over to 19th and C Streets, where you come to the main Department of the Interior, which includes the Park Service and the Department of Indian Affairs.

Its entrance on C Street is decorated with American bison (buffalo) and memorials to President Teddy Roosevelt, the great Rough Rider outdoorsman who created our national park system. The Department's museum is well worth a visit, but you need a reservation. Mystery fans who like Tony Hillerman's Southwest mysteries will appreciate the Native-American artifacts displayed there. During World War II an antiaircraft gun mounted on the roof was accidentally fired and scored a direct hit on the Lincoln Memorial!

Take C Street to 18th Street. Across C Street to the right you can see the red-tiled roof of the Beaux Arts Pan-American Building, now known as the Organization of American States (OAS). It was built in 1910 on the site of two historic D.C. houses: the cottage of David Burnes, who owned much of official Washington's real estate, and the Van Ness House, the Greek Revival mansion built for his daughter.

The OAS headquarters probably was the site of the attempted assassination-cum-shoot-out at the "IAF Building" in Benjamin M. Schutz's *A Tax in Blood* (1987). African-American PI Leo Haggerty, investigating the murder of Malcolm Donnelly and the bombing of the Vietnam Memorial, followed the bloody trail to South American Dr. Rolando

Gutierrez, aka Colonel Bernard Schmidt. The colonel had programmed a boy called Marty Fernandez to murder visiting President General Hortensio Villarosa at a huge IAF reception.

Turn left and walk north on 18th Street toward D Street. On your right is the Daughters of the American Revolution's Constitution Hall built in 1930. In 1939 the DAR refused permission for African-American Marion Anderson to sing there, with the result that First Lady Eleanor Roosevelt got permission for her to sing at the Lincoln Memorial instead.

The main entrance to the DAR headquarters and museum is in Continental Hall, which is connected to Constitution Hall but faces 17th Street. Part of the DAR buildings are on the site of the brick home of Thomas Carberry, a mayor of D.C. in the early 1820s who also served as chairman of the Washington Monument Society.

In Miriam Borgenicht's *Corpse in Diplomacy* (1956), when Fritz Langsdorph's uncle was found murdered under reporter Kate Whipple's bed, Fritz's alibi was that he and a VIP chum had been at a quiet concert at Constitution Hall.

Look at the DAR hall and museum, then continue walking up 18th Street to D Street. Cross D Street to the present headquarters of the American Red Cross. Built in 1917, it occupies the entire block. The Red Cross was begun by Civil War nurse Clara Barton, and there are exhibits from early Red Cross history in the lobby.

Walk past the Red Cross buildings to E Street where you are at the corner of two-block-long Rawlins Park. Cross E Street and walk up 18th Street to New York Avenue. Across New York Avenue to your right at Number 1799 you will find the historic Octagon House. Six-sided, it was built in 1801 on a triangular lot by Colonel John Tayloe, a friend of George Washington. In 1902 the mansion, which had become a boarding house, was purchased by the AIA (the American Institute of Architects) who restored it and made it their headquarters.

During the War of 1812 the French Minister lived there and flew the French flag, so the invading British, who were not at war with France, did not burn it down. Since the British gutted the White House, the Octagon was occupied by President James Madison and his famous hostess wife Dolley for a time and the Treaty of Ghent that ended the war was signed here by the president in the second-floor circular study. According to legend Dolley Madison's ghost likes to haunt the Octagon, where she threw some very special parties.

In Barbara Michaels's (aka Elizabeth Peters) *Shattered Silk* (1986) a necklace of Dolley Madison was on sale at Old Things, the Georgetown antique shop where Karen Nevitt was working. But Dolley's necklace, though historic, was not very valuable, so it probably was not the reason someone broke into the shop and murdered the assistant, Rob, who had written *Legends of Georgetown*.

Visit the Octagon House (museum). Then continue walking north on 18th Street. At E Street across 18th Street is the General Services Administration Building. It was once home to the Interior Department, and the infamous Teapot Dome scandal was cooked up in its dining room during the Harding Administration. Then walk one more block to F Street where you can see the 1825 Ringgold-Carroll House, where Chief Justice John Marshall and several presidents were boarders. Beyond it in the middle of the block is the United Nations headquarters in D.C.

To your right on F Street between 17th and 18th Streets is the elegant French restaurant called Maison Blanche. In Richard Conroy's *Old Ways in the New World* (set in 1976), Henry Scruggs was in charge of getting international folk artists into the country for the Smithsonian Museums. Scruggs took Channel 10's flamboyant anchorwoman Arabella to Maison Blanche to persuade her to cover the murder of Cedric Mahute, an African princeling working at the Smithsonian on a temporary visa. The restaurant was Scruggs's kind of place and Art Buchwald's favorite bistro with walnut paneling, brown-velvet armchairs, elegant crystal chandeliers, and 350 labels on its wine list.

In Lawrence Sanders's *Capital Crimes* (1989), White House Chief of Staff's executive assistant John Tollinger took his ex-wife to lunch there to try to persuade her to forget charismatic presidential confidante Brother Kristos, with whom she was sleeping.

Keep going up 18th Street to G Street, then turn left on G Street and walk to 19th Street. You pass the World Bank Building, which occupies the entire block from 18th to 19th Streets on G Street. In Patricia Moyes's *Black Widower* (1975), British John Colville worked at the World Bank, lured there from the London School of Economics. (Moyes's husband also worked at the World Bank.) Colville and his wife Margaret rented a tiny frame house with a bit of a back garden in Georgetown, which they thought very like London's Chelsea. They entertained Scotland Yard's Chief Superintendent Henry Tibbett and his wife Emily there when they came to solve the Tampican Embassy murders (see Walk 7).

Cross 19th Street and go past the International Monetary Fund. Cross 19th Street and go on to 20th Street. You are at the eastern edge of George Washington University's campus and will find another bronze bust of George Washington marking the corner. At the corner of 20th and G Streets is the United Church—Church of Christ. Built on the site of an earlier church put up in 1833 by Foggy Bottom's Germans, it still has services in both German and English.

George Washington University was founded in 1821, years after George Washington had left some shares of stock to start a college in the capital. Originally a Baptist institution called Columbian College, it changed its name and religious affiliation in 1904, but only moved to Foggy Bottom in 1912. Now it is the second largest landowner in D.C. (after the feds) much of it in Foggy Bottom.

In *Death Is a Tory* (1935) by Keats Patrick, Katherine O'Day was the sister-in-law of "Tom" Collins, one of the reporters investigating the murder of Department of Agriculture Marshall Rich's wife and her lover. "Ka," who lived with the Collinses, said she was studying psychology at George Washington University because when she got her B.A. she had no job offers and too many proposals of marriage!

The block of 20th to 21st Streets, G to H Streets was the university's first quadrangle, designed in appropriate Georgian brick. Walk north on 20th Street to H Street, passing by the university's Law School Complex. Lerner Hall is on the corner of 20th and H and is undoubtedly where Margaret Truman's law professor Mac Smith held forth to his students between murder cases, sometimes even asking their advice. They often asked his.

In Truman's *Murder at the Kennedy Center* (1989), Smith told his class on advanced criminal procedures to watch the televised Kennedy Center Gala for Senator Ewald because he wanted well-rounded lawyers. The class responded by asking him if he would be Ewald's Attorney General. In Truman's *Murder at the National Gallery* (1996), National Gallery curator Luther Mason's son Julian got his art degree at George Washington University.

In Dorothy Sucher's *Dead Men Don't Marry* (1989), shrink Sabina Swift and her assistant Victor Newman were trying to track down Keith Browdy, a good-looking psychopath who had been in the "System" most of his life and loved only his dog. Browdy married middle-aged social workers, got their wills changed, then murdered them. A widowed friend of Vic's mother, Fran O'Donnell, was one of his victims. Her lawyer was a friend of Vic's called Herb Weinstein, who had graduated in the bottom third of his class at George Washington University's law school. He told Vic he had not liked Fran changing her will in favor of her new husband and tried to stop her.

Walk one more block up 20th Street to I (Eye) Street and turn left. At the corner is 2000 Pennsylvania Avenue, a vertical mall made up of old and new redbrick buildings, which has rest rooms and lots of shops and places to eat. It makes a great place to stop near the end of your walk.

If you want to splurge on lunch turn right to 21st Street. About three blocks north between L and M Streets you would find Galileo's. It is one of D.C.'s "power" restaurants, run by Chef Robert Donna. Donna also runs the less formal but excellent "streetfront" i Matti restaurant in Adams-Morgan where we dined with our friends the Garners. Both restaurants serve delicious Italian specialties. But at Galileo's you need not only a reservation, but a jacket and tie, while i Matti is a remodeled storefront that opens up to the sidewalk on warm nights.

In Patricia O'Brien's *The Ladies Lunch* (1994), once a month for fifteen years five powerful D.C. women met at Galileo's for lunch and networking. They always ate in the Wine Room, an alcove reserved for real VIPS. The five were Faith Paige, the White House press secretary; lawyer Sara Marino, about to be appointed a Supreme Court justice; Maggie Stedman, an ex-*Washington Post* investigative reporter who had been offered a huge advance to write a book about her friends; Carol Lundeen, a Maryland congresswoman; and Leona Maccoby, a socialite caterer married to a wealthy broker-cum-White House advisor. After the president died of a heart attack they met as usual, but Faith Paige did not show up. It turned out Faith had committed suicide by jumping off the cliff at the Potomac River's Great Falls.

If you stayed on campus, go left along I (Eye) Street to 21st Street. Across 21st Street you come to the Marvin Center. If you want to explore the sprawling urban campus, go in and get a map of the campus in the University Bookstore in the basement.

If you have had enough walking, stay on I Street to 23rd Street where you pass (Jacqueline) Kennedy Onassis Hall. Like the FBI's J. Edgar Hoover, the First Lady was a student there. Then cross 23rd Street to return to the Foggy Bottom Metro Station to end your walk.

7

GEORGETOWN WALK

BACKGROUND

Georgetown today is considered the most prestigious address in Washington. Older than the District, it is a very independent village, with a mixture of handsome old residential streets and trendy nightspots, restaurants, and shops. Its boundaries are well-defined by Georgetown University on the west, Rock Creek Park on the east, and the Potomac River on the south.

It was founded in 1703 by Scottish immigrant Ninian Beall who called his hilly tract the Rock of Dunbarton after a castle in Scotland. (The name of the famous mansion is misspelled as "Dumbarton.") Another family, named Gordon, established a tobacco plantation there called Rock Creek and in 1751 the Beall and Gordon families got permission from Maryland to establish the village of Georgetown, or the Town of George. Historians are not sure if the "George" being honored was a Beall, a Gordon, or King George II, but it was neither George III nor George Washington!

Like Alexandria, Virginia, Georgetown became a flourishing port with rich and powerful citizens, but Alexandria was larger and more Southern, while Georgetown was an easy commute to the new capital. When George Washington and the District's three new city commissioners met with the landowners to persuade them to sell land for the capital, their historic meeting was held at Suter's Inn, probably in the 1000 block of Wisconsin Avenue.

Georgetown's manor houses like Evermay and Tudor Place were built during the eighteenth century, then in 1789 the first Roman Catholic college in the country, Georgetown University, was founded there. But Washington, D.C., gradually eclipsed its neighbor as "the" place to live, and the Chesapeake and Ohio Canal did not help its economy because the new Baltimore and Ohio Railroad provided cheaper and faster service. Many important residents were Southern sympathizers during the Civil War, and by 1871 D.C. had annexed Georgetown, changing most of its street names and numbers to match D.C.'s. But, according to Patricia Moyes, it kept its independent image and village ways.

Georgetown continued to decline until FDR's New Deal established an ever-growing federal bureaucracy in the 1930s. Bureaucrats and VIPS liked living near the seats of power, and by 1950 the town had recovered so much that the Old Georgetown Act was passed, making it a National Historic District, with reconstruction and new construction subject to review by the Commission on Fine Arts. The 1957 purchase of N Street's Marbury House by young Massachusetts Senator John F. Kennedy made Georgetown not only rich but trendy.

Georgetown has been a popular locale for mysteries from the days of the New Deal when its socialite "cave-dwellers" like Leslie Ford's widowed Grace Latham still lived the antebellum life of the Southern aristocracy. After World War II, an international flavor appeared in thrillers like Robert Ludlum's *The Chancellor Manuscript* (1977), in which a sinister group known as "Inver Brass" met secretly in an unnamed Georgetown mansion. But many writers remain secretive about which Georgetown house is the scene of the crime, while Georgetown's side streets often do *not* have street signs.

This walk is long and hilly. Georgetown has not allowed the Metro System into its territory, but you can stop to return another day by catching a cab on Wisconsin Avenue or M Street. They are Georgetown's major north-south, east-west streets where you also find food and pit stops.

LENGTH OF WALK: About 4½ miles

The walk is divided into two parts which can be done separately. Part One is about three miles. It includes a one-mile walk from the Rosslyn Metro Station across the Key Bridge to Canal Road, then two miles (uphill) from Canal Road to Georgetown University, then east to Wisconsin Avenue and R Street. You can cut the distance by taking a cab to Canal Road. Part Two, which begins at R Street and Wisconsin Avenue and goes to the Washington Circle–Foggy Bottom Metro Station on Pennsylvania Avenue, is another 1½ miles.

See the map on page 199 for the boundaries of this walk and page 281 for a list of the books and detectives mentioned.

TOURS AND INFORMATION

C&O Barge Tours, ninety-minute mule-drawn barge trip with park rangers in period costume. Mid-April–November on Wed. and Sun. 11:00 A.M., 1:00 P.M., and 3:00 P.M. Call 653-5190.*

Georgetown Garden Tour, held annually in early May. Call 333-4953.

Georgetown House Tour, held annually in late April. Call 338-1796.

Georgetown Information Center, 1057 Thomas Jefferson Street. Maps and information. Open April–November. Call 653-5844.

PLACES OF INTEREST

Chesapeake and Ohio (C&O) Canal and Towpath. National park with towpath for hiking, jogging, biking, or boating. Call (301) 739-4200 for information about towpath and Great Falls Park.

Cox's Row, 3327–3339 N Street. Federal row built in 1817 by Georgetown Mayor John Cox.

*The telephone area code for Georgetown, like that of Washington, D.C., is 202.

Dumbarton House, 2715 Q Street. Georgian mansion built c. 1800. Since 1928 headquarters National Society of Colonial Dames of America. Museum. Group tours Tues.–Sat. 10:00 A.M.–12:15 P.M. Donation. Call 337-2288.

Dumbarton Oaks, 1703 32nd Street. 1801 Federal mansion, scene of 1944 Dumbarton Oaks Conference setting up the U.N. Grounds open to the public. ***Mansion:*** Fee April–October, free November–March. ***Art Collections:*** Byzantine and pre-Columbian. Open Tues.–Sun. 2:00 P.M.–5:00 P.M. Closed national holidays and December 24. Call 339-6401.

Evermay, 1623 28th Street. Not open to the public.

Exorcist's Steps, 3600 Prospect Street, just west of the old Street Car Barn. Owned by Georgetown University. 75 steps up—don't fall down!

Francis Scott Key Bridge and Memorial Park, between 34th Street and Key Bridge. Linking Rosslyn, Virginia, with Canal Road, Georgetown. (Site of Key Mansion was 3518 M Street.)

Georgetown Public Library, R Street and Wisconsin Avenue. Georgian-style building with friendly staff and public rest rooms.

Georgetown University, 37th Street and O Street. Oldest Roman Catholic school in the United States; founded by Archbishop John Carroll in 1789. Victorian gothic campus with food and rest rooms. Stop at the main gate information booth at 37th and O Streets for campus map.

Marbury House, 3307 N Street. Redbrick townhouse bought by Senator John F. Kennedy in late 1950s. Not open to the public.

Oak Hill Cemetery, 3001 R Street. Founded in 1849 by banker/art collector W. W. Corcoran on land owned by George Washington's great nephew. Victorian Gothic Gatehouse and chapel. Maps of notable graves at Gatehouse (fee). Open Mon.–Fri. 9:00 A.M.–4:30 P.M. (closed for lunch noon–12:30 P.M.)

Old Stone House, 3051 M Street. Oldest pre-Revolutionary house in Georgetown, built c. 1764. History of haunting. Open daily Memorial Day–Labor Day 9:00 A.M.–5:00 P.M., rest of the year, Wed.–Sun. 9:00 A.M.–5:00 P.M. Closed major holidays. Free. Call 426-6851.

St. John's Episcopal Church, 3240 O Street. Built in 1809. Dolley Madison was a parishioner and Francis Scott Key was a vestryman. Stop by church office (open weekdays 9:00 A.M.–4:30 P.M.) and ask to see the Tiffany window.

Tudor Place, 1644 31st Street. On Q Street between 31st Street and 32nd Street. Neoclassical mansion built in 1816 for Thomas Peter and Martha Custis, Martha Washington's granddaughter. Tours Tues.–Fri. 10:00 A.M., 11:30 A.M., 1:00 P.M., and 2:20 P.M.; Sat. hourly 10:00 A.M.–4:00 P.M. Donation. Reservations advised. Call 965-0400.

Places to Eat

Many do not open until 11:00 A.M. so plan accordingly. (Res.) indicates a restaurant where reservations are recommended. There are also many fast-food places like Roy Rogers on Wisconsin Avenue and M Street.

Blues Alley, Rear 1073 (off Wisconsin Avenue [Res.]). Call 337-4141.

Bistro Lepic, 1736 Wisconsin Avenue. (Res.) Call 333-0111.

Clyde's, 3236 M Street. (Res.) Call 333-9180.

F. Scott's, 1232 36th Street. (Res.) Call 965-1789.

Georgetown Inn, 1523 Wisconsin Avenue. Call 333-0215.

Dean & Deluca, 3276 M Street. Gourmet foodstore/cafe next door to Georgetown Park, 3222 M Street (M and Wisconsin Avenue). Three-level shopping mall with rest rooms. Call 342-2500 or 298-5577.

La Chaumière, 2813 M Street. (Res.) Call 338-1784.

Martin's Tavern, 1264 Wisconsin Avenue. Call 333-7370.

Seasons, The Four Seasons Hotel, 2800 Pennsylvania Avenue. Best afternoon tea in D.C. (Res.) Call 944-2000.

1789, 1226 36th Street at Prospect Street. (Res.) Call 965-1789.

The Tombs, 1226 36th Street (at Prospect Street below ***1789***). No reservations. Call 337-6668.

GEORGETOWN WALK

Begin your walk at the Rosslyn Metro Station in Virginia. Take Lynn Street to the Francis Scott Key Bridge across the Potomac River. The bridge was named for the Maryland author of our national anthem, "The Star-Spangled Banner," written during the War of 1812. His son Barton, U.S. District Attorney, was killed in a duel at Lafayette Park by Congressman Dan Sickles because he was sleeping with Sickles's wife (see Walk 1.) The bridge is a major thoroughfare for cars, hikers, bikers, joggers, and ordinary tourists.

In Tom Clancy's *Patriot Games* (1987), CIA analyst Jack Ryan had tackled an IRA terrorist who threw a grenade at the limo of the Prince and Princess of Wales. He became a hero but his own family was targeted for assassination. The hunt for the killers ended with a stakeout at the Key Bridge with the Prince of Wales there as backup.

In Margaret Truman's *Murder on the Potomac* (1994), when Annabel Reed-Smith joined the board of the National Building Museum, she met members of Tri-S, a theater group dedicated to reenacting historic D.C. crimes. Their current production was about the Sickles-Key affair.

Stop in the middle of the Key Bridge to look south along the Potomac River to the Washington Harbor development, the Watergate Complex, and the Kennedy Center (see Walk 6).

In Leslie Ford's *False to Any Man* (1939), when widowed Grace Latham drove from Alexandria to Georgetown, she saw Washington as a star-spangled city with the white dome of the Capitol and the tall shaft of the Monument. But as Grace crossed the river she passed dirty sidings and belching smokestacks. They are no longer there to spoil the view.

In Nick Carter's *Death of the Falcon* (1974), Nick Carter, or Agent N3 of AXE, had the job of protecting the ex-wife of Shah Hassan of Adabi, whom the Silver Scimitar planned to murder. Carter took Sherima and her friend Candy sightseeing along the Canal Road next to the C&O, then drove northwest to look at the Potomac River's Great Falls (Park).

In Patricia O'Brien's *The Ladies Lunch* (1994), presiden-

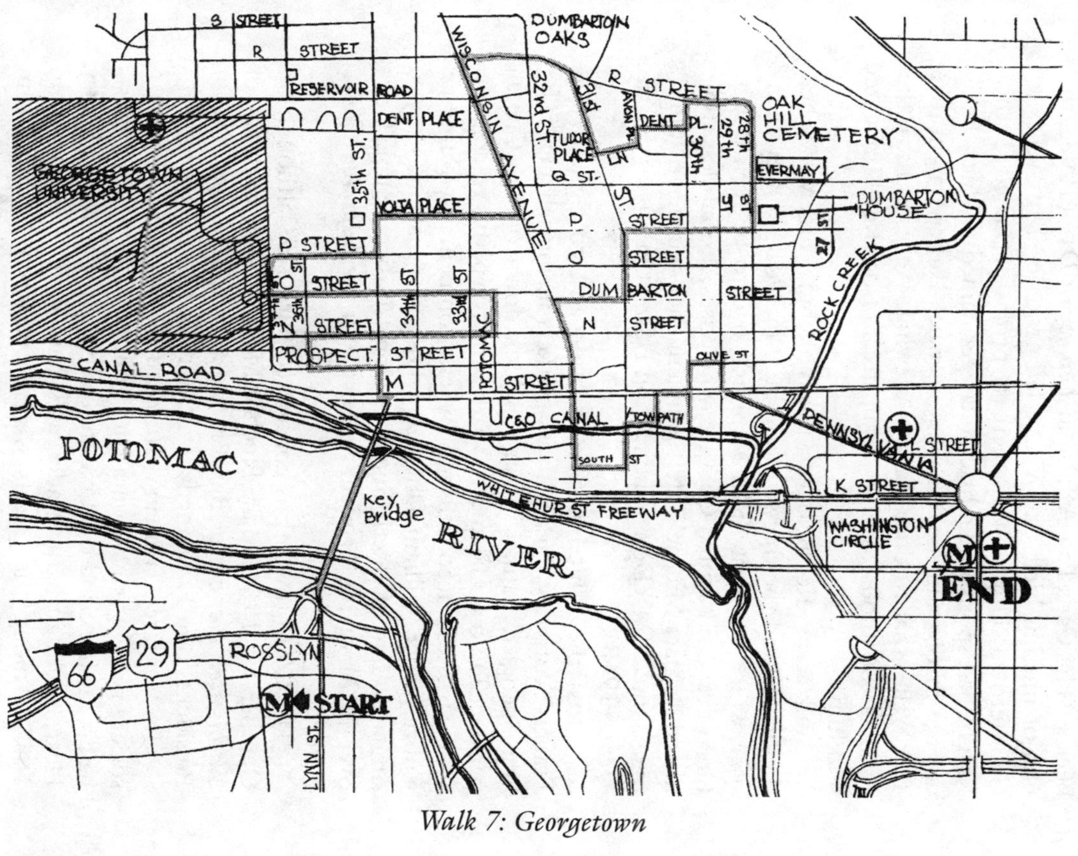

Walk 7: Georgetown

tial press secretary Faith Paige jumped off the cliffs at Great Falls when the president died of a heart attack. In Gary Braunbeck's "The Cat's Paw Affair" in *Danger in D.C.* (1993), the trail of missing First Cat Winnie led groomer Tim Welles to Georgetown University, where a professor called Father Knight had sponsored a black teenager named Rodney. Rodney was involved in the catnaping, so when Father Knight told Tim Welles that Rodney was out crewing, Welles went to the Potomac Boathouse, which was upstream from Key Bridge, to find him.

Walk across Key Bridge to the Whitehurst Freeway. When the bridge and the freeway were built in 1948 the Key Mansion, which stood at 3518 M Street, had to be torn down. One of several haunted Georgetown houses, it doubtless stimulated Barbara Michaels's fertile imagination when she "built" the haunted "MacDougal house" on P Street in *Ammie, Come Home* (1968).

Cross the Whitehurst intersection and go right to the Francis Scott Key Park with its markers memorializing "The Star Spangled Banner." You can look down on the Chesapeake & Ohio Canal and towpath. The towpath's re-creation as a park was accomplished by environmentalist Supreme Court Justice William Douglas, whose personal life story is similar to that of elderly Supreme Court Justice Temple Conover in Margaret Truman's *Murder in the Supreme Court* (1982).

The C&O towpath is considered fairly safe, although on October 13, 1964, Mary Pinchot Meyer, the sister-in-law of *Washington Post* editor Ben Bradlee and reputed girlfriend of President John F. Kennedy, was shot dead there at noon.

In Margaret Truman's *Murder in Georgetown* (1986), a society party was held on a barge on the C&O. Some guests had come in period costumes to celebrate the arrival of Henry Fleet, an English fur trader who landed at Georgetown in 1632. Among the guests were New Jersey Senator John Froelich and his daughter Valerie, a journalism student at Georgetown University. The morning after the party Valerie's body was found in the canal. *Washington Post* crime reporter

Joe Potamos, who was sent to cover the story, became involved with a piano player on the barge and ran afoul of powerful columnist/Georgetown professor George Alfred Bowen.

In Barbara Michaels's *Shattered Silk* (1988), Karen Nevitt was minding the Georgetown house of her Aunt Ruth and Uncle Pat MacDougal. Early summer mornings Karen went jogging on the Canal footpath to lose weight.

In Carey Roberts's *Pray God to Die* (1994), when Congressional aide Caroline McKelvey was found murdered in her D.C. apartment, Congressman Woodward's administrative assistant Alex Shannon's alibi was that he was jogging along the C&O canal with his dog.

Leave Key Park to walk to M Street between 34th and 35th Streets (to the west M Street is called Canal Road). Turn left to walk along Canal Road to 35th Street. Cross 35th Street and walk one block uphill to Prospect Street. Prospect Street once was lined with handsome eighteenth-century mansions perched on the hillside with gardens down to the river. To your right are two such mansions: Quality Hill at number 3425, and Stoddert (Halcyon) House at number 3400. Halcyon House had an underground tunnel to the river, used as part of the Underground Railway.

Turn left and walk past Prospect House at 3508 Prospect Street toward 36th Street. Built in 1788, it was rehabbed by New Dealers, then James Forrestal, the first Secretary of Defense, lived there. It also was the official guest house when the Trumans lived in Blair House during the renovation of the White House.

In Leslie Ford's *Murder in the O.P.M.* (1942), wartime Washington was full of newcomers like Lawrason Hilyard, new head of OPM (Office of Price Management). Hilyard rented a white brick mansion at 37th and Prospect Avenues that friends of Grace Latham had rehabbed. Latham's perennial suitor, Colonel Primrose, had asked Grace to invite him to meet the Hilyards, but before he did, Hilyard's body was found below the Key Bridge in front of the Street Car Barn on M Street.

At 36th Street you reach the back of the Street Car Barn, a big brick building with a tiled roof which fronts on Canal Road. Just past the Car Barn are the infamous "killing steps" in William Blatty's *The Exorcist* (1971). These same stairs, owned by Georgetown University, were used for the film.

In Gary Braunbeck's short story "The Cat's Paw Affair" in *Danger in D.C.* (1993), First Family friend and cat groomer Tim Welles walked to M Street just to look at *The Exorcist*'s seventy-five steep stairs where Jason Miller fell to his death.

Walk down the stairs if you feel like it, then come back up and cross 36th Street. Turn right and cross Prospect Street. At the northwest corner is the upscale restaurant called 1789. In Nick Carter's *Death of the Falcon* (1974), Agent Carter took Queen Sherima and her companion there for dinner. The Tombs, a sort of student rathskeller, is in the basement. Unfortunately, neither place is open for breakfast or a midmorning snack. Just past 1789 at number 3611 Prospect is a nicely preserved two-story house which is the headquarters of the Foundation for the Preservation of Historic Georgetown.

Walk up 36th Street past the Tombs to another Georgetown restaurant called F. Scott's at Number 1232. Named for Roaring '20s role model and author F. Scott Fitzgerald, its decor is Art Deco.

In Margaret Truman's *Murder in the Smithsonian* (1983), after British historian Dr. Lewis Tunney was murdered at a Bicentennial black-tie gala, his Scottish fiancee Heather McBean came over to track down his murderer. She was taken under the wing of Chestertonian eccentric Dr. Evelyn Killinworth, who owned a Georgetown townhouse. Killinworth put Heather McBean there for safety, and since F. Scott's was one of his favorite eating places, he took her and MPD Lieutenant Joe Pearl there to eat and compare notes.

Look on both sides of 36th Street for a somewhat forlorn redbrick Federal house (they are not easy to come by). In Barbara Michaels's *Shattered Silk* (1986), Karen Nevitt visited old Mrs. Ferris, who lived nearby. She sold Karen some vintage clothing which turned out to hold clues to an old murder.

Turn right at the next corner and cross 36th Street to walk four blocks east on brick-paved N Street to Potomac Street. You are surrounded by old Georgetown houses on either side. Most of them look pretty well cared for, in spite of Gar Anthony Haywood's comment in *Bad News Travels Fast* (1995) that this part of Georgetown was charming in a well-worn way, comfortably used, the way a college town should be.

At 34th Street cross N Street and keep going. You are passing Cox's Row, a famous group of five Federal townhouses built around 1790 by Colonel John Cox, the first mayor of Georgetown. In 1824 General Lafayette was a guest at number 3337. Many of these Federal houses have wrought-iron fences to go with the brick sidewalks.

In Spiro Agnew's *The Canfield Decision* (1976), Vice President Porter Canfield was married to a Main Line Philadelphia girl. Instead of living in the official quarters at the Naval Observatory, they bought a Georgetown house near the university, but when his wife Amy looked out the front window and saw some Georgetown students making out she left.

The most famous house on N Street is number 3307 at the corner of 33rd Street. A tall redbrick townhouse with white shutters and black trim built in 1812, it is known as Marbury House. John F. Kennedy bought it for his wife when their daughter Caroline was born, and his brother Bobby, wife, and houseful of kids lived around the corner. The whole gang used to play touch football up and down this part of N Street.

In Mary Higgins Clark's *Stillwatch* (1984), the scene of the crime—both old and new—was a Georgetown mansion at 3000 N Street. This is a nonexistent number near Wisconsin Avenue, but the handsome Federal house Clark described was very like the Kennedy house. It had been the home of Congressman Dean Adams, a friend and contemporary of Senator Jack Kennedy, who had suddenly murdered his wife, nearly killed his small daughter Kerry, then shot himself. When Kerry, now known as Patricia Traymore, returned to live there while producing a television series on Senator Abigail Jennings, who was slated to become vice president, her reappearance caused old scores to come alive again.

Cross 33rd Street on N Street and walk past Smith's Row, built in 1817, to Potomac Street. Turn left on Potomac Street and walk to the corner of O Street. You come to St. John's Episcopal Church at 3240 O Street. This Georgetown parish church, affiliated with St. John's Lafayette Square, was designed by the Capitol architect in 1809 with Frances Scott Key and Thomas Jefferson subscribing to the building fund.

In Carter's *Death of the Falcon* (1974), after dinner at 1789 Carter walked Queen Sherima and her friend Candy past Marbury House where they were attacked by some black guys who jumped out of a station wagon that had been following them. Carter disposed of all four men, then took the women to St. John's Church where they called a cab, leaving Carter to handle the MPD.

Turn left and walk along O Street with its cobblestones and streetcar tracks. You see more Federal townhouses, some being rehabbed. In D.C. mysteries an author often describes a gem of a house "in Georgetown" but gives no address, so you pick your own.

In Elliott Roosevelt's *Murder in the Oval Office* (set in 1936), Alabama Democratic Senator Winstead Colmer was found shot dead inside the locked Oval Office. The First Lady, concerned about his pregnant young widow, went to Senator Colmer's small redbrick house in Georgetown to pay a condolence call.

In Fletcher Knebel and Charles W. Bailey's *Seven Days in May* (1962), when Marine Colonel Martin Casey found out about a plot to kidnap the president, a small but loyal group about the president made plans for overcoming it. Friendly Senator Ray Clark lived in a white painted brick house in Georgetown, but he was kidnaped and taken to Fort Myer where the head of the Secret Service found him locked up in the Stockade. (See Walk 8.)

In Roosevelt's *Murder in the Rose Garden* (set in 1936), Vivian Taliafero (Tolliver), daughter of the late Senator Jefferson Taliafero of Mississippi, ran a salon where she entrapped VIPs by photographing them, then blackmailing them. When

Vivian was found murdered in the White House Rose Garden, some White House staffers and other VIPs were implicated. Taliafero's Federal brick house was on a tree-lined brick street with a cast-iron hitching post. With Secret Service Agent Stanlislaw Szczygiel and MPD Lieutenant Ed Kennelly, FDR's secretary Missy LeHand searched the house for the First Lady who had to give a speech, but the incriminating photographs were not there.

In Joseph Finder's *Extraordinary Powers* (1993), ex-CIA agent Ben Ellison was lured back by the murder of his father-in-law, the head of the CIA. Ellison consulted retired CIA superspy Edmund Moore who lived on N Street in a townhouse with a wrought-iron fence, but soon after Ellison's visit Moore was murdered.

Stay on O Street to 37th Street. You have arrived at the campus of Georgetown University. Georgetown University, founded by the Jesuits in 1789, is the oldest Roman Catholic university in America. Its campus stretches from Prospect Street to your left along 37th Street to Reservoir Road on the north, and backs up to the Potomac River on the west. Across 37th Street you can see a high stone wall and the tops of the towers of the Victorian Healy Building, put up in 1877. Behind the Healy Building is the 1792 Old North Building, still in use.

Cross 37th Street to the university's main entrance at O Street and go inside to explore the campus. There is an information center at the gate where you can get a map. There are public rest rooms in the Healy Building (straight ahead) and in Old North, Maquire Hall (just behind Healy), Blauinger Library, Bunn Intercultural Center, and Leavey Center to your right near Georgetown Hospital. You can also get something to eat.

On Nick Carter's walk with Queen Sherima and her friend Candy they went first to Georgetown University. Carter told them it was two hundred years old and had the world's best international and foreign service studies.

In Charles Goodrum's *Carnage of the Realm* (1979), after the murder of Georgetown History Professor Vandermann, librarian Edward George and history major Steve Carson interviewed Dr. Charter, another coin collector club member, in his university office in one of the antebellum gray stone campus buildings.

In Lawrence Sanders's *Capital Crimes* (1989), when the First Family fell for a charismatic faith healer called Brother Kristos who began to advise the president on policy, Chief of Staff Henry Folsom tried to eliminate Brother Kristos, then left to teach political science at Georgetown University.

In Benjamin M. Schutz's Edgar-winning short story, "Mary, Mary, Shut the Door" in *Deadly Allies* (1992), PI Leo Haggerty was hired by Gina Scolari's uncle to investigate Gina's fiance Derek Marshall. Gina's uncle was sure Marshall was planning matrimony, then murder. Haggerty's staff discovered Marshall was a Georgetown University Law School graduate but the whirlwind romance didn't give them enough time to discredit him. Georgetown University Law School is in downtown Washington at New Jersey Avenue and E Street just west of Union Station. (See Walk 4.) Patricia Cornwall's Chief Medical Examiner Kay Scarpetta went there and met future FBI Special Agent Mark James.

In Marilyn Quayle and Nancy Northcott's *The Campaign* (1996), Georgia's black senator Bob Grant was a presidential hopeful who was being smeared in a campaign orchestrated by the Oval Office. They also implicated his son Bailey, a Georgetown University junior, in a drug bust.

The most likely location for the exclusive Washington Day School in James Patterson's *Along Came a Spider* (1992) is somewhere west of Georgetown University. (It also might be Sidwell Friends School—see Walk 5.) Two children, Maggie Rose Dunne, daughter of a movie star, and Michael "Shrimpie" Goldberg, son of the secretary of the treasury, were kidnaped by a teacher named Gary Soneji. MPD African-American homicide detectives Alex Cross and his buddy John Simpson were called to the scene and then found themselves giving D.C.'s media-minded black Mayor Carl Monroe a ride back. Cross drove from the school to Canal Road and took it to the Whitehurst Freeway just before the Key Bridge.

On Reservoir Road at the northern end of Georgetown

University campus is the Georgetown University Hospital. In R. B. Dominic's *Epitaph for a Lobbyist* (1974), NPA lobbyist Shirley Knapp was murdered after being accused of paying some congressman fifty thousand dollars. Then her secretary Barbara Underwood was attacked while visiting the suspected congressman and taken to Georgetown University Hospital.

In Margot J. Fromer's medical mysteries, *Scalpel's Edge* (1991) and *Night Shift* (1993), Amanda Knight was Director of Nursing at J.F.K. Memorial Hospital, where staff and/or patients were "routinely" murdered. According to Fromer, J.F.K. Hospital was located in Georgetown whose narrow streets were clogged with students and restaurants were expensive, and its location on Reservoir Road makes it a Georgetown University Hospital look-alike.

In Benjamin M. Schutz's *Embrace the Wolf* (1985), African-American PI Leo Haggerty, hired to locate the father of twin girls who had been kidnaped, went north of Reservoir Road on 38th Street to an old row house with pebbled glass and a wrought-iron door. There, he interviewed a hooker named Joceyln who had been left seriously injured and blind from an attack by the kidnaper.

Explore the campus, then walk past Copley Hall and turn right to walk past an old walled cemetery and come out of the campus at P and 37th Street.

In *State Department Cat* (1945), Mary Plum commented that Georgetown was a sane and sober community except for its passion for chairs which may not be sat upon and antique bottles, bellows, and tuning forks. In Plum's mystery Nancy Patterson and George Stair, a candidate for the Foreign Office, went (by night) to the Georgetown home of Mrs. Warrenden, a narrow wooden structure next to a brick house of the 1880 period. George left Nancy in the car but when he didn't return, Nancy got hold of her uncle who called the cops. Nancy's Uncle Wade also lived near P Street in a very old brick house set in an ancient garden with a long narrow porch pillared with exquisite wrought iron. There was a fanlight over the door, eighteenth-century shutters, and a Chinese ghost who visited the garden by moonlight. After they "visited" the

Warrenden house, George and Nancy spent the night at Uncle Wade's, where in the morning the secretary of state came to call.

Turn right to walk along cobblestoned P Street to 35th Street. Then turn left and go one block north to Volta Place. Syndicated columnist Walter Lippmann and his wife lived at 1527 E. 35th Street in inventor Alexander Graham Bell's old home before they moved "up" to 3525 Woodley Road, where they gave famous parties. (See Walk 5.) Lippmann matches the prototype of media VIPS that appear in D.C. mysteries by Leslie Ford, John Ehrlichman, Margaret Truman, et al.

One block north of Volta Place is Q Street. In Anne Morice's *Murder in Mimicry* (1977), British actress Tessa Crichton, wife of Scotland Yard Chief Inspector Robin Crichton, came to D.C. with a play at the Kennedy Center. She stayed with an American friend at Number 1312A Erskine Lane "between P and Q Street" near Wisconsin Avenue in a dreamy little brick and timber house perched eight steps above the sidewalk. It might have been Volta Place. Alger Hiss, the convicted Russian spy, also lived on Volta Place once.

Turn right on Volta Place and walk to 34th Street. At 1537 34th Street you see an unusual brick building known as the Volta Bureau, built by Alexander Graham Bell for the American Association for the Teaching of Speech to the Deaf. Cross 34th Street to walk along the south side of Volta Place. In the middle of the block is a tiny enclave called Pomander Walk with ten tiny, pastel-colored houses that have been lovingly restored. It makes a plausible (but not perfect) site for Carolyn Wheat's story "The Black Hawthorn" in *Danger in D.C.* (1993). Wheat's story was set in a block of redbrick Georgian townhouses around a square, but there are no real "English" squares in Georgetown. In Wheat's story British Mrs. Simpson-Phelps asked her next door neighbor Nikki to cat-sit while she went to the UK on a visit. Since Mrs. Simpson-Phelps had welcomed Nikki and her spouse, making scones and showing her the family heirloom, a Chinese ginger jar in a deep rich black, Nikki agreed. But the day before Mrs.

Simpson-Phelps was due home, Nikki found her house a shambles and the Black Hawthorn vase broken.

Look at Pomander Row, then keep walking along Volta Place, crossing first 33rd Street, then 32nd Street. Keep your eyes out for a small two-story brick house. In Ross Thomas's *Ah, Treachery!* (1994), the "Little Rock crowd" had just been elected, but someone had ripped off fund-raiser Millicent Altford. Altford hired ex-Major Edd "Twodees" Partain to ride shotgun while she tried to recover the stolen funds. Chums of Partain ran a storefront operation called VOMIT—Victims of Military Intelligence Treachery—at 3219 Volta Place in a small yellow brick house. In real life this is the address of an old friend of Patricia Moyes who writes historical fiction.

In Janice Law's *Backfire* (1994), Anna Peters had settled down to run Executive Security, which made the homes and offices of D.C. VIPs safe from bugs, break-ins, and other Capital habits. Anna was hired to investigate a fire and the death of entrepreneur Joe Skanes's invalid wife and to find an alibi for Maria Rivas, the maid. Anna discovered that Skanes had a longtime mistress, Natalie Welsung, whom he kept in a nice little house in Georgetown filled with objets d'art.

Walk to Wisconsin Avenue, Georgetown's major north-south road. At 3230-16 Volta Place the former police station has been converted into a classy residential enclave which the architect called "Fantasy Federal." It was once home to the seventh precinct's police station. In Leslie Ford's *The Simple Way of Poison* (1937), Colonel John Primrose, Grace Latham, and Randall Nash's second wife and daughter came home from the traditional Georgetown Christmas Assembly to find Nash poisoned in his ancestral house on Beall Street. The Georgetown police, who seemed to know Colonel Primrose, came from their Seventh Precinct Headquarters on Volta Place. In Ford's 1942 *Murder in the O.P.M.*, the Georgetown police also came to the C&O Canal scene of the crime from Volta Place.

In Patricia Moyes's *Black Widower* (1975), at the reception for Tampica's new ambassador Sir Edward Ironmonger,

African-American activist Franklin D. Martin picketed the embassy. His protest march began at the Georgetown "Pig" (Police) Station on Volta Place, but at the embassy, the guests just stepped over the sitting demonstrators because in Washington they were part of its scenic charm.

If you want to quit now for the day, turn right and walk two blocks down Wisconsin Avenue to O Street. On Wisconsin south of O Street there are plenty of mysterious places to stop and eat, then find a cab. To finish Part One, turn left on Wisconsin Avenue and head uphill to Q Street. Then walk up Wisconsin to Dent Place.

In *Black Widower*, although she deplored the high cost of Georgetown living, Moyes made it clear she loved its village atmosphere. She described Wisconsin Avenue as a great shopping street with pavement-squatting hippies in outrageously colorful outfits like harbingers of spring, and trendy boutiques, making it D.C.'s answer to London's Chelsea. (See *Mystery Reader's Walking Guide: London.*) Moyes's choice for lunch, the French Market, has closed and moved to Chevy Chase. But this part of Dent Place west of Wisconsin Avenue would be the place to find 3320 Dent, whose garden has been featured on the annual Garden Tour.

Continue walking up Wisconsin to Reservoir Road, passing by the Corcoran School of Art. Founded in 1890 it is the only D.C. professional school of art and design; it is named for the wily, but courtly old banker W. W. Corcoran who appeared in Sarah Booth Conroy's *Refinements of Love* (set in 1885).

Cross Wisconsin Avenue at Reservoir Road and walk one more block to R Street, passing by the wrought-iron fence around the Georgetown (Branch) Library on R Street. The library is housed in a handsome '30s redbrick Georgian style mansion. There are rest rooms in the basement and public phones if you decide it is time to call a cab. The staff are very pleasant, curious but not critical when we descended upon them, loaded down with camera, tape recorder, maps, clipboard, a script, and pedometers. When we complained that the French Market had closed, they recommended a small French bistro nearby, so we returned to Wisconsin Avenue and walked one block north to tiny Bistro Lepic at 1736 Wisconsin Avenue. We walked in sans tie, jacket, skirt, or reservation, but the young maitre d' seated us and served us charmingly. Most of the customers looked well-heeled in three-piece suits and little black dresses. On the eastern side of Wisconsin we could have gone to Mexican Restorante Agajutla instead.

Farther north on Wisconsin Avenue is the USSR's skyscraper Embassy. In Margaret Truman's *Murder in Georgetown* (1986), megadeveloper Marshall Jenkins was building a high-rise condo on Wisconsin Avenue across the street from the Embassy. But Georgetown settlers did not like high-rises, and security forces like the FBI did not want anyone snooping on their snooping on the Russians, with the result that *Washington Post*'s crime reporter Joe Potamos was nearly tossed off the roof.

This is the end of Part One of the Georgetown Walk. If you want to stop at this point, take Wisconsin Avenue to your right back to R Street. Either hail a cab or return to the Georgetown Public Library to call a cab from there.

Begin the second part of the Georgetown Walk by going left on R Street to 32nd Street. You reach the main entrance to the mansion known today as Dumbarton Oaks at 1703 32nd Street between R and S Streets. The garden entrance is at 31st and R Streets.

A brass plaque on Dumbarton Oaks' wrought-iron fence says that the Rock of Dunbarton was granted by Queen Anne to Colonel Ninian Beall. In 1801 Senator William Dorsey of Maryland bought twenty-two acres from the Beall family to build the Federal-style brick mansion. By the 1830s "Oakly" had become the home of Vice President John C. Calhoun and his wife, but because they snubbed the wife of President Jackson's Secretary of War, Calhoun never got to run for president. In 1860 Edward Linthincum added two Victorian wings and renamed it "The Oaks." Finally in 1920 diplomat Robert Bliss and his wife, Mildred, bought the estate and renamed it "Dumbarton Oaks," misspelling the original name.

The Blisses added the stately Music Room, for which Igor Stravinsky wrote the "Dumbarton Oaks Concerto" for their thirtieth wedding anniversary. They also created the formal gardens and began a collection of Byzantine artifacts. When they moved to California they gave most of the estate to Harvard University, then in 1963 they added their pre-Columbian collection and built it a special museum on the grounds.

The grounds of Dumbarton Oaks belong to the National Park Service and are open daily. But if possible you should also tour the mansion, the Byzantine and pre-Columbian collections, and the formal gardens.

Dumbarton Oaks was the site of the famous 1944 Dumbarton Oaks Conference when distinguished representatives of Britain, China, the United States, and the USSR met in the Music Room (for its calming effect) to plan the United Nations Organization. The media was banned! The UN charter they devised was officially ratified in San Francisco the following year.

A different approach to world government occurred in Robert Ludlum's *The Chancellor Manuscript* (1977) when the group known as Inver Brass met secretly at a porticoed mansion in tree-lined Georgetown. The six men sat around a circular table in a wood-paneled room with a Franklin stove in which they burned their agendas. They voted to assassinate FBI Director J. Edgar Hoover and steal his files, but half of them—M through Z—turned out to be missing!

In Margaret Truman's *Murder at the National Gallery* (1996), Annabel Reed-Smith ran her own Georgetown pre-Columbian gallery on Wisconsin Avenue. After a former client charged in and destroyed one of her best pieces, Steve Jordan of MPD's Art Squad asked Reed-Smith's help with a sting operation to recover three objects stolen from Dumbarton Oaks: a were-jaguar, black basalt serpent, and gold monkey.

Come out of Dumbarton Oaks and cross R Street at 32nd Street. Turn left and walk along R Street to 31st Street. You are now in the classy half of Georgetown where you see many mansions with coach houses and large gardens or grounds. It is a delightful neighborhood to walk through, and the best part is that you are walking downhill toward the river! But there are very few street signs.

Turn right on 31st Street to walk down to Tudor Place at number 1644. The brick and stucco mansion with its circular portico was designed for Thomas Peter and his wife Martha Custis Peter, one of Martha Washington's granddaughters; it has family pieces from Mount Vernon. The house stayed in the Peters family until 1983 when it was opened to the public.

It, too, could be the meeting place of Ludlum's Inver Brass in *The Chancellor Manuscript* (1977), and according to Barbara Michaels (aka Elizabeth Peters), was one of her models for the mansion of the fabulous (and eccentric) Mrs. Jackson MacDougal. In Michaels's *Ammie, Come Home* (1968), after Ruth Bennett met her niece Sara's Georgetown University professor Pat MacDougal, he took Ruth to meet his mother. "Mrs. Mac" was holding a seance at her Georgetown mansion, which was almost invisible except for its chimneys because of the trees and high wall that enclosed its grounds. It was staffed with old retainers and Alexander, the ugliest (and worst-tempered) dog in Georgetown. "Mrs. Mac" herself, one of Washington's most famous hostesses, looked like an Egyptian mummy and greeted Ruth and her son wearing a silvery caftan.

In Patricia Moyes's author's note in *Black Widower* (1975), she insisted that Oxford Gardens, Exeter Place, and Maycroft House were all fictional. But Moyes lived in Georgetown when her husband worked at the World Bank and enjoyed its village atmosphere—and knew its houses. All three of her fictional mansions resemble Tudor Place, but her friend Helen Lillie Marwick who still lives in Georgetown insists the real model is Evermay. Lillie's next novel, *The Shadow Queen*, will be set in present-day Georgetown with a contemporary plot to put a Mary Queen of Scots look-alike back on the Scottish throne!

When retired Tampican Bishop Barrington's wife Prudence took the (fictional) Chevy Chase Episcopal Ladies's Club on the (real) Georgetown Garden Tour, Henry Tibbett and his wife Emily followed them and chased the Bishop's wife into the Maycroft House maze to save her from the murderer. Tudor Place does not have a maze but it does have a circular garden and its grounds occupy a city block.

Tudor Place could also be the Georgetown mansion refurbished by society hostess ex-movie star Dotty Waring (aka Elizabeth Taylor who lived on S Street?) in Walter J. Sheldon's *Rites of Murder* (1984). Roman Catholic Bishop Burdock attended one of her parties—and played the piano—hoping to meet VIPS who had enjoyed the services of murdered call girl Laureen Triplett. The bishop had helped Triplett's daughter get into an exclusive parochial school.

After admiring Tudor Place, cross 31st Street to Avon Lane. Then turn right to take Avon Lane to Avon Place which runs back to R Street. But only take Avon Place to Dent Place, then go left on Dent Place back to 30th Street.

This enclave of restored Federal townhouses have come up in the world since Leslie Ford wrote *Murder in the O.P.M.* (1942). When Grace Latham and Colonel Primrose came to Dent Place, they found a charming little street with old-fashioned lights but the small two-story redbrick houses had been converted into apartments, where penniless social climber ex-Count Stanley (Stanislaus) Woland(sky) lived.

Cross R Street at 30th Street to walk along the wrought-iron fence of Oak Hill Cemetery to its Italianate Gatehouse built in 1839. Along the south side of R Street are a number of handsome houses, one lived in by "Mr. Republican," Senator Robert Taft of Ohio, another at number 2920 is the home of the *Washington Post* owner Katherine Graham of Watergate and Pentagon Papers fame.

In Ross Thomas's *If You Can't Be Good* (1973), Carolyn Ames, the daughter of Senator Robert Ames who was caught accepting a big bribe, lived on R Street near Oak Hill Cemetery in "a hell of a nice little pad" with a wood-burning fireplace and a big kitchen. Syndicated D.C. columnist Frank Size hired Decatur Lucas to find out why the wealthy senator took the bribe, but before Lucas could talk to Carolyn, she was blown up by a bomb.

If you have time, buy a map of the notable graves at the Gatehouse, then go inside to see the Victorian mausoleums and Gothic Revival chapel. This very exclusive cemetery was given to the city by W. W. Corcoran, who bought the land from a great-nephew of Washington, and is buried there himself. Other notables include the Van Ness family, who owned most of Foggy Bottom; Truman's secretary of state, Dean Acheson; and Lincoln's secretary of war, Edwin M. Stanton.

In G. J. A. O'Toole's *The Cosgrove Report* (set in 1867), when Secretary Stanton found out the body of Lincoln assassin John Wilkes Booth was missing, he hired Pinkerton agent Nicholas Cosgrove to find Booth—dead or alive.

In George P. Pelecanos's *Down by the River Where the Dead Men Go* (1995), after PI Nick Stefanos found a dead young African-American man by the Anacostia River, he drove to Dumbarton Oaks because it was his favorite spot in his hometown. He went into Rock Creek Park to sit on a bench and watch the creek flow as cars drove by. Then Stefanos walked to the iron fence that surrounded Oak Hill Cemetery to look at the place where privileged people had privileged places to rest.

Stay on R Street past Oak Hill Cemetery to 28th Street. Turn right on 28th Street to walk down to Q Street. Halfway there at number 1623 you pass Evermay, another historic mansion. A redbrick Georgian built in 1801 with a high brick fence and wrought-iron gates, Evermay is still in private hands, but the Georgetown Garden Tour's tea party usually takes place here. Evermay certainly could be the model for Moyes's Maycroft House in *Black Widower* (1975), and for Barbara Michaels's MacDougal mansion in *Ammie, Come Home* (1968).

In addition, in Margaret Truman's *Murder at the Kennedy Center* (1989), Senator Kenneth Ewald lived in a stately two-story redbrick mansion with a wrought-iron fence on upper 28th Street with a grand view of Dumbarton Oaks. After the body of Senator Ewald's staffer Andrea Feldman was found near the Kennedy Center, his friend Mackensie Smith reluctantly became the defense lawyer for Ewald's son Paul, who was accused of the murder.

Look across 28th Street where you can just see Mackall Square, hidden by trees and walls. It could be the Georgetown square where British war bride Mrs. Simpson-Phelps lived with her four beloved cats and heirloom vase in Carolyn Wheat's story "The Black Hawthorn" in *Danger in D.C.* (1993).

When you reach Q Street (if there is no street sign, just

assume the next east-west street *is* Q Street) go left partway down Q Street to another historic mansion called Dumbarton House at Number 2715. Yet another Federal-style mansion called Bellevue, it was relocated here in 1915 when Q Street was extended across Rock Creek to connect Georgetown with Kalorama. In 1928 the National Society of Colonial Dames bought it, renamed it Dumbarton House, and turned it into the society's headquarters with a museum which is open to the public. Of course Dumbarton House, too, could be the mansion in Barbara Michaels's and Patricia Moyes's mysteries. Take your pick!

In spite of the gracious homes located here, in Mark Olshaker's *The Edge* (1994), homicide detective Sandy Mansfield was called to the scene of the crime in a seedy redbrick apartment house on Q Street on the far eastern fringe of Georgetown. The terribly mutilated victim was Sarah Hazeltine, who had worked in a gallery called Conway on P Street.

In Ann Ripley's *Mulch* (1994), President Jack Fairchild wanted inventor/arms trader Peter Hoffman to be undersecretary of defense because his secretary was too dovish. To get the job, Hoffman needed a clean sheet but he had a love nest in a Q Street row house where he had already killed one mistress. Now he murdered another and put her body parts into leaf bags for pickup. (See Walk 8.)

Walk back on Q Street to 28th Street and head south toward P Street. At Number 2803 at the corner of P Street look at Reuben Daw's Fence, made entirely of musket barrels from the Mexican War of 1848 and very appropriate for a mystery walk!

Turn right to walk along P Street toward Wisconsin Avenue. You are now in mystery maven Leslie Ford's territory, where her main characters have lived in the same house since kingdom come. Widowed Grace Latham's house was somewhere in the next block on P Street. Grace lived there with her two sons, overseen by Lilac, her housekeeper, who knew—or was related to—all the other African-American servants (known then as "darkies") in Georgetown. Grace was the epitome of the Mary Roberts Rinehart heroine who might have prevented murder "had she but known." According to Grace the reason she never married retired Colonel John Primrose, who lived across the street, was simple: he had never asked her, and she felt he would be terribly embarrassed if she asked him! Others suspected his "batman" Sergeant Phineas Buck was the real reason.

One of the trickiest problems with the Ford mysteries is her imaginary Beall Street—a nice Georgetown name—which Ford located as "backing up" to P Street. Possible locations would be two short streets: Poplar Street, which runs from 28th to 27th Streets half a block south of P Street or Orchard Lane, which turns into West Lane Keys two blocks at 30th Street just north of P Street. But when Ford wrote that Beall Street ran into Wisconsin Avenue, she also may have been renaming O, Q, or Dumbarton Streets! Then once she wrote that Colonel Primrose's address was 2491 P Street, which would mean that he and Grace Latham really lived in Rock Creek Park, much the way Rex Stout put Nero Wolfe's 35th Street brownstone in the Hudson River!

To further confuse her fans, in *All for the Love of a Lady* (1943), Molly and Cass Crane had bought a small house which was the second to last on Beall Street, almost at Rock Creek and approached by 26th Street. (This makes P Street and Beall Street the same street.) Molly had fixed it up while Cass was away spying. When Cass came home a body was found in the derelict house next door and everyone thought Cass did it. Intriguingly, the evidence about those murders (found by Grace) came from conversations recorded on the hard disks which predated tapes.

In Leslie Ford's *The Simple Way of Poison* (1937), Grace Latham walked from Wisconsin Avenue to the Beall Street residence of Randall Nash and his wife Iris, which backed up to Latham's home on P Street. There Randall Nash told them all a nasty story about a Beall ancestor who had built the house using mahogany brought in his own ships and had married his children's governess. His secretary was an Oxford grad and one night the wife and secretary supposedly ran off with her body servant, a slave girl of sixteen. But when they graded

Beall Street for a sewer system, Randall Nash's father found a vault at the back of his lot with three skeletons inside—the missing wife, secretary, and slave girl.

After hearing this Christmasy tale, Grace went home to finish wrapping presents. When Lilac told her that Col. Primrose had called she looked across P street to his yellow brick house, built by a Colonel John Primrose attached to Washington's staff.

Keep an eye out for a yellow brick house while walking along P Street past Secretary of State Dean Acheson's house at 2805 P Street. When you cross 29th Street look for Barbara Michaels's redbrick Bennett-MacDougal house in *Ammie, Come Home* (1968). Ruth Bennett had inherited the Georgian house that had been in her family since the Revolutionary War. It had a hanging staircase like Octagon House and a strangely cold living room! Her niece Sara, who was staying with her and going to Georgetown University, became possessed by a Revolutionary War relative, Ammie (Amanda), whose father Douglass Campbell had disapproved of Ammie's suitor, Captain Anthony Doyle.

The same house and family reappeared in Michaels's *Shattered Silk* (1986) but now it was only two blocks off M Street. Michaels described it as a Federal house with the classic balance of windows and exterior ornament and an iron gate. Sara's younger sister Karen Nevitt was house-sitting while she worked for her friend Julie. Finally, in Michaels's *Stitches in Time* (1995), Rachel Grant became possessed by a Civil War slave girl called Rachel by way of a bride's quilt which had been handed down in the family until Rachel bought it. She took it to the Bennett-MacDougal house, now occupied by Ruth's niece Kara (aka Karen) and her husband.

Keep walking along very mysterious P Street to 31st Street, then turn left to walk to O Street. On the corner is the Victorian Christ Episcopal Church. Cross O Street to walk down 31st Street another block to Dumbarton Street. About a block and a half to your left at 2820 Dumbarton Street there is a mansion that once put terror in the hearts of all D.C. It was the office/home of syndicated columnist Drew Pearson who wrote "Washington Merry Go-Round" beginning in

1932. Pearson specialized in attacking world-famous politicians, socialites, diplomats, and the media. The column later reappeared in the *Washington Post*, written by Jack Anderson, for whom James Grady of *Six Days of the Condor* (1974) worked as a legman. In Ross Thomas's mysteries you also meet a VIP columnist Frank Size who controls people and events.

In John Ehrlichman's *The Company* (1977), there was a 1785 white farmhouse at 2990 N Street owned by columnist Arthur Perrine. Perrine liked to pretend that he had inherited the house from his family but was actually a Jewish kid from Chicago. Perrine preferred to invite sources to lunch but when he got a tip the FBI were investigating members of the White House staff, he went to Pittsburgh for the inside dope. This was a ploy to get Perrine out of his house so the FBI could bug it for paranoid President Monckton, but CIA Director Martin's spies caught the White House in the act and used the information to blackmail President Monckton.

Walk along on Dumbarton Street to Wisconsin Avenue where you are back in trendy shopping territory. In Michaels's *Shattered Silk* (1986), Karen Nevitt walked to work from her Aunt Ruth's house on P Street through the traffic maelstrom of Wisconsin Avenue. Ten years earlier, as a Georgetown University student, Karen had loved Georgetown's eclectic liveliness, the bars and fortunetellers rubbing shoulders with chic boutiques, vendors selling cheap chains, the elegant antique shops sandwiched in between Peoples' Drugs and McDonald's, but now she found it tawdry and unappealing. Karen was heading for Julie's antique shop called Old Things on a side street off Wisconsin. Julie's other employee, Rob, was a blond ladykiller who wrote a book on Georgetown legends that prompted break-ins at the store and the MacDougal house.

Cross Wisconsin at Dumbarton Street and go to the Georgetown Inn which is in the middle of the block between O and N Streets. The Georgetown Inn is a small Colonial-style building with a tiny lobby with no place to sit. Its restaurant called The Four Georges has closed, but it was a popular rendezvous for mystery characters.

In Jeffrey Archer's *Shall We Tell the President?* (1977; rev.

ed. 1985), the conspirators planning to assassinate the president met there on Thursday, February 24, 1981. The FBI found out about the conspiracy from a Greek illegal immigrant waiter who served them lunch. When it turned out that a senator was involved, FBI Special Agent Marc Andrews was given the job of finding the restaurant and discovering which senator it was.

In Margaret Truman's *Murder on Capitol Hill* (1981), lawyer Lydia James, who had been asked by the widow of murdered Senator Caldwell to serve as special counsel for Senator MacLoon's committee looking into his death met her lover Clarence Foster-Sims for brunch in the George II Room. Lydia lived nearby in a brownstone which she later found out was bugged.

In Susan Moody's *Penny Black* (1984), black photographer Penny Wannawake was the daughter of British Lady Helena Hurley and her African husband, UN Ambassador Dr. Wanawake of Senangaland. When her boarding-school chum Marfa was murdered, Penny took a room at the Georgetown Inn while she investigated the murder. As she walked back to the hotel a car started up suddenly on Wisconsin Avenue, knocking Penny down.

In Gary A. Braunbeck's story "The Cat's Paw Affair" in *Danger in D.C.* (1993), cat groomer Tim Welles stayed there. Welles, who grew up with First Lady Karen Ryan, was in town to groom First Cat Winnie for the Inauguration.

Leave the Georgetown Inn to walk down Wisconsin Avenue and cross N Street to Martin's Tavern. In Truman's *Murder on Capitol Hill* (1981), Martin's Tavern opened the day Prohibition ended. It was a quintessential Georgetown hangout, with dark wooden booths, veteran waiters, and a long oak bar and restaurant where Special Counsel Lydia James met her assistant Ginger to plan the investigation of the murder of Senator Cale Caldwell. The two women met in the Dugout, but someone was spying on them because when she left, Ginger was mugged.

Go one more block to Prospect Avenue and cross it to the Roy Rogers, which might be a good place to stop, too. In

Archer's *Shall We Tell the President?* (1977), when FBI Special Agent Marc Andrews went to pick up Dr. Elizabeth Dexter who had given emergency care to the immigrant Greek waiter, he drove by the Roy Rogers. Andrews was heading for Dexter's small Georgian brick townhouse on 30th Street, probably paid for by her father the senator.

Look around for the pre-Columbian art gallery run by Truman's Annabel Reed-Smith in *Murder at the National Gallery* (1996). Its centerpiece was a baked clay double-faced female figure called Tlatilco, which a former client in one of her divorce cases broke.

Walk one more block to M Street. Cross M Street and turn right to the Georgetown Park, a mall put into an old tobacco warehouse-cum-trolley car barn which backs up to the C&O Canal. Built in 1981, it has specialty shops, an Indian Craft Shop sponsored by the Department of the Interior, and rest rooms. You can also get a snack at indoor/outdoor Dean & DeLuca's.

Just beyond Georgetown Park at number 3236 you come to Clyde's. In Benjamin M. Schutz's *A Tax in Blood* (1987), African-American PI Leo Haggerty was hired to determine if the "suicide" of Malcolm Donnelly was really murder. His investigations turned out to be related to the random bombing at the Vietnam Wall and led Haggerty to a Georgetown doctor named Gutierrez. He met his significant other Samantha at Clyde's, a turn-of-the-century saloon look-alike where they had a drink at the bar, then ate dinner, but broke up for the evening because Haggerty had to go to 14th Street to interview a hooker. Haggerty commented that hookers were named for a Civil War General Hooker who forgot to leave his camp followers in D.C. when he left with his troops.

If you walked past Clyde's to Potomac Street and turned right one block north to Prospect Street, you might find artist Nina Bibesco's art gallery, the Firebird, in a small two-story brick building with bright blue trim. In Carey Roberts's *Touch a Cold Duck* (1989), British art patron Theo DeLise had bought it for Nina before he was found murdered in her house on Volta Place.

Turn right to walk along M Street to Wisconsin Avenue. Somewhere along here in Max Allan Collins's story "Catgate" in *Danger in D.C.* (1993) was the Gentleman's Club, a glittering chrome and mirrored wonderland where Senator Rawson picked up girls. When one called Vicki became a problem, he murdered her, then picked up Sheila who turned out to be Vicki's sister. Sheila used his cat, Tricky Dick, to bug the senator's pad.

At the corner of M and Wisconsin across the street you see the landmark golden dome and clock of the Riggs Bank. Cross Wisconsin Avenue. On the southeast corner is Nathan's, a seafood pasta restaurant popular with the three-piece suit crowd.

Turn right to walk down Wisconsin to tiny Blues Alley at Rear 1073 (Wisconsin Avenue) where you will find a small jazz supper club which claims to be the oldest in the nation. Internationally famous, the club is located in an eighteenth-century coach house, and its brick walls are hung with photographs of the jazz greats who have performed there from Ella Fitzgerald to Dizzy Gillespie to present-day Wynton Marsalis, who often does his Christmas gig here.

It was in a similar coach house south of M Street that alcoholic and eccentric Lavinia Fawcett lived and wrote blackmail notes in Leslie Ford's *The Simple Way of Poison* (1937).

In Margaret Truman's *Murder on Capitol Hill* (1981), Lydia James and her music teacher-cum-lover Clarence Foster-Sims went to Blues Alley after a concert at the new Caldwell Performing Arts Center (Kennedy Center?) because neither of them particularly liked Haydn.

In Carey Roberts's *Touch a Cold Duck* (1989), MPD homicide detective Anne Fitzhugh went to Blues Alley to interview sax player Misha Courbois, who was a suspect in the murder of Margot Farley, the dead Theo DeLise's girlfriend.

A little south of Blues Alley on Wisconsin you come to Houston's. In Truman's *Murder at the National Gallery* (1996), National Gallery curator Luther Mason took his artist son Julian to eat hickory-smoked hamburgers and feathery onion rings at Houston's because Julian refused to dress appropriately for better places.

Return to M Street and cross M Street to walk toward 31st Street. If you have time, turn left on 31st Street to walk to Booked Up at 1209 31st Street. Owned by Marcia Carter and Larry McMurtry, the author of *Lonesome Dove*, this bookstore has old, rare books and modern first editions in a mellow atmosphere with bookcases lining the walls.

While a terrific place to browse, Booked Up is not in an old white clapboard house like Weatherall's Rare & Used Books in Marcy Heidish's *The Torching* (1992). Weatherall's had been started by Alice Grey's Celtic grandmother before Georgetown was restored, renovated, and chic. Sixty-five years later the store became the scene of mysterious fires, related to a story of a Maryland woman possessed by the devil in 1738, with its modern-day murders somehow entwined with that grim past. Heidish does suggest, however, that Weatherall's is a clone of the Francis Scott Key Bookstore.

Return to M Street and cross 31st Street to keep walking along M Street until you reach the Old Stone House at number 3051. Built in 1765, it is believed to be the oldest house in Georgetown, and the only one that predates the Revolutionary War. Rumor has it that this house is haunted by ghosts from all periods of Georgetown history.

Cross M Street to Jefferson Street which goes to the C&O Canal. You pass a modern building called the Foundry which has a restaurant, shops, and galleries, together with the terminal for canal boat tours. At the end of Jefferson along the canal's towpath there is also a group of tiny worker houses now used for shops and homes. Built cheaply for the Irish navvies who dug the canal, these little redbrick houses look enough like slave quarters to make them appropriate housing for President Lockwood's Chief of Staff Julian Hubbard. Hubbard, a Yalie and member of the secret Shelley Society, lived with his young wife Emily in a small house filled to the brim with Empire furniture and Hubbard heirlooms in Charles McCarry's *Shelley's Heart* (1995).

Turn left to walk back up Jefferson to M Street, then turn right to 30th Street. Cross M Street and walk up 30th Street one block north to Olive Street. Turn right and walk one block on Olive Street past what is called the "narrowest house" in Georgetown.

Somewhere in this pleasant residential area "near M Street" was the Pleydels' elegant eighteenth-century Federal mansion in Helen MacInnes's *I and My True Love* (1952). State Department big shot Pleydel had rehabbed it in the '50s before Georgetown became—in his words—too trendy. Pleydel was a total snob, who kept the house and his wife Sylvia for appearances's sake.

This is also a good place for Dorothy Sucher's Sabina Swift to live and work. A shrink who was the owner of a detective agency, Swift was married to Professor Bruno Herschel, a theoretical physicist, and her home office was on a side street off M Street in a Federal-style house of weathered pink brick with black shutters. It had two wings, one containing the office, the other, her studio. Her legman Victor (Vic) Newman had a key to the office wing and went there to tell Swift about his mother's old friend Fran O'Donnell, who had died in a weird accident, in *Dead Men Don't Marry* (1989).

Just north of you on the 3000 block of N Street are some of the best examples of Federal-style architecture in D.C. Although this street was a Southern bastion during the Civil War, it was the probable site of the old redbrick building where Lincoln's Secretary Seward (who purchased Alaska) once lived. Much later it housed the select Serpentine Club in James Z. Alner's *The Capital Murder* (c. 1935). One summer night five members of the club, including Trevor Stoke, an epidemiologist, were sitting in its quaint, walled garden on N Street, telling ghost stories about the Octagon House, when the head of the Metropolitan Police Department told them a woman's body had been found in a house on Q Street, and the group decided to solve the murder themselves.

Turn right on 29th Street and walk back to M Street. Cross M Street to take Pennsylvania Avenue to the Four Seasons Hotel located along Rock Creek Park and the C&O

Canal. This is one of D.C.'s grand hotels where you may want to stop. Its Garden Terrace serves English afternoon tea with scones and Devonshire cream—just right for footsore mystery buffs—and it is also home to the elegant Seasons Restaurant.

In Margaret Truman's *Murder on Capitol Hill* (1981), when Clarence Foster-Sims took Lydia James there, he told her she must stiffen her backbone with both the Senate committee and the Caldwell family because he and she were "Scotsmen." Lydia corrected Foster-Sims by saying they were "Scotspeople."

The Seasons would also be a likely venue for the French chefs featured and murdered in Phyllis Richman's restaurant mystery, *The Butter Did It* (1997), where restaurant columnist Chas Wheatley had to solve the death of her former lover Chef Laurence Levain with the help of gourmet detective Homer Jones.

As an alternative Patricia Moyes recommended La Chaumière, "with genuine provincial French cooking." It is just across from the Four Seasons Hotel. If you are too tired to walk any more, catch a cab. Otherwise, take Pennsylvania Avenue across Rock Creek on the M Street Bridge. Stay on Pennsylvania Avenue to Washington Circle and turn right on 23rd Street one block to the Foggy Bottom Metro Station to end the walk.

8

ARLINGTON CEMETERY AND ALEXANDRIA WALKS

Arlington National Cemetery

BACKGROUND

Arlington National Cemetery is located in Arlington, Virginia, directly across the Potomac River from Washington, D.C. In 1608 Captain John Smith sailed up the Potomac and recorded an Indian tribe living there. Later much of the area was owned by the Alexander family, for whom Alexandria was named.

The cemetery itself was part of the land left George Washington Custis by his father, on which he built his Greek Revival mansion overlooking D.C. Robert E. Lee was a cousin of the Custises and married their only daughter, Mary, who inherited the estate. In 1863 the Union took over Lee's mansion, Arlington House, and used it as a military headquarters for the defense of Washington. Soon afterward Secretary of War Edwin Stanton approved the establishment of a military cemetery on the grounds, and the first soldier, Private William Christman of Pennsylvania, was buried there on May 13, 1864.

While there was vindictiveness in the takeover of the Lee mansion and the fact that the first graves were placed in Mrs. Lee's rose garden, Quartermaster General Montgomery Meigs who was in charge of the cemetery—and many others fighting for the Union—considered Robert E. Lee a traitor. In 1883 when the Supreme Court decided that the Lee estate should be returned to its owner, the family accepted a sum of money rather than the land, and Arlington became the United States's official national cemetery.

Today Arlington Cemetery has 612 acres and holds over 200,000 graves of military personnel and their dependents. Any day you visit the cemetery, you may see a military funeral taking place with a horse-drawn, flag-covered caisson, followed by a military band and honor guard. Only two presidents, John F. Kennedy and William H. Taft, who was both president and chief justice of the Supreme Court, are buried there, but there are many other memorials like the Tomb of the Unknowns (formerly the Unknown Soldier), the memorial for the space shuttle *Challenger*'s crew, and those for individual American heroes like Admiral Richard Byrd, Medgar Evers, and Joe Louis (Barrow).

LENGTH OF WALK: About 2¼ miles

The walk goes from Arlington Metro Station to Arlington House (Lee/Custis Mansion), the Tomb of the Unknowns, and back to the gate. Possible side trips can be made either by metro or by car.

The Visitor Center on Memorial Drive has maps of the cemetery, information about individual grave sites and points of interest, and the rest rooms. You may purchase a Tourmobile ticket which lets you get off at all the major sights, reboarding when ready. You can also park your car there or get a senior citizen pass to drive inside the cemetery. (Car passes are also available for those whose loved ones are buried there.)

See the map on page 231 for the boundaries of this walk and page 284 for a list of the books and detectives mentioned.

PLACES OF INTEREST

Arlington House (Robert E. Lee Memorial). Home of Robert E. Lee, who married Martha Washington's great-granddaughter Mary Custis. Small museum and slave quarters. Rest rooms available. Tours given by park rangers in pre–Civil War costumes. Open daily 9:30 A.M.–4:30 P.M. October–March, until 6:00 P.M. April–September. Closed December 25 and January 1. Free. Call 557-0613.*

Arlington Memorial Bridge, symbolically linking the North and South. Goes across the Potomac river from the base of the Lincoln Memorial to Lee's estate at Arlington House. Dedicated by President Herbert Hoover on January 16, 1932.

Grave of Joe Louis (Barrow), longest holder of the title of World Heavyweight Champion (1937–1949).

Grave of President John F. Kennedy, most visited grave in cemetery. Eternal flame lit by Jacqueline Kennedy at the Arlington Cemetery burial service on November 25, 1963.

Grave of Robert F. Kennedy, marked by white cross on the hill below Arlington House left of his older brother's grave.

Grave of Pierre L'Enfant, designer of the capital.

Iwo Jima Statue (Marine memorial), just outside the cemetery gates to your left. Modeled after an Associated Press photograph, it is the largest cast bronze statue in the world.

Lookout Point, uphill from Kennedy graves. Best view of the capital.

Netherlands Carillon. Gift from the Netherlands for American help during and after World War II. You can climb the tower to see the forty-nine bells being rung.

Tomb of the Unknowns. Began with an unidentified World War I soldier whose body was buried here on Armistice Day, November 11, 1921. Then unknown soldiers from World War II, Korean War, and Vietnam were added. Special honor guard on duty 24 hours a day.

*The telephone area code for Arlington and Alexandria is 703.

Places to Eat

There are no places to eat at Arlington National Cemetery. See suggested side trips or head to Alexandria.

— ARLINGTON CEMETERY WALK —

Begin your walk at the Arlington Cemetery Metro Station. Stop to look up at Arlington House, the colonnaded mansion of Robert E. Lee, behind which is a Confederate cemetery. Then look back across the Arlington Memorial Bridge to the Lincoln Memorial. The bridge was built because on November 11, 1921 (Armistice Day), when the official procession was bringing the Unknown Soldier to his tomb from the Capitol rotunda there was a terrible traffic jam. Dignitaries had to wait for hours to get across the 14th Street Bridge with the result that funds for the new bridge were voted that same day. The bridge was completed by 1932 and opened by President Herbert Hoover. Its location connecting the Lincoln Memorial with Lee's mansion was intended to reunite the North and the South.

Take Arlington Memorial Drive to the Visitors Center on your left where there is a big public parking lot. Inside you can get a copy of the walking map and if you are a senior citizen, handicapped, or have a relative buried there, a blue vehicle pass to drive into the cemetery and park almost anywhere. If you know the relative's name they will look him up and give you a specially marked map. You can also get a pass for the Tourmobile. The Visitor Center is also useful as a pit stop both coming and going.

Come out of the Visitor Center and take Memorial Drive to the Memorial Gate. In Diplomat's *Murder in the State Department* (1930), there was a wild chase across the unfinished Arlington Bridge. Dennis Tyler, Chief of CPI (State Department's Secret Service), was driven by his good friend Japanese Commander Akechi Kanemitsu, a samurai naval

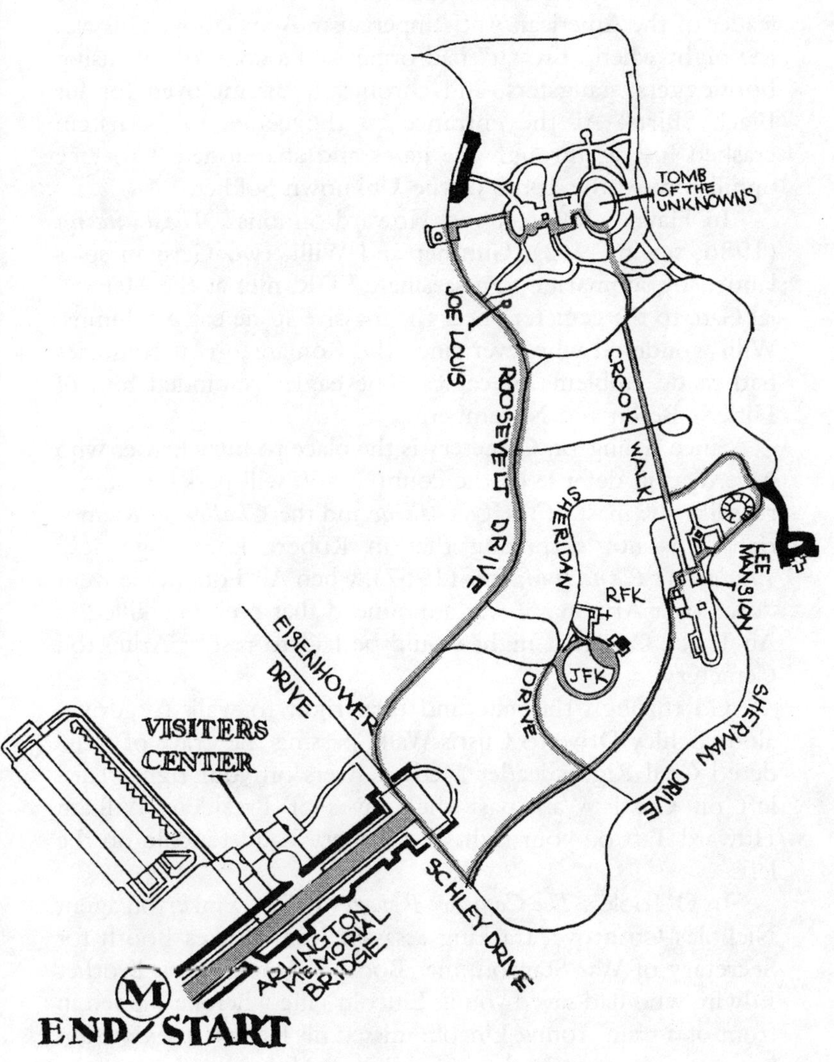

Walk 8: Arlington National Cemetery

attaché at the Imperial Japanese Embassy. They were chasing Ivan Bernstein, a gangster comrade of "Clovis Brown," the leader of the American Anti-Imperialism Association. This was the night when "Brown" had organized a coup d'etat, using bootleggers, gangsters, and chronically unemployed for his Black Shirts! At the entrance to the cemetery Bernstein crashed his car through the gates and abandoned it to race uphill toward the Tomb of the Unknown Soldier.

In Haynes Johnson and Howard Simons's *The Landing* (1986; set in 1942), Gunther and Willi, two German spies landed by submarine to assassinate FDR, met at the Memorial Gate to the cemetery near the massive stone eagle columns. Willi wondered why, ever since the Romans, great countries had made emblems of eagles. The eagles reminded him of Hitler's Berlin and Nuremberg.

Since Arlington Cemetery is the place to bury heroes who have died in defense of the country, you will pass by memorials like the mast of the USS *Maine* and the *Challenger* Memorial. It is not surprising that in Robert J. Serling's *The President's Plane Is Missing* (1967), when Air Force One went down over Arizona, it was announced that everyone killed in Air Force One that night would be laid to rest at Arlington Cemetery.

Go through the gate and turn right to walk (or drive) along Schley Drive to Custis Walk, passing the grave of murdered Civil Rights leader Medgar Evers on your right. Turn left on Custis Walk past the graves of President William Howard Taft on your right and Robert Todd Lincoln on the left.

In O'Toole's *The Cosgrove Report* (1979), Pinkerton agent Nicholas Cosgrove, tracking assassin John Wilkes Booth for Secretary of War Stanton, met Booth's famous actor brother Edwin, who had saved young Lincoln's life when he slipped in front of a train. Young Lincoln missed his father's assassination but was present at both Garfield's and McKinley's!

At Sheridan Drive, which is closed to vehicles and tour buses, walk uphill to the grave of President John F. Kennedy on the hillside below the Lee Mansion. Robert F. Kennedy's grave is just beyond JFK's on the slope of the hill.

In Jeffrey Archer's 1977 version of *Shall We Tell the President?* on Inauguration Day, January 20, 1981, president-elect Edward M. (Ted) Kennedy went to Arlington National Cemetery to visit the graves of his brothers JFK and RFK, and met Bobby's widow Ethel. Shortly after his inauguration the FBI discovered that there was a conspiracy to assassinate EMK when he went to the Capitol to push for gun control on March 10.

Rachel Cannon's *The Anniversary* (1996) opened with the ceremonial burial of the first woman president, Melanie Lombard, who was shot three days after her inauguration. On the anniversary of her death Vice President Danny Court decided to go for her activist agenda and called her old friends to help. But the result was a series of murderous attacks that threatened to destroy Lombard's "Wonder Woman" image.

After visiting the Kennedy graves, go back to Sheridan Drive to take Custis Walk up to the Arlington House Museum. On the way you pass the grave of Mary Randolph, a direct descendant of Pocahontas and a cousin of Jefferson and Lee. At the top you come first to Lookout Point and the grave of Pierre L'Enfant overlooking the capital city he designed, then Lee's mansion.

Built by George Washington Parke Custis, it was filled with memorabilia from Mount Vernon, but in 1864 War Secretary Stanton authorized the use of the grounds as a military cemetery and the estate was not returned to Robert E. Lee's son Washington Custis Lee until 1883. The Lees never came back because the estate had become a graveyard. It was declared the nation's Robert E. Lee Memorial in 1925.

Take a self-guided tour of the house as well as the museum, then go into the garden and follow a brick pathway that leads to a graveyard where over two thousand Confederate and Union soldiers were buried in what is now called the Tomb of the Unknown Civil War Dead.

In Johnson and Simons's *The Landing* (1986), the Nazi

spies Gunther and Willi walked away from the tourists to a grove of Scotch pines with a memorial to the Civil War dead. Gunther told Willi, who was a double agent, that his cover was broken, and they had a vicious fight which Gunther won. He then dumped Willi's body in an open gravesite.

Take the pathway left to Sherman Drive past the Tomb of the Unknown Civil War Dead and go downhill toward the Old Amphitheater. Find Crook Walk and take it to your right to the great white temple which is the new Memorial Amphitheater with the Tomb of the Unknowns.

This Amphitheater's cornerstone was laid by President Woodrow Wilson in 1915 and it was dedicated on Memorial Day 1920. On the east side of the amphitheater is the Tomb of the Unknowns. Originally it held the unidentified body of a World War I soldier, but the tomb now holds the bodies of soldiers killed in World War II, and the Korean and Vietnam Wars as well. It has a twenty-four-hour honor guard of a single soldier who takes twenty-one steps, pauses twenty-one seconds facing the tomb, then repeats the process in the other direction. (The number twenty-one represents a twenty-one-gun salute, the highest honor that can be given to anyone.) The changing of the guard takes place every half hour in summer, every hour in winter, and every two hours by night.

In Diplomat's *Murder in the State Department* (1930), gangster Ivan Bernstein had raced uphill to the Tomb of the Unknown Soldier where he was shot dead by the honor guard on duty when he did not stop as ordered. (Captain Dennis Tyler had put the entire Armed Services of the country on high alert.) But Bernstein had winged Tyler and shot his Japanese friend Kanemitsu, who dropped dead at the Tomb.

In Elliott Roosevelt's *Murder in the Executive Mansion* (set in 1939), the King and Queen of England arrived for a state visit. President and Mrs. Roosevelt escorted the royal couple to Arlington National Cemetery where King George VI placed a wreath on the Tomb of the Unknown Soldier. During their visit First Lady Eleanor was preoccupied with solving the murder of Lucinda Robinson, a White House staffer who had been recruited for a Nazi spy ring.

Watch the Changing of the Guard, then walk down the wide steps to take the path to Roosevelt Drive at the foot of the Tomb. Turn left on Roosevelt Drive to return to the cemetery entrance. Shortly after you cross a driveway, you find the simple, brown granite marker for Technical Sergeant (and world-famous African-American prize fighter) Joe Louis (Barrow).

In Elliott Roosevelt's *Murder in the Rose Garden* (1989; set in 1936), the president had gone sailing, but First Lady Eleanor had stayed in Washington to investigate the murder of Vivian Taliafero and to campaign. She was told by her African-American advisor, college president Mary McLeod Bethune, to invite a young black athlete to the White House because photos taken with him would be good publicity. Eleanor met the shy young man in the Red Room where she served him lemonade and told Mr. Barrow (Joe Louis) that she knew he would win the championship!

In Keats Patrick's *Death Is a Tory* (1935), gossip columnist Sally Shaftoe and Congressman Gil Lightfoot, investigating the murder of Marshall Rich's wife and her lover, came to Arlington Cemetery. The Department of Agriculture had an experimental farm there and Rich was a professor on loan to the Department, trying to grow Dust Bowl–resistant crops. Then they went to the jail to visit Rich, who had confessed to the double murder.

In Ross Thomas's *Twilight at Mac's Place* (1990), the full-dress military funeral of former CIA operative-cum-con man Steadfast Haynes was attended by his son Granville, his mistress Isabelle Gelinet, a retired CIA analyst called Gilbert Undean, and Tinker Burns, a buddy from the Foreign Legion who flew in on the Concorde. When the bugler finished playing taps, and the folded flag was handed to his son, the four retired to Mac's Place near Dupont Circle to reminisce. But Steady had made dummy copies of his memoirs which were found, with the result that only his son Granville managed to stay alive with the help of the two old proprietors of Mac's Place, McCorkle and Padillo.

Walk back along Roosevelt Drive. You will cross Wilson,

McClellan, and Weeks Drives before you come to Eisenhower Drive. Take Eisenhower Drive left to the Memorial Gate to end this walk at the Arlington Cemetery Metro Station.

If you want to do suggested side trips or the Alexandria Walk now, be sure to make a stop at the Visitor Center before you take the Metro since there are no rest rooms in the Metro stations.

If you want to stop and/or have something to eat, turn left outside Memorial Gate to take Jefferson Davis Highway to Marshall Drive. Take a left on Marshall Drive until you reach the Netherlands Carillon, a gift from the Dutch for our help during World War II. Take the pathway to the Marines' memorial, known as the Iwo Jima Statue, whose bronze sculpture was copied from a prize-winning photograph.

To your left beyond the cemetery is Fort Myer. In Fletcher Knebel and Charles W. Bailey's *Seven Days in May* (1962), "Gentleman Jim" Scott, chief of the Joint Chiefs of Staff, lived on the post at Fort Myer. After he got wind of the plot to kidnap the president, Colonel Martin (Jiggs) Casey drove past General Scott's home to give him the news. But he saw the car of California Senator Prentice parked there, which made Jiggs suspicious because Senator Prentice had given away the fact he knew about the secret Red Alert. By Monday morning Casey called the White House and asked to see the president.

Circle the Iwo Jima Statue to your left to find the path to Meade Street. Take Meade Street past Arlington Boulevard to the junction of Fort Myer Drive and Lynn Street in Rosslyn. You'll find a number of motels and places to eat nearby. Then take Lynn Street to the Rosslyn Metro Station to end this part of the walk.

In Margaret Truman's *Murder at the Kennedy Center* (1989), law professor Mac Smith and his Great Dane Rufus had found the body of Andrea Feldman, one of Senator Kenneth Ewald's staff. It turned out that she had been sleeping with the Senator's son Paul, who routinely took her to the Buccaneer Motel in Rosslyn, Virginia.

In Jerome Doolittle's *Head Lock* (1993), PI Tom Bethany

flew down from Boston to go with his mistress Hope Edwards when she had an abortion. Director of the Washington Bureau of the ACLU, Hope had chosen an Arlington County clinic they supported on Glebe Road, but the day was complicated by media attention when the Reverend Howard Orrin led a violent demonstration by his Life Force pro-life organization there.

In Nessen and Neuman's *Knight and Day* (1995), Jerry Knight, conservative talk-show host of the All Talk Network lived in Rosslyn. When his show ended Knight always walked the two miles from his studio in D.C. to his penthouse apartment there. It may just be coincidence, but TV talk-show host Larry King lives in an all-glass complex behind the Iwo Jima Monument near Fort Myer.

In Gar Anthony Haywood's *Bad News Travels Fast* (1995), the senior Loudermilks had parked their beloved Airstream trailer Lucille in the Nation's Best Trailer Park in Arlington. They hoped to see the sights in D.C., but their activist son Eddie got arrested for murder, so both the Capitol (Hill) police and MPD cops broke into their trailer. (This appears to be a mythical trailer park.)

Possible Side Trips

The following mystery sites may be reached by Metro.

Pentagon: Headquarters of the Department of Defense, built in 1947. Largest office building in the world. Take escalator from Pentagon Metro Station directly into the building. Photo ID needed. Guided tours every half hour 9:30 A.M.–3:30 P.M. Mon.–Fri. Free. Call (703) 695-1776.

Take the Metro Blue Line from the Arlington National Cemetery Station one stop to the Pentagon Station. Get off here if you want to take the guided tour of the Pentagon or just walk around the enormous five-sided building. The second Pentagon stop is Pentagon City, where you will find a shopping mall and places to eat.

The huge Pentagon houses the Armed Forces's top commanders, not only the Secretary of Defense but the Joint

Chiefs of Staff (Army, Navy, and Air Force), combining under one roof all the branches of the original Department of War. Built during World War II, the concrete and limestone structure is the largest single-structure office building in the world. Inside there are five concentric circles enclosing a five-acre central courtyard and about eighteen miles of corridors. Some twenty thousand people work here in shifts round the clock. Stories abound of people getting lost.

In Mary Plum's *Susanna, Don't You Cry* (1946), two disabled World War II vets were sent to Iowa where an old resort hotel was supposed to be an R and R facility. But its former owner turned up dead in the lake. The Pentagon's Major Humboldt was on the scene in Iowa, but completely clueless.

In Knebel and Bailey's *Seven Days in May* (1962), when Marine Colonel Casey was on Sunday duty at the Pentagon he got a call from an old friend who was running a base in Texas so secret no one had heard of it. Then a telegram came for General Scott about a horse race bet and Casey became suspicious.

In R. B. Dominic's (aka Emma Lathen) *Epitaph for a Lobbyist* (1974), lobbyist Shirley Knapp was murdered for paying a congressman fifty thousand dollars for his vote. Her secretary Barbara Underwood pretended she knew more than she really did about the bribe, hoping to make a fast buck because her husband was a dumb career naval officer who worked at the Pentagon.

Margaret Truman's *Murder at the Pentagon* (1992) gives an excellent armchair tour through the Pentagon, circle by circle. In her mystery, the chief engineer of the Pentagon's Project Safekeep (an antimissile system) was murdered at a purple water fountain during a Pentagon picnic in the center courtyard. Major Margit Falk, who had just joined the Secretary of Defense's General Counsel Staff, became the defense attorney for CIA agent Captain Robert Cobol who was accused of the murder; she consulted her old law professor Mac Smith.

In Tom Clancy's *The Hunt for Red October* (1984), there was a top-level discussion at the Pentagon about capturing the maverick USSR sub. It was peacetime so the president wouldn't allow them to kill the crew, but CIA analyst Jack Ryan came up with a plan for hiding her.

In Jeremiah Healy's *The Staked Goat* (1986), Boston PI John Cuddy, trying to find out why his old Vietnam buddy Al Sachs was murdered Vietcong style, called on a mutual buddy, Colonel J. T. Kivens, who worked at the Pentagon. J.T. agreed to let Cuddy look at Sachs's war record, but when Cuddy showed up at the Pentagon to read the files, he was kidnaped and taken outside D.C. to be "questioned."

Return to the Metro Pentagon Station and take the Blue Line south past the next stop:

Crystal City. In Billie Sue Mosiman's short story, "Talk Shows Just Kill Me" in *Danger in D.C.* (1993), a prisoner named Buddy had been interviewed by Roger Spencer, who wrote a book about the murder Buddy had committed. When Spencer's book was on the bestseller list he appeared on the Larry King Show broadcast from Crystal City. Buddy called in when Roger was on the show but got cut off, so he stole a Lincoln and, with the help of his skinny white cat named Cat, kidnaped Roger.

Stay on the Metro Blue Line to the next stop:

Washington National Airport (off George Washington Memorial Parkway and Route 1). If you have time, get off and explore the airport. There are so many mysterious characters that go in and out of this airport that only a few can be mentioned. Unless there is a specific mention of either Dulles or Baltimore (BWI) airports, for D.C. this is it.

In Leslie Ford's *The Simple Way of Poison* (1937), Grace Latham was shopping in Georgetown when she heard an airplane overhead and looked up to see it fly past to the new airport.

In R. B. Dominic's (aka Emma Lathen) *Epitaph for a Lobbyist* (1974), a couple returning from a Caribbean vacation found the body of lobbyist Shirley Knapp in the airport's parking garage.

In Robert A. Carter's *Final Edit* (1994), Nicholas Barlow, CEO of his family publishing company, flew into National Airport for the annual ABA (American Booksellers Association)

Convention. Barlow arrived on Memorial Day weekend on the shuttle from New York with Sidney Leopold, his editor-in-chief, and they proceeded to the Shoreham Hotel because that was where Nicholas had always stayed with his dad (see Walk 5).

The following mystery sites can be reached only by car.

CIA (Central Intelligence Agency): George Washington Memorial Parkway at Langley, Virginia.

The CIA was created by the National Security Act of 1947 to prevent the United States from being caught flat-footed at another Pearl Harbor. It is known by its employees as "the Company," and most of its work is research and intelligence gathering.

Unfortunately for mystery fans, the CIA, like Scotland Yard, is not open to the general public. You may drive past its grounds but unless you have special spy-police-academic connections and set it up ahead of time, you will not get inside.

To drive by, take the Washington Memorial Parkway left along the Potomac River to the cloverleaf where you can get Route 193 (the Georgetown Pike). Take the Georgetown Pike west until you see the sign for the Central Intelligence Agency at Langley, Virginia.

"The Company" is omnipresent in D.C. mysteries. Dorothy Gilman's *The Unexpected Mrs. Pollifax* (1966) was one of the earliest, in which, bored by bridge and garden clubs, Emily Pollifax went to Washington, got a letter of introduction to the CIA from her congressman, and took a bus to Langley where she told them she had come to volunteer as a spy. Since Director Carstairs needed a tourist to go to Mexico as a courier, Emily became improbably embroiled in a series of adventures abroad.

In Sam Greenlee's *The Spook Who Sat by the Door* (1969), Dan Freeman was a token black recruited to help a senator get reelected. During training Freeman liked the woods around the vast, ugly marble and granite building, combining the worst of neoclassical and modern government, but he finally quit to go organize gang violence in Chicago.

In Robert Ludlum's *The Osterman Weekend* (1972), the

CIA told New Jersey newspaper man John Tanner his closest friends and neighbors were all members of a Communist cell called Omega, but there turned out to be double-crossers on all sides.

In 1973 former CIA operative George O'Toole wrote *An Agent on the Other Side*, which described the psychics used to contact USSR Oleg Penkovsky at the time of the Soviet invasion of Czechoslovakia in 1968. In Joseph Finder's account of corruption in the CIA, *Extraordinary Powers* (1993), parapsychological experiments were still being performed.

In James Grady's famous *Six Days of the Condor* (1974), Grady claimed CIA agent Ronald Malcolm's (aka Condor) branch of the CIA existed as Department 17, located in an old building behind the Capitol (really the FBI's intelligence unit at 215 Pennsylvania Avenue SE). Their job was to analyze spy stories and mysteries to see if the mysteries described new ploys for their agents or appeared to have had access to classified information.

In John Ehrlichman's *The Company* (1977), when President Anderson (aka LBJ) who succeeded after the plane-crash death of President William Arthur Curry (aka JFK) told the nation that he would not seek reelection, everyone scrambled to protect his butt. CIA Director William Martin had obeyed an order by Curry to assassinate Father Julio Benitimes, who was leading a South American invasion that failed, and he needed to bury its Primula Report so that president-elect Monckton (aka Nixon) would not destroy the image of President Curry—and Director Martin.

In Margaret Truman's *Murder in the CIA* (1987), when CIA agent Barrie Mayer died of a heart attack, fellow agent Collette Cahill was sure Mayer's death was a hit. Cahill knew there were a lot of good people at the CIA who cared about the country, but their definition of the "right thing" got blurred.

In Ross Thomas's *Twilight at Mac's Place* (1990), the CIA high command had the impossible task of convincing the world that Steadfast (Steady) Haynes had not been one of their own—and getting their hands on his memoirs.

In William Safire's *Sleeper Spy* (1995), investigative reporter Irving Fein made use of an old CIA source to flush out a USSR sleeper (spy) left in place from the Cold War. His discovery eliminated the spook and a lot of other people and afterward Fein met with Dorothy Barclay, the CIA's Director of Intelligence, to bury the hatchet. Even at Langley, they met secretly at little Marcy Park (where the body of "Friend of Bill" Vincent Foster was found).

End these side trips by returning to the National Airport Metro Station. You can continue with Part Two by taking the Metro to Alexandria or call it quits for the day.

Alexandria

BACKGROUND

Alexandria was incorporated in 1749 by John Alexander, one of many Scottish merchants who established it as a thriving port on the Potomac River that rivaled New York and Boston. It was laid out in a grid with typical eighteenth-century street names: King, Queen, Prince, Duke, Cameron (for Virginia's Lord Fairfax, Baron of Cameron), Fairfax, Royal, Pitt, and, of course, Washington and Lee. Alexandria played an important part in the lives of both George Washington—who surveyed it and kept a townhouse here—and Robert E. Lee, who grew up here. The tobacco warehouses and commercial buildings were located along the river while the Scots built charming colonial and Georgian mansions uphill with a river view.

Alexandria's political and economic importance in colonial times was great, but in 1791 when the District of Columbia was established it became a part of the capital. "Freed" from the District in 1847, Alexandria was occupied by Union forces during the Civil War; later, when railroads became the main carriers, it began a long decline. The torpedo factory on the waterfront built during World War I improved the economy, but it was really the New Deal and World War II that brought back prosperity when D.C.'s professional class moved across the river to renovate and restore the working-class houses and warehouses and the merchants' colonial and Georgian mansions.

Old Town Alexandria was placed on the National Register of Historic Places in 1969, then a twenty-year urban renewal program, the Gadsby Project, completed in 1981, helped to preserve and restore the historic Old Town.

Length of Walk: 3½ to 4 miles

This walk is from the King Street Metro Station to Old Town and back, or about three miles if you begin at King and Columbus Streets.

It makes sense to take a cab or a DASH bus from the King Street Metro Station to Columbus Street. If you drive take Patrick Street (Route 1) and turn left at King Street to find one of the many public parking places in Old Town.

See the map on page 247 for the boundaries of this walk and page 284 for a list of the books and detectives mentioned.

Places of Interest

Captain's Row, 100 block of Prince Street (Lee to Union Street) where sea captains built houses. The cobblestoned street was laid by Revolutionary War Hessian prisoners of war.

Carlyle House, 121 N. Fairfax Street. Built in 1753 by Scottish merchant John Carlyle and General Braddock's headquarters for the French and Indian War. Tours every half hour. Open Tues.–Sat. 10:00 A.M.–4:30 P.M., Sun. noon–4:30 P.M. Fee. Call 549-2997.*

Christ Church (Episcopal), 118 N. Washington Street. Built in 1773. Open weekdays and Sat. 9:00 A.M.–4:00 P.M., Sun. 2:00 P.M.–4:30 P.M. Free. Call 549-1450.

City Hall, 300 Cameron Street. Built 1873. In earlier days this half-square contained Court House, Market Hall, two fire engine houses, schoolhouse, jail, stocks, and pillory!

Friendship Firehouse (rehabbed nineteenth century), 107 Alfred Street. Open Fri.–Sat. 10:00 A.M.–4:00 P.M., Sun. 1:00 P.M.–4:00 P.M. Donation. Call 838-3891.

Gadsby's Tavern Museum, 134 Royal Street. Tours. Open October–March Tues.–Sat. 11:00 A.M.–4:00 P.M., Sun. 1:00 P.M.–4:00 P.M. Fee. Call 838-4242.

Gentry Row, 200 block of Prince Street. Brick-paved, has homes of merchants and Revolutionary War patriots.

George Washington Masonic National Memorial, 101 Callahan Drive at King Street (west of Amtrak Station). Observation deck on ninth floor and furnishing from first Alexandrian Masonic lodge. Open daily 9:00 A.M.–5:30 P.M. Tours at 9:30 A.M., 10:30 A.M., 11:30 A.M., 1:00 P.M., 2:00 P.M., 3:00 P.M., 4:00 P.M. Free. Call 683-2007.

Lee Corner, at Washington and Oronoco Streets, where several other Lee family homes stood. Those remaining are:

- ***Lee-Fendell House***, 614 Oronoco Street. Home of Richard Henry Lee, signer of the Declaration of Independence, and Henry "Light Horse Harry" Lee. Open Tues.–Sat. 10:00 A.M.–4:00 P.M., Sun. noon–4:00 P.M. Fee. Call 548-1789.
- ***Robert E. Lee's Boyhood Home***, 607 Oronoco Street. Nineteenth-century townhouse. Open Mon.–Sat. 10:00 A.M.–4:00 P.M., Sun. 10:00 A.M.–4:00 P.M. Closed December 15–February 1 except for Sunday nearest January 19, when it is open for Lee's birthday celebration. Fee. Call 548-8454.

Lloyd House, 220 N. Washington Street. Georgian house built in 1797, now part of Alexandria Library. Free. Open Mon.–Sat. 9:00 A.M.–5:00 P.M.

*The telephone area code for Arlington and Alexandria is 703.

Lyceum, 201 Washington Street. Built in 1839. Now a museum and art gallery. Open Mon.–Sat. 10:00 A.M.–5:00 P.M., Sun. noon–5:00 P.M. Free. Call 838-4994.

Market Square (Tavern Square), behind City Hall; the block of Cameron to King Streets between Royal and Fairfax Streets.

Old Presbyterian Meeting House, 321 Fairfax Street. Gathering place for Scottish patriots during Revolution. Tomb of Unknown Soldier of the American Revolution in corner of churchyard. Open weekdays 9:00 A.M.–5:00 P.M. Free. Call 549-6670.

Ramsay House, 221 King Street. Probably the oldest house in Alexandria, built for first Lord Mayor William Ramsay. Now Alexandria's Convention & Visitors Bureau. Get free twenty-four-hour parking stickers, brochures, maps, walking & bus tours. Open daily 9:00 A.M.–5:00 P.M. Call 838-4200.

Stabler-Leadbeater Apothecary Shop, 105–107 Fairfax Street. Second-oldest "drugstore" in the country; patronized by Washington and Lee families. Open Mon.–Sat. 10:00 A.M.–4:00 P.M., Sun. 1:00–5:00 P.M. Fee. Call 836-3713.

Torpedo Factory Arts Center, 105 Union Street. Former munitions plant converted to artists' studios and galleries. Open daily 10:00 A.M.–5:00 P.M. Free.

PLACES TO EAT

Old Town has many places to drop in for coffee or a sandwich as you explore.

Gadsby's Tavern Museum, 134 N. Royal Street. Alexandria's most historical eatery has many mystery connections! Reservations recommended at dinner. Call 548-1288.

Radio Free Italy, 5 Cameron Street. Part of a waterfront dining complex with takeout food and an upstairs restaurant with windows on the harbor. Call 683-0361.

South Austin Grill, 801 King Street at Columbus Street. No reservations. Popular, so try for off-hours.

Also consider taking one of the Potomac River cruises like the *Dandy* (listed under "Possible Side Trips") where you can eat brunch, lunch, or dinner and pretend to be a Virginia planter.

ALEXANDRIA WALK

Begin your walk at the King Street Metro Station behind the Amtrak Railroad Station. You are on the western edge of the historic district and the present-day suburbanlike city with condos, hotels, elegant housing subdivisions, and high rise office buildings, which stretches to Fairfax County. To visit the western part of Alexandria take King Street straight west to Route 395 and turn left (south) to Duke Street, then take Duke Street to Beauregard Street.

In Benjamin M. Schutz's *All the Old Bargains* (1985), black PI Leo Haggerty met Samantha Clayton playing racquetball at his local health club and drove her home to Beauregard and King. Samantha was a freelance writer who gave Leo a hand with Randi Benson, a teenage runaway he had been hired to find.

In Ann Ripley's *Mulch* (1994), the Eldridges lived still farther out in a wooded Fairfax County subdivision. Bill, who "worked at State," was really a CIA agent. His wife Louise was "into" organic gardening with dire results when she collected some body parts in leaf bags. One of their new neighbors was gunrunner Peter Hoffman, whom the president wanted for Deputy Secretary of Defense. Hoffman's office was in Alexandria.

In David Baldacci's *Absolute Power* (1996), lawyer on the run Jack Graham hid out from the Secret Service in a motel on the outskirts of Alexandria, hoping to reestablish contact with Middleburg detective Seth Frank.

In Norma Johnston's (aka Nicole St. John) young adult series *The Carlisle Chronicles* (1986), the Carlisle family lived on Prince Street in Alexandria's Old Town. Because their Foreign Service family often moved to new posts around the world, the four kids went to private schools called Cheltenhem and Evesham, which shared grounds, classes, and teachers. The Carlisle kids had to take the King Street bus to get to school, which sounds as if their schools were located like Alexandria's Episcopal High School on the grounds of Virginia Theological Seminary. The model, however, was Friends School in D.C.

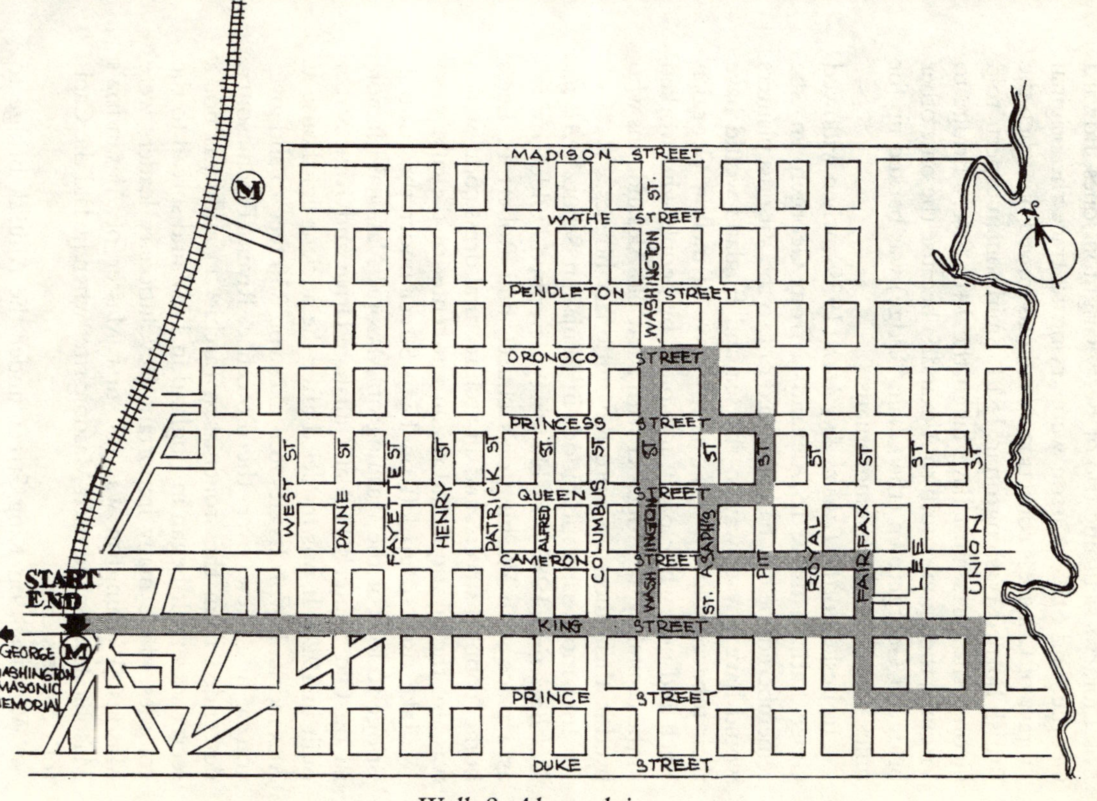

Walk 8: Alexandria

In Charles Goodrum's *The Best Cellar* (1987), the Werner-Bok Library's sleuthing trio of Betty Crighton Jones, Edward George, and Steve Carson were trying to trace the original Library of Congress collection which was moved out when the British burned Washington in 1814. Smithsonian experts told George the carts must have taken the 14th Street Bridge to Virginia, then gone south to Alexandria because the only other bridge at Georgetown (the Chain Bridge) was backed up for miles with fleeing Washingtonians.

In Leslie Ford's *False to Any Man* (1939), when widowed Grace Latham drove to Alexandria from Georgetown, she remembered the city had been laid out so the Virginia planters would have a waterway to the sea and England would have their tobacco. Now it was a sleepy town of mellow Georgian brick and new white paint, inhabited by people who worked in the capital by day, together with a few old Alexandrians who lived in their ancestors's pre-Revolutionary houses.

In a more sarcastic mood, in Benjamin Schutz's *All the Old Bargains* (1985), PI Haggerty described "Olde Towne" as a place with Washington's church and Robert E. Lee's home, cobbled streets, and an architectural dress code, which was also the boutique and restaurant center of the city.

Take time to go left on King Street under the Amtrak Bridge to look at the Washington Masonic National Memorial on Old Shuter's Hill at Callahan Drive and King Street built in 1923. It was modeled after the ancient lighthouse at Alexandria, Egypt. Its elevator takes you 330 feet up and gives you a fine view over the Potomac River. Freemasonry, descended from the stonemason (architect) guilds, is not a secret society. It began in England in 1717 and spread to the colonies where many important Revolutionary leaders were Masons. Washington was the first Master of Alexandria's Masonic Lodge and used Masonic rites when he laid the Capitol's cornerstone.

Walk back on King Street under the Amtrak bridge to Diagonal Road, where it crosses Daingerfield Road to head down King Street to Old Town. It is a mile to Columbus Street, so consider catching a cab at the King Street Metro Station or the Amtrak Station, or taking either DASH bus number A.T. 2 (red) or A.T. 5 (yellow). If you drove, take King Street to St. Asaph Street where there are public parking lots. At the Ramsay House Visitors Center at Fairfax Street you can also get a free parking pass good for twenty-four hours.

If you are walking, go nine blocks down King Street, crossing both Henry and Patrick Streets (Route 1) to Alfred Street. To your left at 107 S. Alfred Street just before Prince Street you see the historic Friendship Firehouse. It housed the first volunteer fire-fighting group in the country, established in 1774. This building was put up in 1855 and restored by the City of Alexandria in 1992.

In Ford's *False to Any Man* (1939), Grace Latham, who had gotten up to let a cat in, saw a fire at the Candler's carriage house and called the fire department. Then she went across the street just in time to help discover Karen Lunt's body inside.

Go look at the fire house, then walk one more block on King Street to Columbus Street. At King Street and Columbus Street on the southeast corner there is a mysterious-sounding restaurant/bar called Scotland (Yard) House, but it is open only for dinner. Across the street the South Austin Grill with Tex-Mex food is open for lunch but usually busy.

Turn left on Columbus Street and walk one block to Cameron Street. You are walking on brick sidewalks like those in Georgetown, surrounded by handsome old houses. Keep an eye out for a likely-looking Federal house with a coach house for Leslie Ford's Candler family who lived on fictional Chatham Street (probably Pitt Street). Pitt was the family surname of the Earls of Chatham, whose father and son both were Prime Ministers, and Leslie Ford liked to make up streets with local historical significance like Beall Street in Georgetown. (See Walk 7.)

Part way down the block you reach the wrought-iron gate and grounds of redbrick Christ Church with its handsome tower. Built in 1773, this Georgian landmark was attended by George Washington and Robert E. Lee, and there are silver markers on their pews. To go inside the church you have to walk through the grounds, which include a historic graveyard. The official entrance is on Washington Street.

Cross Cameron Street and walk two more blocks past Queen Street and Princess Street to Oronoco Street (named for the original tobacco wharf). Turn right on Oronoco and go one block to Washington Street. You are at "Lee Corner" where on either side there once were Lee family houses. At the white clapboard Federal Lee-Fendau Home at 614 Oronoco, built in 1785, Robert E. Lee's father, "Light Horse Harry" Lee, wrote Alexandria's farewell to George Washington when he left to become president. Robert E. Lee's boyhood home, the Potts-Fitzhugh House, is across Oronoco Street at number 607.

Visit the Lee Museums, then turn right on Washington Street to walk back to Princess Street. Turn left at Princess Street to go one block to St. Asaph and go right to look at Number 311 which is a flounder house. In Norma Johnston's series *The Carlisle Chronicles*, the Carlisle family live in a flounder house, which was one room wide and four stories high with no windows on one side to avoid the tax on glass.

Stay on St. Asaph to Queen Street. Cross Queen Street and turn right to go one block to Washington Street. At the southwest corner of Queen and Washington Streets at number 220 there is an elegant mansion known as the Lloyd House with a classic Georgian redbrick facade and white trim. Originally it was a tavern built by John Wise in 1797, where Benjamin Hallowell, Robert E. Lee's tutor, had his school. Then in 1832 John Lloyd, one of Alexandria's Scottish merchants, who was married to a Lee cousin, bought the house, and his family stayed there until 1918. Tradition says that Robert E. Lee stopped here on his way to take command of the Confederate Army. Now a branch of the Alexandria Library specializing in genealogy and Virginia history, it once had outbuildings including a coach house, so it's a contender for the Doyle-Candler House in Ford's *False to Any Man* (1939).

Walk along Washington Street back to Cameron Street. Cross Cameron Street to the main entrance to Christ Church and go see the Washington and Lee family pews. Then go left on Cameron Street back to St. Asaph's Street. The City Jail, built in 1831, used to be located at 403 St. Asaph's. Before that, the jail was housed at City Hall in Market Square.

In Elliott Roosevelt's *Murder in the Rose Garden* (1989; set in 1936), Washington hostess Vivian Taliafero (pronounced Tolliver), daughter of the late senator, was found murdered in the Rose Garden. Since FDR had left on a sailing cruise First Lady Eleanor worked with the Secret Service and MPD to solve the crime. They discovered that Vivian ran a salon where she also slept with her guests while her partner Joe Bob Skaggs photographed them. Skaggs lived in Alexandria in a run-down Georgian brick house where Eleanor and her confederates found his body and the missing photographs. When the Alexandria police caught Sally Partridge burglarizing Skaggs's house she was put in one of the three cells for women at the City Jail, where Eleanor insisted on interviewing her.

Cross St. Asaph and continue on Cameron to Pitt Street. Number 508 was George Washington's townhouse where he had his business office. This is not the original but one reconstructed recently. One block to your right at King Street and Pitt there is a Super Crown bookstore.

Walk one more block on Cameron to Royal Street. The famous Gadsby Tavern Museum and the City Hotel are at 134 Royal. Gadsby's Tavern probably was built on the site of Charles Mason's 1752 ordinary (or inn). By 1792 there were two buildings, both managed by John Gadsby until 1808. The City Hotel, a three-story building put up in 1792, had a ballroom on the second floor and the guest list for its assemblies and recitals included the first six presidents and the Marquis de Lafayette (the District's most popular guest). The city now owns both buildings; they contain a museum and a restaurant with authentic Georgian decor which serves appropriate food and drink. The fact that this inn was once "Charles Mason's Ordinary," and that George Mason was an Alexandrian VIP, makes it likely that Leslie Ford meant Gadsby's Tavern when Colonel John Primrose stayed at the "George Mason Hotel" in *False to Any Man* (1939).

In Charles Goodrum's *Carnage of the Realm* (1979), the

Werner-Bok's Betty Crighton Jones and her beau Steve Carson picked up Yale librarian Edward George at National Airport and drove him to Alexandria. George noted that the town became more and more remorselessly Georgian, with banks with colonial drive-in windows! They went to Gadsby's Tavern to meet with Dr. Vandermann, a member of a coin collector's club which met there, but that same night Dr. Vandermann was murdered. The trio next met with other coin club members, several of whom were also murdered.

After visiting and/or eating at the Gadsby Tavern Museum, cross Royal Street to City Hall, which shares a city block with the open Market Square. The square where General Braddock drilled his troops for the French and Indian War in 1755 once contained the market house, courthouse, two fire engine houses, a schoolhouse, jail, stocks, and a pillory.

In Goodrum's *Carnage of the Realm* (1979), after George met with coin club member Paul Barrow at Gadsby's Tavern, he wandered out into Market Square where he sat and thought about the fact that Barrow had said nothing should be done about the murders of his fellow coin club members.

In Ford's *False to Any Man* (1939), Grace Latham drove to the corner of Prince and (fictional) Chatham Street and turned up to Royal Street looking for a parking place. She then went to City Hall across from the old Gadsby Tavern to meet eccentric Isabel Doyle. Isabel told her that Judge Candler's office was on Fairfax Street near King Street. Had she but known that Isabel Doyle once wanted to marry Judge Candler, Grace might have thought twice about meeting that dotty lady.

Return to Cameron Street and turn right to Fairfax Street. Cross Fairfax Street and turn right to walk toward King Street where you come to the elegant Carlyle House with its wrought-iron gate at number 121. Built in 1753 by Scottish merchant John Carlyle, a friend of George Washington's who married Sarah (Sally) Fairfax of Belvoir, it is elegantly Palladian in style with formal gardens like the Governor's Palace at Williamsburg, and originally overlooked the river.

Carlyle House's fifteen minutes of fame came in 1755

when General Braddock used it as his headquarters and held the Governor's Council with five colonial governors there. The general asked them for military advice on the coming campaign, while the governors told him that Americans would not pay more taxes to support his army. With a young George Washington along, Braddock learned his military lesson at Fort Pitt; by passing the Stamp Act, the British Crown learned about Americans' view of taxes.

In Goodrum's *Carnage of the Realm* (1979), Crighton Jones and Edward George had met coin club member Paul Barrow in front of the Carlyle House. Barrow, a historian, said Carlyle was a penniless Scotch clerk who got rich in Alexandria and married one of the Fairfax girls! George replied that the Fairfaxes had multiplied like rabbits all over Virginia.

Continue along Fairfax, passing cobblestoned Ramsay Alley (there are a number of alleys in Old Town). A townhouse at number 113 has a carriage (coach) house in back like the houses in Leslie Ford's *False to Any Man* (1939).

Walk to the corner of King and Fairfax, where you come to the Ramsay House, which is Alexandria's official Visitors Center and full of useful people and information. This is Alexandria's oldest house, built around 1724 and moved to this location later. It once faced the Potomac River so its owner could watch his own ships sail in and out of the harbor.

In Norma Johnston's young adult mystery *Carlisle's Hope* (1986), the Carlisle family's flounder house was off King Street on a side street like Ramsay Alley. Teenage Jessamyn Carlisle enjoyed walking home from her school bus stop on King Street along the centuries-old cobbled street beneath the gas lampposts, past the boutiques and prim Federal townhouses and tourists. Johnston's actual model was the home of Washington's doctor.

After visiting Ramsay House, turn left at the corner of King and Fairfax and walk to Lee Street. You pass rows of colonial and Federal houses, some grand and some not. In *False to Any Man* (1939), Ford placed the Candler ancestral mansion, now owned by the upstart Irish lawyer Philander Doyle, and the Candlers' present-day establishment across the street from each other on "Chatham Street," which was just below Lee Street overlooking the dingy wharves and warehouses of the riverfront. That would make "Chatham Street" Union Street. While Leslie Ford never relocated public buildings, she was very fond of "reorganizing" street names. (See Walk 7.).

In *The King Is Dead on Queen Street* (1945), a murder occurred at a wartime "block party" of the Queen Street Steak and Chowder Society two blocks to your left on the 200 block of Queen Street. Francis Bonnamy explained that the 200 block of Queen really had no charmingly restored group of old Alexandria houses, but there really were thousands of military and civilian newcomers in the D.C. area. Among them were famous moviemaker Joe Long, known as the King, and his long-time partner Chic Short, who had houses on Queen Street. The enigmatic Peter Shane, who had taught criminology at the University of Chicago, and his faithful friend Francis Bonnamy lived there, too. During the party the King, a grandstander whom everyone hated, went upstairs to get a new cello string. Someone in the group strung a wire across the bottom of the steep stairs, so the King tripped, killing himself. No one but his dog grieved.

Walk past the Ramsay House on King Street and go one block east to Union Street, which was the main commercial warehouse area. At the corner of Union and King Streets Number 6 was an early nineteenth-century brick and stone warehouse.

In Benjamin Schutz's *All the Old Bargains* (1985), PI Haggerty and his sidekick 'Nam veteran Arnie Kendall tracked missing teenager Randi Benson who was mixed up in a kiddie porn ring to a warehouse south of King between Union Street and the Potomac River. They entered by different routes just in time to keep the bad guys from filming Randi having sex, then murdering her on camera.

Turn left on Union Street to walk to the Torpedo Factory Art Center at 105 N. Union Street. Built by the Navy in 1918 it now houses two hundred artists and a gallery. Past the factory to your left at Cameron Street there is a waterfront dining complex where you can eat and look at the river.

Look at the art gallery and get something to eat, then return to King Street. Cross King Street and walk to Prince Street. Turn right on Prince Street and walk uphill along the rough, cobblestoned block called "Captain's Row" with its group of small, old houses built for sea captains and crews.

Then cross Lee Street to the 200 block of Prince Street, known as Gentry Row. With a bricked pavement and handsome residences, it is considered one of the best examples of eighteenth-century houses in Virginia. On the corner is the Athens, a Greek Revival building, built in 1850 to be a bank. This is another excellent street for houses with carriage houses à la Leslie Ford.

Walk one more block up Prince Street to Fairfax Street and cross Fairfax. Turn left and walk along Fairfax to Duke Street. One block to your left you can see the Old Presbyterian Meeting House built in 1774; George Washington's memorial service was held here.

Walk back along Fairfax Street to King Street. Just before you reach King Street you come to the Stabler-Leadbeater Apothecary Shop at 105–107 Fairfax, founded in 1792. It remained a drugstore until 1933. Today it is a museum with a collection of handblown glass and medical implements. It was patronized by the Washingtons, and Robert E. Lee was there when J. E. B. Stuart brought him the War Department's order to march to Harper's Ferry to put down John Brown's insurrection, which ended with "John Brown's Body" and the Civil War.

Return to King Street. If you drove, walk up King Street to your parking lot or get a cab to return to the King Street Metro Station to end your walk. You also may walk up King Street all the way to the King Street Metro Station or take the DASH bus A.T. 2 (red) or A.T. 5 (yellow) back.

Possible Side Trips

Potomac River. By boat: *The Spirit of Washington* has dinner cruises down the Potomac to Alexandria; *The Potomac Spirit* cruises to Mount Vernon. Both daily (except Mon.)

March–October. Depart Pier 4 at 6th and Water Streets SW. Reservations. Call 554-8000.

The Dandy has lunch, dinner, and evening cruises from Alexandria that take you past D.C.'s shoreline to Georgetown University. Daily March–October. Departs Prince Street Pier. Reservations. Set-price meal/cruise. Call 683-6076.

Mount Vernon. By car: sixteen miles from D.C., eight miles from Alexandria by Washington Memorial Highway south along the Potomac or inland via Route 1.

By Tourmobile: from Arlington National Cemetery.

By boat: *The Potomac Spirit* (see above).

The Washington family owned the property from 1674 but it was not until 1735 that George's father moved his family there. George's half-brother Lawrence, who married a Fairfax, became the owner in 1740 and renamed it for his hero Admiral Vernon. When Lawrence Washington died in 1752 George took over the estate's management for Lawrence's widow; he became its owner in 1761. Between serving his country as general and president, Washington lived there the rest of his life and was buried there in 1799.

In Elliott Roosevelt's *Murder in the Executive Mansion* (set in 1939), President and Mrs. Roosevelt took the King and Queen of England on the presidential yacht *Potomac* to Mount Vernon where King George VI laid a wreath at the tomb of George Washington (who probably never expected that honor!). This was the famous visit on which the Roosevelts also introduced the royal couple to hot dogs.

In Margaret Truman's *Murder on Capitol Hill* (1981), Virginia Senator Cale Caldwell, the Senate Majority Leader, was murdered with an ice pick at a party given in his honor by his wife Veronica. After his murder D.C. lawyer Lydia James, a friend of the family, was asked to come to the Caldwell estate four miles from Mount Vernon. It was a wide handsome two-story residence on thirty acres of meadowland and woods, occupied by police and press. Veronica Caldwell asked James to serve as the Special Counsel to the Senate Committee investigating Senator Caldwell's death.

The following sites can be reached by car.

Woodlawn Plantation: From Mount Vernon drive west three miles on Route 235, then follow the signs to Woodlawn, the handsome brick Georgian house and estate of Eleanor (Nelly) Parke Custis, Washington's step-granddaughter and his nephew Lawrence Lewis, built on land Washington gave them when they married in 1799. After the family sold it in 1846, the estate was cut up and the house owned by a variety of people until in 1957 it became the property of the National Trust for Historic Preservation. Woodlawn Plantation, obviously, could also be the home of the late Senator Cale Caldwell in Truman's *Murder on Capitol Hill* (1981).

Gunston Hall: From Mount Vernon or Woodlawn take Route 1 south about three miles, then follow the signs. Or take Route 395/95 out of Alexandria.

Gunston Hall, built in 1755, was the home of the noted Alexandrian George Mason, a fourth-generation American and friend of George Washington. A member of the Virginia House of Burgesses, a delegate to the Constitutional Convention of 1787, and founder of the Fairfax militia, he disliked political life and preferred to influence others privately through his writing. He drafted a number of important documents which served as models for more famous ones, such as the Fairfax Resolves (1774) and the Virginia Declaration of Rights (1776), whose words about life, liberty, and the pursuit of happiness were echoed by his friend and protégé Thomas Jefferson in the Declaration of Independence. Mason objected to the Constitution because it contained no Bill of Rights and did not call for the immediate abolition of the slave trade. His efforts led to the passage of the first ten amendments, known as the Bill of Rights. Mason died in 1791 but the house remained in his family until 1866. In 1912 it was privately purchased, restored, and donated to the Commonwealth of Virginia to be administered by the Colonial Dames of America.

Like many Tidewater mansions, at Gunston Hall there is a small frame schoolhouse on the south side with a pathway that leads to a walled family grave where Mason and his wife are buried. In *The Best Cellar* (1987), Charles Goodrum claimed he had reconstructed Mount Vernon's neighbor, the Fairfax family's Belvoir Manor, which burned to the ground in 1783, as the hiding place for the books, but the original Library of Congress collection might have been hidden here, too. It, too, was near Washington on the river, with a cellar dug out to make the bricks for the house and to keep food and wine cool.

The mysterious disappearance of University of Virginia grad student Durance Steele led the Werner-Bok trio to investigate the possibility that the original Library of Congress books were not lost but hidden in some Tidewater plantation basement like this.

Williamsburg: Take Route 95 from Richmond.

The colonial capital of Virginia from 1699 to 1779 and its cultural center, Williamsburg is located on the peninsula between the James and York rivers. Originally part of a protective palisade across the peninsula to protect the original settlement at Jamestown, the College of William and Mary opened there in 1693. By 1699 the town itself was named Williamsburg for William III. The center of political and cultural activity until the capital was moved to Richmond in 1779, the town fell into decline until the rector of Bruton Parish Church invited John D. Rockefeller, Jr., to visit and sold him the idea of letting the past teach the future. Beginning in 1926 more than six hundred buildings were torn down or moved while two hundred were rebuilt and over one hundred restored, turning an area a mile long and half a mile wide into colonial America.

The principal street is Duke of Gloucester Street, with the College at one end and the Capitol at the other. Along the streets are other famous sites: the Governor's Palace, Raleigh Tavern, the Gaol (jail) and Courthouse, and Bruton Parish Church.

Leslie Ford's *The Town Cried Murder* (1939) was set in Williamsburg during the period when the town was being rebuilt by the Rockefellers. There were several families of old gentry like the Yardleys with ("darkie") servants and little money. Ford's story gives you an idea what it was like to live through the restoration.

A generation later to celebrate the Bicentennial in 1976, Barbara Michaels's *Patriot's Dream* takes place in two periods: 1776 and 1976, showing what it was like then and now as Jan Wilde visited her elderly aunt and uncle in the Wilde family house on Duke of Gloucester Street and became "possessed" by her eighteenth-century ancestors. Michaels's mystery is also a great armchair tour of the town.

In Patricia Cornwell's *All That Remains* (1992), *Washington Post* reporter Abby Turnbull, a friend of Richmond's Chief Medical Examiner Kay Scarpetta, who was following the serial killer case, went to Williamsburg to investigate the Dealer's Room. It was a bookstore in the new Merchant's Square run by oddball loner Steven Spurrier, who was very friendly with both FBI and CIA types from nearby Camp Peary.

Jamestown: Follow the signs from Williamsburg to the James River.

In Leslie Ford's *The Town Cried Murder* (1939), the local boy who made good once proposed to Miss Lucy there when she was seventeen, but left town when she refused him. At the end of the mystery the couple went for a drive along the James River to Jamestown, taking his son Bill and Faith Yardly along. They crossed College Creek and the pottery shed on the rickety bridge to the island where the first permanent English colonists in America landed, got out of the car, and went through the turnstile and past the statue of Pocahontas to the ivy-covered ruin of the church where he proposed again.

In Barbara Michaels's *Patriot's Dream* (1976), her latter-day heroine Jan Wilde and her wimpy suitor Richard Blake, a Vietnam vet in retreat from reality, went there on a picnic. They looked at the low mounds left of the foundations of first settlement and commented on the nearby information center and Jamestown Park with replicas of the ships and souvenir shops. In the 1990s we also have Disney's *Pocahontas*.

In 1983 my friend Mary Craig, a president of Mystery Writers of America, published a historical novel about Jamestown called *Lyons Pride* (1983). The first of a series, it was the story of a first (founding) family of Virginia who came over during Puritan Cromwell's reign.

In Goodrum's *The Best Cellar* (1987), historian Steve Carson was doing a dig in Davenport Hundred, a stockaded plantation across from Jamestown. He told Crighton the dig was being done by Williamsburg veterans who roared along: photograph, survey, measure, grid, strip, sieve, bottle, strip, sieve, photograph—everybody laughing and never missing a grain of sand.

Richmond: Take Route 64 west from Williamsburg to Richmond or take Route 95 from Alexandria.

This is where Dr. Kay Scarpetta, chief medical examiner (aka coroner), works in Patricia Cornwell's mysteries. It is also the capital of Virginia and closely associated with the Grand Master of Mystery, Edgar Allan Poe. The Edgar Allan Poe Museum at 1914–1916 E. Main Street is open all year except Christmas Day. Call (804) 648-5523.

Charlottesville: Take Route 66, then 29 out of Alexandria.

This is Thomas Jefferson's town with the University of Virginia and his home Monticello. In murder this area has become the turf of Rita Mae Brown and Sneaky Pie Brown (her feline coauthor) who live in nearby Crozet. In Brown and Sneaky Pie's mystery *Wish You Were Here* (1990), people kept getting postcards of the cemetery with the sentiment "wish you were here" on them, then turning up dead. In these mysteries the animals talk to one another and their conversations are written into the tale. They include Mrs. Murphy, postmistress Mary Minor Haristeen's gray cat, and Tee Tucker, a Welsh corgi, who helped "Harry" Haristeen solve murders.

In their *Murder at Monticello* (1994), you get a grand tour of present-day Monticello, both as a tourist haven and the home of a fictional Jefferson descendant, James Madison Randolph.

In Charles Goodrum's *The Best Cellar* (1987), the murdered graduate student Durance Steele who snooped about Tidewater basements was getting her Ph.D. from the University of Virginia, where she had met tour guide Grace Fairchild and stolen her thesis idea.

SPECIAL HELPS

Authors, Books, and Sleuths by Walk

WHITE HOUSE/DOWNTOWN WALK: AUTHORS AND BOOKS

Adams, Zach, *Pursuit* (1996)

Adler, Warren, *Immaculate Deception* (1991)

Agnew, Spiro, *The Canfield Decision* (1976)

Anonymous (Joe Klein), *Primary Colors* (1996)

Archer, Jeffrey, *Shall We Tell the President?* (1977; rev. ed. 1985)

Armstrong, Charlotte, *Alibi for Murder* (1955)

Baldacci, David, *Absolute Power* (1996)

Beinhart, Larry, *American Hero* (1993)

Bowen, Michael, *Faithfully Executed* (1992)

Box, Edgar (aka Gore Vidal), *Death Before Bedtime* (1953)

Buckley, William F., *The Story of Henri Tod* (1984)

Cain, James, *The Institute* (1976)

Carlson, P. M. "The Father of the Bride" in Greenberg and Nevins, *Mr. President, Private Eye* (1989)

Carter, Nick, *Death of the Falcon* (1974)

Carter, Robert A., *Final Edit* (1994)

Clancy, Tom, *Clear and Present Danger* (1989); *The Hunt for Red October* (1984)

Clark, Mary Higgins, *My Gal Sunday* (1996)

Cohen, William S., and Thomas B. Allen, *Murder in the Senate* (1993)

Conroy, Richard Timothy, *The India Exhibition* (1992); *Mr. Smithson's Bones* (1993)

Conroy, Sarah Booth, *Refinements of Love* (1993)

Cornwell, Patricia, *All That Remains* (1992)

D'Amato, Barbara, *Killer.app* (1996)

Diplomat, *Murder in the State Department* (1930)

Dominic, R. B. (aka Emma Lathen), *Epitaph for a Lobbyist* (1974)

Douglas, Carole Nelson, "Sax and the Single Cat" in *Danger in D.C.* (1993)

Drury, Allen, *Advise and Consent* (1959)

Eberhart, Mignon G., *The Man Next Door* (1942)

Ehrlichman, John, *The Company* (1977)

Ford, Leslie, *The Murder of A Fifth Columnist* (1940); *Washington Whispers Murder* (1953)

Forsyth, Frederick, *The Devil's Alternative* (1980)

Goodrum, Charles, *The Best Cellar* (1987)

Gordons, the, *Power Play* (1965)

Gorman, E. J. *The First Lady* (1995)

Grady, James, *Hard Bargains* (1984); *Runner in the Street* (1984)

Greenberg, Martin H., and Ed Gorman, eds., *Danger in D.C.* (1993)

Greenfield, Jeff, *The People's Choice* (1995)

Greenlee, Sam, *The Spook Who Sat by the Door* (1969)

Haywood, Gar Anthony, *Bad News Travels Fast* (1995)

Himmel, Richard, *Lions at Night* (1979)

Holton, Hugh, *Chicago Blues* (1996)

James, Leigh, *The Capitol Hill Affair* (1975)

Johnson, Haynes, and Howard Simons, *The Landing* (1986)

King, Nina, and Robin Winks, *Crimes of the Scene* (1997)

Knebel, Fletcher, and Charles W. Bailey, *Seven Days in May* (1962)

Lee, John, *The Ninth Man* (1976)

Ludlum, Robert, *The Chancellor Manuscript* (1977)

Lutz, John, "The President's Cat Is Missing" in *Danger in D.C.* (1993)

MacInnes, Helen, *I and My True Love* (1952)

Mason, Van Wyck, *The Washington Legation Murders* (1935)

McCarry, Charles, *Shelley's Heart* (1995)

McGerr, Pat, *Pick Your Victim* (1946)

Michaels, Barbara (aka Elizabeth Peters), *Shattered Silk* (1986)

Mikulski, Barbara, and Marylouise Oates, *Capitol Offense* (1996)

Nessen, Ron, and Johanna Neuman, *Knight and Day* (1995)

O'Toole, G. J. A., *The Cosgrove Report* (1979)

Patrick, Keats, *Death Is a Tory* (1935)

Patterson, Richard North, *The Lasko Tangent* (1979)

Paul, Barbara, "Close but No Cigar" in *Danger in D.C.* (1993)

Pelecanos, George P., *The Big Blowdown* (1996); *Down by the River Where the Dead Men Go* (1995)

Pierson, Eleanor, *Murder Without Clues* (1942)

Plum, Mary, *State Department Cat* (1945)

Quayle, Marilyn, and Nancy Northcott, *The Campaign* (1996)

Revell, Louisa, *The Men with Three Eyes* (1955)

Richman, Phyllis, *The Butter Did It* (1997)

Ripley, Ann, *Mulch* (1994)

Roberts, Carey, *Pray God to Die* (1994)

Roosevelt, Elliott, *A First Class Murder* (1991); *Murder in the Blue Room* (1990); *Murder in the Oval Office* (1989); *Murder in the Rose Garden* (1989); *The White House Pantry Murder* (1987)

Safire, William, *Full Disclosure* (1987); *Sleeper Spy* (1995)

Sanders, Lawrence, *Capital Crimes* (1989)

Schafer, Edith Nalle, *Literary Circles of Washington* (1993)

Serling, Robert J., *The President's Plane Is Missing* (1967)

Stout, Rex, *The Doorbell Rang* (1965)

Thomas, Ross, *Ah Treachery!* (1994); *Cast A Yellow Shadow* (1967); *If You Can't Be Good* (1973); *The Porkchoppers* (1972); *Twilight at Mac's Place* (1990)

Travers, Robert, *The Apartment on K Street* (1972)

Truman, Margaret, *Murder at the FBI* (1985); *Murder at the National Gallery* (1996); *Murder in the Smithsonian* (1983); *Murder in the White House* (1980); *Murder on the Potomac* (1994)

Zencey, Eric, *Panama* (1995)

WHITE HOUSE/DOWNTOWN WALK: SLEUTHS

Special Agent Marc Andrews   Archer
Nick Carter   Carter
Colonel Martin (Jiggs) Casey   Knebel and Bailey
Chicago Police Commander Larry Cole   Holton
Nicholas Cosgrove   O'Toole
Detective Don Dakota   Roberts
Jane Day   Nessen and Neuman
Naval Lieutenant Harry Eaton   Johnson and Simons
Ron Fairbanks   Truman
Irving Fein   Safire
Detective Fiona FitzGerald   Adler
Chief of Capitol Police Jeff Fitzgerald   Cohen and Allen
Detective Anne Fitzhugh   Roberts
Seth Frank   Baldacci
Dan Freeman   Greenlee
Edward George   Goodrum
Jack Graham   Baldacci
Senator Bob Grant   Quayle and Northcott
John Hadley   Pierson
Captain Mac Hanrahan   Truman
Congressman Glenn Holden   the Gordons
Jerry Knight   Nessen and Neuman
Grace Latham   Ford
Dottie and Joe Loudermilk   Haywood
Decatur Lucas   Thomas
Heather McBean   Truman

Cyril "Mac" McCorkle Thomas
Richard Michaelson Bowen
Adam Munro Forsyth
Captain Hugh North Mason
Blackford Oakes Buckley
Chris Paget Patterson
Dr. Lloyd Palmer Cain
Major Edd Partain Thomas
Colonel John Primrose Ford
John Rankin Grady
Pete Robbins McGerr
Eleanor Roosevelt Roosevelt
Dr. Jack Ryan Clancy
Congressman Ben Safford Dominic
Peter Cutler Sargeant III Box
Chief Medical Examiner Kay Scarpetta Cornwell
Henry Scruggs Conroy
Nick Sherman Grady
George Stair Plum
Special Agent Reggie Stanton Holton
Nick Stefanos Pelecanos
Cora Steffani Armstrong
John Tollinger Sanders
Dennis Tyler Diplomat
H. A. L. Tyson Archer
Special Agent Martin Walsh Adams
Chas (Charlotte Sue) Wheatley Richman
Nero Wolfe Stout

East Mall: Museums Walk: Authors and Books

Brawner, Dan, "A Taste for the Good Life" in *Danger in D.C.* (1993)

Collins, Max Allan, *Stolen Away* (1991)

Conroy, Richard Timothy, *The India Exhibition* (1992); *Mr. Smithson's Bones* (1993); *Old Ways in the New World* (1994)

Coonts, Stephen, *Under Siege* (1990)

Crawford, Dan, "Under Separate Cover" in *Alfred Hitchcock Magazine* (July 1990)

D'Amato, Barbara, "Freedom of the Press" in *Danger in D.C.* (1993)

Goodrum, Charles, *The Best Cellar* (1987); *Carnage of the Realm* (1979); *Dewey Decimated* (1977)

Grady, James, *Hard Bargains* (1984)

Greenberg, Martin H., and Ed Gorman, eds., *Danger in D.C.* (1993)

Haywood, Gar Anthony, *Bad News Travels Fast* (1995)

Healy, Jeremiah, *The Staked Goat* (1986)

Hillerman, Tony, *Talking God* (1989)

Johnson, Haynes, and Howard Simons, *The Landing* (1986)

Lee, Wendi, "Indiscreet" in *Danger in D.C.* (1993)

Michaels, Barbara (aka Elizabeth Peters), *Smoke and Mirrors* (1989)

Morice, Anne, *Murder in Mimicry* (1977)

Patrick, Keats, *Death Is a Tory* (1935)

Rinehart, Mary Roberts, *The Man in Lower Ten* (1909)

Rogers, Bruce Holland, "Enduring as Dust" in *Danger in D.C.* (1993)

Sanders, Lawrence, *Capital Crimes* (1989)

Thomas, Ross, *The Brass Go-Between* (1969)

Truman, Margaret, *Murder at the National Gallery* (1996); *Murder in the Smithsonian* (1983)

Wheat, Carolyn, "The Black Hawthorn" in *Danger in D.C.* (1993)

EAST MALL: MUSEUMS WALK: SLEUTHS

Lawrence Blakely   Rinehart

Steve Carson   Goodrum

Officer Jim Chee Hillerman

Tessa and Chief Inspector Robin Crichton (Scotland Yard) Morice

John Cuddy Healy

Edward George Goodrum

Captain Jake Grafton Coonts

Captain Mac Hanrahan Truman

Nathan (Nate) Heller Collins

Betty Crighton Jones Goodrum

Lieutenant Joe Leaphorn Hillerman

Dottie and Joe Loudermilk Haywood

Louise Lee

Cat Marsala D'Amato

Heather McBean Truman

Nikki Wheat

John Rankin Grady

Annabel Reed-Smith and Mac Smith Truman

Philip St. Ives Thomas

Henry Scruggs Conroy

John Tollinger Sanders

West Mall: Monuments Walk: Authors and Books

Baldacci, David, *Absolute Power* (1996)

Chizmar, Richard T., "A Capital Cat Crime" in *Danger in D.C.* (1993)

Cohen, William S., and Thomas B. Allen, *Murder in the Senate* (1993)

Conroy, Richard, *The India Exhibition* (1992)

Crider, Bill, "Code Red: Terror on the Mall" in *Danger in D.C.* (1993)

Crowther, Peter, "Dumb Animals" in *Danger in D.C.* (1993)

Diplomat, *Murder in the Embassy* (1930); *Murder in the State Department* (1930)

Ford, Leslie, *Washington Whispers Murder* (1953)

Goode, Bill, *The Senator's Nude* (1947)

Grady, James, *Runner in the Street* (1984); *Six Days of the Condor* (1974)

Haywood, Gar Anthony, *Bad News Travels Fast* (1995)

Healy, Jeremiah, *Rescue* (1995)

Hynd, Noel, *Truman's Spy* (1990)

Johnson, Haynes, and Howard Simons, *The Landing* (1986)

Kraus, Krandall, *The President's Son* (1986)

Lee, John, *The Ninth Man* (1976)

MacInnes, Helen, *I and My True Love* (1952)

Mason, Van Wyck, *The Washington Legation Murders* (1935)

Michaels, Barbara (aka Elizabeth Peters), *Patriot's Dream* (1976)

Mikulski, Barbara, and Marylouise Oates, *Capitol Offense* (1996)

Moyes, Patricia, *Black Widower* (1975)

Nessen, Ron, and Johanna Neuman, *Knight and Day* (1995)

Pelecanos, George P., *The Big Blowdown* (1996)

Roberts, Carey, *Pray God to Die* (1994)

Roosevelt, Elliott, *Murder in the Rose Garden* (1989); *The White House Pantry Murder* (1987)

Safire, William, *Full Disclosure* (1977)

Schutz, Benjamin M., *A Tax in Blood* (1987)

Truman, Margaret, *Murder on Capitol Hill* (1981)

WEST MALL: MONUMENTS WALK: SLEUTHS

Special Agent Tom Buchanan Hynd

John Cuddy Healy

Detective Don Dakota Roberts

Jane Day Nessen and Neuman

Chief of Capitol Police Jeff Fitzgerald Cohen and Allen

Detective Anne Fitzhugh Roberts

Senator Eleanor Gorzack Mikulski and Oates

Jack Graham Baldacci

Leo Haggerty Schutz
Storey Hawke Goode
Lydia James Truman
Pete Karras Pelecanos
Jerry Knight Nessen and Neuman
Grace Latham Ford
Dottie and Joe Loudermilk Haywood
Ronald Malcolm (aka Condor) Grady
Captain Hugh North Mason
Colonel John Primrose Ford
John Rankin Grady
Eleanor Roosevelt Roosevelt
Chief Inspector Henry Tibbett Moyes
Lieutenant Robert Turner MacInnes
Dennis Tyler Diplomat

CAPITOL HILL WALK: AUTHORS AND BOOKS

Adler, Warren, *Immaculate Deception* (1991)

Agnew, Spiro T., *The Canfield Decision* (1976)

Archer, Jeffrey, *Shall We Tell the President?* (1977; rev. ed. 1985)

Baldacci, David, *Absolute Power* (1996)

Banks, Carolyn, *The Girls on the Row* (1983)

Bonnamy, Francis, *Dead Reckoning* (1943)

Borgenicht, Miriam, *Corpse in Diplomacy* (1956)

Bowen, Michael, *Corruptly Procured* (1994); *Washington Deceased* (1990)

Box, Edgar (aka Gore Vidal), *Death Before Bedtime* (1953)

Breen, Jon L., "Rachel and the Bookstore Cat" in *Danger in D.C.* (1993)

Cain, James M., *The Institute* (1976)

Carlson, P. M., *Bad Blood* (1991); *Murder in the Dog Days* (1991)

Clancy, Tom, *Executive Orders* (1996); *The Hunt for Red October* (1984)

Clark, Mary Higgins, *Stillwatch* (1984)

Coffin, Geoffrey, *Murder in the Senate* (no date; c. 1935)

Cohen, William S., and Thomas B. Allen, *Murder in the Senate* (1993)

Conroy, Richard Timothy, *The India Exhibition* (1992); *Old Ways in the New World* (1994)

Conroy, Sarah Booth, *Refinements of Love* (1993)

Coonts, Stephen, *Under Siege* (1990)

Cornwell, Patricia, *All That Remains* (1992); *Body of Evidence* (1991)

D'Amato, Barbara, "Freedom of the Press" in *Danger in D.C.* (1993)

Dominic, R. B. (aka Emma Lathen), *Epitaph for a Lobbyist* (1974); *Murder in High Place* (1970); *Murder Out of Commission* (1976); *Murder Sunny Side Up* (1968); *There Is No Justice* (1971)

Drury, Allen, *Advise and Consent* (1959)

Finder, Joseph, *Extraordinary Powers* (1993)

Ford, Leslie, *Date with Death* (1959); *The Girl from the Mimosa Club* (1957); *Trial by Ambush* (1961)

Goode, Bill, *The Senator's Nude* (1947)

Goodrum, Charles, *The Best Cellar* (1987); *Carnage of the Realm* (1979); *Dewey Decimated* (1977)

Gordons, the, *Power Play* (1965)

Grady, James, *Hard Bargains* (1984); *Runner in the Street* (1984); *Six Days of the Condor* (1974)

Greenberg, Martin H., and Ed Gorman, eds., *Danger in D.C.* (1993)

Greene, Douglas G., *John Dickson Carr, The Man Who Explained Miracles* (1995)

Greenlee, Sam, *The Spook Who Sat by the Door* (1969)

Grimes, Martha, *The Horse You Came in On* (1993)

Grisham, John, *The Pelican Brief* (1992)

Hammett, Dashiell, *The Continental Op* (1992); *The Glass Key* (1989)

Hatvary, George Egon, *The Murder of Edgar Allan Poe* (1997)

Haywood, Gar Anthony, *Bad News Travels Fast* (1995)

Hillerman, Tony, *The Fly on the Wall* (1971)

Johnson, Haynes, and Howard Simons, *The Landing* (1986)

Knebel, Fletcher, and Charles W. Bailey, *Seven Days in May* (1962)

Lee, Barbara, *Death in Still Waters* (1995)

Lerner, Preston, *Fools on the Hill* (1995)

Ludlum, Robert, *The Chancellor Manuscript* (1977)

MacLeod, Charlotte, *Had She But Known, A Biography of Mary Roberts Rinehart* (1994)

Marlowe, Stephen, *The Lighthouse at the End of the World* (1995)

Mason, Van Wyck, *The Washington Legation Murders* (1935)

McCarry, Charles, *Shelley's Heart* (1995)

Michaels, Barbara (aka Elizabeth Peters), *Smoke and Mirrors* (1989)

Mikulski, Barbara, and Marylouise Oates, *Capitol Offense* (1996)

Moore, William, *The Last Surprise* (1990)

O'Toole, G. J. A., *The Cosgrove Report* (1979)

Patrick, Keats, *Death Is a Tory* (1935)

Patterson, James, *Along Came a Spider* (1992)

Pelecanos, George P., *Down by the River Where the Dead Men Go* (1995)

Peters, Elizabeth, *The Murders of Richard III* (1974)

Pierson, Eleanor, *Murder Without Clues* (1942)

Plum, Mary, *Death of a Redhaired Man* (1950); *Susanna, Don't You Cry* (1946)

Poe, Edgar Allan, "Murders in the Rue Morgue" in *Edgar Allan Poe Selected Tales* (1980)

Quayle, Marilyn, and Nancy Northcott, *The Campaign* (1996); *Embrace the Serpent* (1992)

Revell, Louisa, *The Men with Three Eyes* (1955)

Rinehart, Mary Roberts, *The Man in Lower Ten* (1909)

Roberts, Carey, *Pray God to Die* (1994)

Roberts, Kelsey, *Legal Tender* (1993)

Roosevelt, Elliott, *Murder and the First Lady* (1984); *Murder in the Blue Room* (1990); *Murder in the Executive Mansion* (1995); *Murder in the Oval Office* (1989); *Murder in the Rose Garden* (1989); *Murder in the West Wing* (1993); *The White House Pantry Murder* (1987)

Roudybush, Alexandra, *A Sybaritic Death* (1972)
Schafer, Edith Nalle, *Literary Circles of Washington* (1993)
Stern, Aaron Marc, *Death Takes a Paying Guest* (1947)
Swanson, Jean, and Dean James, *By a Woman's Hand* (1994)
Tey, Josephine, *The Daughter of Time* (1952)
Thomas, Ross, *Ah Treachery!* (1994); *If You Can't Be Good* (1973)
Titchener, Louise, *Homebody* (1993); *Mantrap* (1994)
Travers, Robert, *The Apartment on K Street* (1972)
Truman, Margaret, *Murder at the National Cathedral* (1990); *Murder in the House* (1997); *Murder in the Supreme Court* (1982); *Murder in the White House* (1980); *Murder on Capitol Hill* (1981)
Wilson, F. Paul, *The Select* (1994)

Capitol Hill Walk: Sleuths

Ross Allen   Pierson
Special Agent Marc Andrews   Archer
Lawrence Blakely   Rinehart
Tim Brown   Wilson
Jeff Carmichael   Lerner
Steve Carson   Goodrum
Colonel Martin (Jiggs) Casey   Knebel and Bailey
Officer Jim Chee   Hillerman
"Tom" Collins   Patrick
Continental OP   Hammett
Nicholas Cosgrove   O'Toole
John Cotton   Hillerman
Antoinette Credella   Titchener
Deputy Chief of Detectives Alex Cross   Patterson
Detective Dan Dakota   Roberts
Sally Dunphy   Titchener
C. Auguste Dupin   Hatvary, Poe, Marlowe

Eve Elliott Lee
Ben Ellison Finder
Ron Fairbanks Truman
Detective Anne Fitzhugh Roberts
Detective Fiona FitzGerald Adler
Chief of Capitol Police Jeff Fitzgerald Cohen and Allen
Dan Freeman Greenlee
Edward George Goodrum
Senator Eleanor Gorzack Mikulski and Oates
Jack Graham Baldacci
Senator Bob Grant Quayle and Northcott
Erin Hartsock Michaels
Storey Hawk Goode
Rachel Hennings Breen
Elsie Mae Hunt Stern
Caitlin Jeffrey Roberts
Betty Crighton Jones Goodrum
John Keefer Travers
Lieutenant Joe Leaphorn Hillerman
Brett Leighton Truman
Dottie and Joe Loudermilk Haywood
Decatur Lucas Thomas
Ross Macalaster McCarry
Ronald Malcolm (aka Condor) Grady
Cat Marsala D'Amato
Russell McGarvey Moore
Richard Michaelson Bowen
Tim Mulligan Stern
Captain Hugh North Mason
Dr. Lloyd Palmer Cain
John Rankin Grady
Eleanor Roosevelt Roosevelt
Dr. Jack Ryan Clancy

Maggie Ryan Carlson
Nate Ryan Ford
Congressman Ben Safford Dominic
Peter Cutler Sargeant III Box
Chief Medical Examiner Kay Scarpetta Cornwell
Henry Scruggs Conroy
Darby Shaw Grisham
Dr. Jonas Smith Ford
Mackensie Smith Truman
Nick Stefanos Pelecanos
Inspector Scott Stuart Coffin
Jerry Vale Plum
Katherine Whipple Borgenicht

DUPONT CIRCLE/EMBASSY ROW WALK: AUTHORS AND BOOKS

Adler, Warren, *Immaculate Deception* (1991)
Agnew, Spiro, *The Canfield Decision* (1976)
Anonymous (Joe Klein), *Primary Colors* (1996)
Anthony, Evelyn, *The Avenue of the Dead* (1982)
Baldacci, David, *Absolute Power* (1996)
Borgenicht, Miriam, *Corpse in Diplomacy* (1956)
Bowen, Michael, *Washington Deceased* (1990)
Box, Edgar (aka Gore Vidal), *Death Before Bedtime* (1953)
Brawner, Dan, "A Taste for the Good Life" in *Danger in D.C.* (1993)
Breen, Jon L., "Rachel and the Bookstore Cat" in *Danger in D.C.* (1993)
Bush, Barbara, *A Memoir* (1994)
Carlson, P. M., *Bad Blood* (1991)
Carter, Robert A., *Final Edit* (1994)
Charteris, Leslie, *The Saint Steps In* (1943)

Clancy, Tom, *Executive Orders* (1996); *Patriot Games* (1987)

Cohen, William S., and Thomas B. Allen, *Murder in the Senate* (1993)

Collins, Max Allan, *Stolen Away* (1991)

Conroy, Richard Timothy, *Mr. Smithson's Bones* (1993); *Old Ways in the New World* (1994)

Conroy, Sarah Booth, *Refinements of Love* (1993)

Coonts, Stephen, *Under Siege* (1990)

Cornwell, Patricia, *All That Remains* (1992)

D'Amato, Barbara, *Killer.app* (1996)

Davey, Jocelyn, *A Capitol Offense* (1956)

Diplomat, *Murder in the Embassy* (1930)

Dominic, R. B. (aka Emma Lathen), *Epitaph for a Lobbyist* (1974); *Murder in High Place* (1970); *Murder Out of Commission* (1976)

Doolittle, Jerome, *Head Lock* (1993)

Drury, Allen, *Advise and Consent* (1959)

Eberhart, Mignon G., *The Man Next Door* (1942)

Ford, Leslie, *All for the Love of a Lady* (1943); *The Murder of a Fifth Columnist* (1940); *Washington Whispers Murder* (1953)

Goodrum, Charles, *The Best Cellar* (1987); *Carnage of the Realm* (1979)

Grady, James, *Hard Bargains* (1984); *Runner in the Street* (1984); *Six Days of the Condor* (1974)

Greenfield, Jeff, *The People's Choice* (1995)

Haywood, Gar Anthony, *Bad News Travels Fast* (1995)

Healy, Jeremiah, *Rescue* (1995)

Johnson, Haynes, and Howard Simons, *The Landing* (1986)

Keating, H. R. F., *Crime and Mystery: The 100 Best Books* (1987)

Law, Janice, *The Big Payoff* (1976)

MacInnes, Helen, *I and My True Love* (1952)

MacLeod, Charlotte, *Had She But Known, A Biography of Mary Roberts Rinehart* (1994)

Mason, Van Wyck, *The Washington Legation Murders* (1935)

McCarry, Charles, *Shelley's Heart* (1995)

Moody, Susan, *Penny Black* (1984)

Moyes, Patricia, *Black Widower* (1975)

Nessen, Ron, and Johanna Neuman, *Knight and Day* (1995)

Olshaker, Mark, *The Edge* (1994)

Patrick, Keats, *Death Is a Tory* (1935)

Patterson, James, *Along Came a Spider* (1992)

Pelecanos, George P., *Down by the River Where the Dead Men Go* (1995)

Pierson, Eleanor, *Murder Without Clues* (1942)

Plum, Mary, *Death of a Redhaired Man* (1950)

Quayle, Marilyn, and Nancy Northcott, *The Campaign* (1996); *Embrace the Serpent* (1992)

Revell, Louisa, *The Men with Three Eyes* (1955)

Rinehart, Mary Roberts, *The Circular Staircase* (1908); *The Man in Lower Ten* (1909)

Roberts, Carey, *Pray God to Die* (1994)

Roosevelt, Elliott, *Murder and the First Lady* (1984); *Murder in the Blue Room* (1990); *Murder in the Oval Office* (1989); *Murder in the Rose Garden* (1989); *The White House Pantry Murder* (1987)

Roudybush, Alexandra, *A Sybaritic Death* (1972)

Sanders, Lawrence, *Capital Crimes* (1989)

Schutz, Benjamin M., *Embrace the Wolf* (1985)

Sheldon, Walter J., *Rites of Murder* (1984)

Stern, Aaron Marc, *Death Takes a Paying Guest* (1947)

Sucher, Dorothy, *Dead Men Don't Marry* (1989)

Thomas, Ross, *If You Can't Be Good* (1973)

Truman, Margaret, *Murder at the National Cathedral* (1990); *Murder at the National Gallery* (1996); *Murder in the Smithsonian* (1983); *Murder in the White House* (1980); *Murder on Embassy Row* (1984)

Valentine, Paul, *Crime Scene at "O" Street* (1989)

Viorst, Judith, *Murdering Mr. Monti* (1994)

Dupont Circle/Embassy Row Walk: Sleuths

Clover Adams Conroy

Tom Bethany Doolittle

Steve Blake and Maida Lovell Eberhart

Bishop Paul Burdock Sheldon

Capitol Police Captain Jeff Carmichael Cohen and Allen

Steve Carson Goodrum

"Tom" Collins Patrick

John Cuddy Healy

Detective Don Dakota Roberts

Jane Day Nessen and Neuman

Detective Fiona FitzGerald Adler

Detective Anne Fitzhugh Roberts

Edward George Goodrum

Captain Jake Grafton Coonts

Davina Graham Anthony

Senator Bob Grant Quayle and Northcott

John Hadley Pierson

Leo Haggerty Schutz

Captain Mac Hanrahan Truman

Nate Heller Collins

Detective Dewey Hudlow Valentine

Elsie Mae Hunt Stern

Detective Magnus Johnson Valentine

Betty Crighton Jones Goodrum

Jerry Knight Nessen and Neuman

Brenda Kovner Viorst

Grace Latham Ford

Dottie and Joe Loudermilk Haywood

Decatur Lucas Thomas

Sandy Mansfield Olshaker

Heather McBean Truman
Richard Michaelson Bowen
Captain Sal Morizio Truman
Tim Mulligan Stern
Vic Newman Sucher
Captain Hugh North Mason
Anna Peters Law
Colonel John Primrose Ford
John Rankin Grady
Annabel Reed-Smith Truman
First Lady Eleanor Roosevelt Roosevelt
President John (Jack) Ryan Clancy
Maggie Ryan Carlson
Congressman Ben Safford Dominic
Peter Cutler Sargeant III Box
Chief Medical Examiner Kay Scarpetta Cornwell
Henry Scruggs Conroy
Mac Smith Truman
Nick Stefanos Pelecanos
Sabina Swift Sucher
Simon Templar (The Saint) Charteris
Douglas Travers Dominic
Dennis Tyler Diplomat
Ambrose Usher Davey
Jerry Vale Plum
Penny Wannawake Moody
Katherine Whipple Borgenicht

FOGGY BOTTOM WALK: AUTHORS AND BOOKS

Adams, Zach, *Pursuit* (1996)
Archer, Jeffrey, *Shall We Tell the President?* (1977; rev. ed. 1985)
Baldacci, David, *Absolute Power* (1996)
Borgenicht, Miriam, *Corpse in Diplomacy* (1956)

Bowen, Michael, *Worst Case Scenario* (1996)

Buckley, William F., Jr., *Mongoose R.I.P.* (1987)

Cain, James, *The Institute* (1976)

Carter, Nick, *Death of the Falcon* (1974)

Clancy, Tom, *The Hunt for Red October* (1984)

Clark, Mary Higgins, *Stillwatch* (1984)

Conroy, Richard, *Old Ways in the New World* (1994)

Ehrlichman, John, *The Company* (1977)

Fleming, Ian, *Diamonds Are Forever* (1956)

Goode, Bill, *The Senator's Nude* (1947)

Grady, James, *Runner in the Street* (1984)

Hallahan, William H., *Catch Me, Kill Me* (1977)

Haywood, Gar Anthony, *Bad News Travels Fast* (1995)

Heidish, Marcy, *The Torching* (1992)

Hynd, Noel, *Truman's Spy* (1990)

Kimball, Stephen, *Death Duty* (1996)

Michaels, Barbara (aka Elizabeth Peters), *Shattered Silk* (1986)

Morice, Anne, *Murder in Mimicry* (1977)

Moyes, Patricia, *Black Widower* (1975)

O'Brien, Patricia, *The Ladies Lunch* (1994)

Patrick, Keats, *Death Is a Tory* (1935)

Quayle, Marilyn, and Nancy Northcott, *Embrace the Serpent* (1992)

Richman, Phyllis, *The Butter Did It* (1997)

Ripley, Ann, *Mulch* (1994)

Roosevelt, Elliott, *Murder in the Rose Garden* (1989)

Sanders, Lawrence, *Capital Crimes* (1989)

Schutz, Benjamin M., *A Tax in Blood* (1987)

Sucher, Dorothy, *Dead Men Don't Marry* (1989)

Thomas, Ross, *If You Can't Be Good* (1973)

Travers, Robert, *The Apartment on K Street* (1972)

Truman, Margaret, *Murder at the Kennedy Center* (1989); *Murder at the National Cathedral* (1990); *Murder at the National Gallery* (1996); *Murder in Georgetown* (1986); *Murder in the White House* (1980); *Murder on Capitol Hill* (1981)

Foggy Bottom Walk: Sleuths

Special Agent Marc Andrews Archer
James Bond (Agent 007) Fleming
Special Agent Tom Buchanan Hynd
FBI Director T. C. Carson Travers
Nick Carter Carter
"Tom" Collins Patrick
Tessa Crichton Morice
Bill Eldridge Ripley
Ron Fairbanks Truman
Detective Seth Frank Baldacci
Jack Graham Baldacci
Senator Bob Grant Quayle and Northcott
Leo Haggerty Schutz
Storey Hawk Goode
Lydia James Truman
Special Agent Hazel Loomis Clancy
Dottie and Joe Loudermilk Haywood
Decatur Lucas Thomas
CIA Director William Martin Ehrlichman
Richard Michaelson Bowen
Karen Nevitt Michaels
Blackford Oates Buckley
Dr. Lloyd Palmer Cain
Joe Potamos Truman
John Rankin Grady
Annabel Reed-Smith Truman
Jack Ryan Clancy
Henry Scruggs Conroy
Mac Smith Truman
Sabina Swift Sucher
Chief Inspector Henry Tibbett Moyes
John Tollinger Sanders

Special Agent Martin Walsh   Adams
Chas (Charlotte Sue) Wheatley   Richman
Katherine Whipple   Borgenicht

GEORGETOWN WALK: AUTHORS AND BOOKS

Agnew, Spiro, *The Canfield Decision* (1976)
Alner, James Z., *The Capital Murder* (c. 1935)
Archer, Jeffrey, *Shall We Tell the President?* (1977; rev. ed. 1985)
Blatty, William Peter, *The Exorcist* (1971)
Braunbeck, Gary A., "The Cat's Paw Affair" in *Danger in D.C.* (1993)
Carter, Nick, *Death of the Falcon* (1974)
Clancy, Tom, *Patriot Games* (1987)
Clark, Mary Higgins, *Stillwatch* (1984)
Collins, Max Allan, "Catgate" in *Danger in D.C.* (1993)
Conroy, Sarah Booth, *Refinements of Love* (1993)
Cornwell, Patricia, *All That Remains* (1992)
Dominic, R. B. (aka Emma Lathen), *Epitaph for a Lobbyist* (1974)
Ehrlichman, John, *The Company* (1977)
Finder, Joseph, *Extraordinary Powers* (1993)
Ford, Leslie, *All for the Love of a Lady* (1943); *False to Any Man* (1939); *Murder in the O.P.M.* (1942); *The Simple Way of Poison* (1937)
Fromer, Margot J., *Night Shift* (1993); *Scalpel's Edge* (1991)
Goodrum, Charles, *Carnage of the Realm* (1979)
Greenberg, Martin H., and Ed Gorman, eds., *Danger in D.C.* (1993)
Haywood, Gar Anthony, *Bad News Travels Fast* (1995)
Heidish, Marcy, *The Torching* (1992)
Knebel, Fletcher, and Charles W. Bailey, *Seven Days in May* (1962)
Law, Janice, *Backfire* (1994)
Ludlum, Robert, *The Chancellor Manuscript* (1977)
MacInnes, Helen, *I and My True Love* (1952)
McCarry, Charles, *Shelley's Heart* (1995)

Michaels, Barbara (aka Elizabeth Peters), *Ammie, Come Home* (1968); *Shattered Silk* (1986); *Stitches in Time* (1995)

Moody, Susan, *Penny Black* (1984)

Morice, Anne, *Murder in Mimicry* (1977)

Moyes, Patricia, *Black Widower* (1975)

O'Brien, Patricia, *The Ladies Lunch* (1994)

Olshaker, Mark, *The Edge* (1994)

O'Toole, G. J. A., *The Cosgrove Report* (1979)

Patterson, James, *Along Came a Spider* (1992)

Pelecanos, George P., *Down by the River Where the Dead Men Go* (1995)

Plum, Mary, *State Department Cat* (1945)

Quayle, Marilyn, and Nancy Northcott, *The Campaign* (1996)

Richman, Phyllis, *The Butter Did It* (1997)

Ripley, Ann, *Mulch* (1994)

Roberts, Carey, *Pray God to Die* (1994); *Touch a Cold Duck* (1989)

Roosevelt, Elliott, *Murder in the Oval Office* (1989); *Murder in the Rose Garden* (1989)

Sanders, Lawrence, *Capital Crimes* (1989)

Schutz, Benjamin M., *Embrace the Wolf* (1985); "Mary, Mary, Shut the Door," in Robert J. Randisi and Marilyn Wallace, *Deadly Allies* (1992); *A Tax in Blood* (1987)

Sheldon, Walter J., *Rites of Murder* (1984)

Sucher, Dorothy, *Dead Men Don't Marry* (1989)

Thomas, Ross, *Ah, Treachery!* (1994); *If You Can't Be Good* (1973)

Truman, Margaret, *Murder at the Kennedy Center* (1989); *Murder at the National Gallery* (1996); *Murder in Georgetown* (1986); *Murder in the Smithsonian* (1983); *Murder in the Supreme Court* (1982); *Murder on Capitol Hill* (1981); *Murder on the Potomac* (1994)

Wheat, Carolyn, "The Black Hawthorn" in *Danger in D.C.* (1993)

Georgetown Walk: Sleuths

Steve Carson Goodrum
Nick Carter Carter
Colonel Martin (Jiggs) Casey Knebel and Bailey
Nicholas Cosgrove O'Toole
Tessa Crichton Morice
Detective Alex Cross Patterson
Ben Ellison Finder
Detective Anne Fitzhugh Roberts
Edward George Goodrum
Senator Bob Grant Quayle and Northcott
Alice Grey Heidish
Leo Haggerty Schutz
Lydia James Truman
Betty Crighton Jones Goodrum
Amanda Knight Fromer
Grace Latham Ford
Dottie and Joe Loudermilk Haywood
Decatur Lucas Thomas
Detective Sandy Mansfield Olshaker
Heather McBean Truman
Major Edd "Twodees" Partain Thomas
Nancy Patterson and George Stair Plum
Anna Peters Law
Joe Potamos Truman
Colonel John Primrose Ford
Annabel Reed-Smith Truman
Eleanor Roosevelt Roosevelt
Jack Ryan Clancy
Chief Medical Examiner Kay Scarpetta Cornwell
Detective John Simpson Patterson

Mac Smith Truman
Nick Stefanos Pelecanos
Sabina Swift Sucher
Pat Traymore Clark
Penny Wanawake Moody
Chas (Charlotte Sue) Wheatley Richman

ARLINGTON/ALEXANDRIA WALKS: AUTHORS AND BOOKS

Archer, Jeffrey, *Shall We Tell the President?* (1977; rev. ed. 1985)

Baldacci, David, *Absolute Power* (1996)

Bonnamy, Francis, *The King Is Dead on Queen Street* (1945)

Brown, Rita Mae, and Sneaky Pie Brown, *Murder at Monticello* (1994); *Wish You Were Here* (1990)

Cannon, Rachel, *The Anniversary* (1996)

Carter, Robert A., *Final Edit* (1994)

Clancy, Tom, *The Hunt for Red October* (1984)

Conroy, Sarah Booth, *Refinements of Love* (1993)

Cornwell, Patricia, *All That Remains* (1992)

Craig, Mary Shura, *Lyon's Pride* (1983)

Diplomat, *Murder in the State Department* (1930)

Dominic, R. B. (aka Emma Lathen), *Epitaph for A Lobbyist* (1974); *Murder Out of Commission* (1976)

Doolittle, Jerome, *Head Lock* (1993)

Ehrlichman, John, *The Company* (1977)

Finder, Joseph, *Extraordinary Powers* (1993)

Ford, Leslie, *False to Any Man* (1939); *The Simple Way of Poison* (1937); *The Town Cried Murder* (1939)

Gilman, Dorothy, *The Unexpected Mrs. Pollifax* (1966)

Goodrum, Charles, *The Best Cellar* (1987); *Carnage of the Realm* (1979)

Grady, James, *Six Days of the Condor* (1974)

Greenlee, Sam, *The Spook Who Sat by the Door* (1969)

Haywood, Gar Anthony, *Bad News Travels Fast* (1995)
Healy, Jeremiah, *The Staked Goat* (1986)
Johnson, Haynes, and Howard Simons, *The Landing* (1986)
Johnston, Norma (aka Nicole St. John) *Carlisles All* (1986)
Knebel, Fletcher, and Charles W. Bailey, *Seven Days in May* (1962)
Ludlum, Robert, *The Osterman Weekend* (1972)
Michaels, Barbara (aka Elizabeth Peters), *Patriot's Dream* (1976)
Mosiman, Billie Sue, "Talk Shows Just Kill Me" in *Danger in D.C.* (1993)
Nessen, Ron, and Johanna Neuman, *Knight and Day* (1995)
O'Toole, G. J. A., *An Agent on the Other Side* (1973); *The Cosgrove Report* (1979)
Patrick, Keats, *Death Is a Tory* (1935)
Plum, Mary, *Susanna, Don't You Cry* (1946)
Ripley, Ann, *Mulch* (1994)
Roosevelt, Elliott, *Murder in the Executive Mansion* (1995); *Murder in the Rose Garden* (1989)
Safire, William, *Sleeper Spy* (1995)
Schutz, Benjamin M., *All the Old Bargains* (1985)
Serling, Robert J., *The President's Plane Is Missing* (1967)
Thomas, Ross, *Twilight at Mac's Place* (1990)
Truman, Margaret, *Murder at the Kennedy Center* (1989); *Murder at the Pentagon* (1992); *Murder in the CIA* (1987); *Murder on Capitol Hill* (1981)

Arlington/Alexandria Walks: Sleuths

Tom Bethany Doolittle
Francis Bonnamy Bonnamy
CIA Operative Collette Cahill Truman
Steve Carson Goodrum
Colonel Martin (Jiggs) Casey Knebel and Bailey
Nicholas Cosgrove O'Toole
John Cuddy Healy

Jane Day Nessen and Neuman
Irving Fein Safire
Edward George Goodrum
Jack Graham Baldacci
Leo Haggerty Schutz
Mary Haristeen Brown
Lydia James Truman
Betty Crighton Jones Goodrum
Jerry Knight Nessen and Neuman
Grace Latham Ford
Joe and Dottie Loudermilk Haywood
Ronald Malcolm (aka Condor) Grady
Mrs. Murphy and Tee Tucker Brown
Mrs. Emily Pollifax Gilman
Colonel John Primrose Ford
Eleanor Roosevelt Roosevelt
Congressman Ben Safford Dominic
Chief Medical Examiner Kay Scarpetta Cornwell
Professor Peter Shane Bonnamy
Mac Smith Truman
John Tanner Ludlum
Dennis Tyler Diplomat

BIBLIOGRAPHY

This is a complete list of the books used to write this guide. It includes not only all the mysteries mentioned but also other guides and histories I found helpful.

Adams, Zach. *Pursuit*. New York: Onyx (Penguin), 1996.

Adler, Warren. *Immaculate Deception*. New York: Zebra Books, 1991.

Agnew, Spiro T. *The Canfield Decision*. Chicago: Playboy Press, 1976.

Alner, James Z. *The Capital Murder*. London: Hurst & Blackett, Ltd.

Anonymous (Joe Klein). *Primary Colors*. New York: Random House, 1996.

Anthony, Evelyn. *The Avenue of the Dead*. New York: New American Library, 1982.

Archer, Jeffrey. *Shall We Tell the President?* New York: Viking Press, 1977, rev. ed. 1985.

Armstrong, Charlotte. *Alibi for Murder*. New York: Pocket Books, 1955.

Baldacci, David. *Absolute Power*. New York: Warner Books, 1996.

Banks, Carolyn. *The Girls on the Row*. New York: Fawcett Crest, 1983.

Beinhart, Larry. *American Hero*. New York: Ballantine, 1993.

Bergheim, Laura. *The Washington Historical Atlas*. Rockville, MD: Woodbine House, 1992.

Blatty, William Peter. *The Exorcist*. New York: Harper & Row, 1971.

Bonnamy, Francis. *Dead Reckoning*. New York: Penguin, 1943.

———. *The King Is Dead on Queen Street*. New York: Duell, Sloan and Pearce, 1945.

Borgenicht, Miriam. *Corpse in Diplomacy*. London: Panther Books, 1956.

Bowen, Michael. *Corruptly Procured*. New York: St. Martin's, 1994.

———. *Faithfully Executed*. New York: St. Martin's, 1992.

———. *Washington Deceased*. New York: St Martin's, 1990.

———. *Worst Case Scenario*. New York: Crown, 1996.

Box, Edgar (Gore Vidal). *Death Before Bedtime*. New York: Vintage Books (Random House), 1953.

Breen, Jon L. "Rachel and the Bookstore Cat," in *Danger in D.C.* New York: Ivy Books, 1993.

Brown, Rita Mae, and Sneaky Pie Brown. *Murder at Monticello*. New York: Bantam, 1994.

———. *Wish You Were Here*. New York: Bantam, 1990.

Buckley, William F., Jr. *Mongoose R.I.P.* New York: Random House, 1987.

———. *The Story of Henri Tod*. New York: Doubleday, 1984.

Cain, James. *The Institute*. New York: Mason/Charter, 1976.

Cannon, Rachel. *The Anniversary*. New York: Random House, 1996.

Carlson, P. M. *Bad Blood*. New York: Doubleday (Bantam, Dell), 1991.

———. "The Father of the Bride; or A Fate Worse Than Death," in Greenberg and Nevins, *Mr. President, Private Eye*. New York: Ballantine, 1989.

———. *Murder in the Dog Days*. New York: Bantam, 1991.

Carter, Nick. *Death of the Falcon*. New York: Award Books, 1974.

Carter, Robert A. *Final Edit*. New York: Mysterious Press, 1994.

Charteris, Leslie. *The Saint Steps In*. New York: Doubleday Doran, 1943.

Chase, Elaine Raco, and Anne Wingate. *Amateur Detectives*. Cincinnati, Ohio: Writer's Digest Books, 1996.

Clancy, Tom. *Clear and Present Danger*. New York: Berkley, 1990.

———. *Executive Orders*, New York: Putnam, 1996.

———. *The Hunt for Red October*. New York: Berkley, 1984.

———. *Patriot Games*. New York: Berkley, 1987.

Clark, Mary Higgins. *My Gal Sunday*. New York: Simon & Schuster, 1996.

———. *Stillwatch*. New York: Dell, 1984.

Coffin, Geoffrey. *Murder in the Senate*. London: Hurst & Blackett, c. 1935.

Cohen, Senator William, and Thomas B. Allen. *Murder in the Senate*. New York: St. Martin's, 1993.

Collins, Max Allan. *Stolen Away*. New York: Bantam, 1991.

Conroy, Richard Timothy. *The India Exhibition*. New York: St. Martin's, 1992.

———. *Mr. Smithson's Bones*. New York: St. Martin's, 1993.

———. *Old Ways in the New World*. New York: St. Martin's, 1994.

Conroy, Sarah Booth. *Refinements of Love*. New York: Pantheon, 1993.

Coonts, Stephen. *Under Siege*. New York: Pocket Books, 1990.

Cornwell, Patricia D. *All That Remains*. New York: Avon, 1993.

———. *Body of Evidence*. New York: Avon, 1991.

Cox, Ethelyn. *Historic Alexandria Virginia Street by Street*. McLean, VA: EPM Publications, 1976

Craig, Mary Shura. *Lyon's Pride*. New York: Jove, 1983.

Crawford, Dan. "Under Separate Cover," in *Alfred Hitchcock Magazine*, July 1990.

Dale, Alzina Stone. *Dorothy L. Sayers, the Centenary Celebration*. New York: Walker, 1993.

D'Amato, Barbara. "Freedom of the Press," in *Danger in D.C.* New York: Ivy Books, 1993.

———. *The Doctor, the Murder, the Mystery*. Chicago: Noble Press, 1992.

———. *Killer.app*. New York: Forge, 1996.

Davey, Jocelyn. *A Capitol Offense*. New York: Knopf, 1956.

Diplomat, *Murder in the Embassy.* New York: Jonathan Cape & Harrison Smith, 1930.

———. *Murder in the State Department.* New York: Jonathan Cape & Harrison Smith, 1930.

Dominic, R. B. (aka Emma Lathen). *Epitaph for a Lobbyist.* New York: Doubleday, 1974.

———. *Murder in High Place.* New York: Doubleday Crime Club, 1970.

———. *Murder Out of Commission.* New York: Doubleday Crime Club, 1976.

———. *Murder Sunny Side Up.* London: Abelard-Schuman, 1968.

———. *There Is No Justice.* New York: Doubleday, 1971.

Doolittle, Jerome. *Head Lock.* New York: Pocket Books, 1994.

Drury, Allen. *Advise and Consent.* New York: Doubleday, 1959.

Eberhart, Mignon G. *The Man Next Door.* New York: Random House, 1942.

Ehrlichman, John. *The Company.* New York: Pocket Books, 1977.

Finder, Joseph. *Extraordinary Powers.* New York: Ballantine, 1993.

Fleming, Ian. *Diamonds Are Forever.* New York: Macmillan, 1956.

Ford, Leslie, *All for the Love of a Lady.* New York: Scribner's, 1943.

———. *Date with Death.* New York: Scribner's, 1959.

———. *False to Any Man.* New York: Scribner's, 1939.

———. *The Girl from the Mimosa Club.* New York: Scribner's, 1957.

———. *Murder in the O.P.M.* New York: Popular Library, 1942.

———. *The Murder of a Fifth Columnist.* New York: Scribner's, 1940.

———. *The Simple Way of Poison.* New York: Scribner's, 1937.

———. *The Town Cried Murder.* New York: Scribner's, 1939.

———. *Trial by Ambush.* New York: Scribner's, 1961.

———. *Washington Whispers Murder.* New York: Dell, 1953.

Forsyth, Frederick. *The Devil's Alternative.* New York: Viking, 1980.

Fromer, Margot J. *Night Shift.* New York: Diamond Books, 1993.

———. *Scalpel's Edge*. New York: Diamond Books, 1991.

Gilman, Dorothy. *The Unexpected Mrs. Pollifax*. New York: Fawcett Crest, 1966.

Goode, Bill. *The Senator's Nude*. Chicago: Ziff Publishing, 1947.

Goodrum, Charles A. *The Best Cellar*. New York: Harper & Row, 1987.

———. *Carnage of the Realm*. New York: Crown, 1979.

———. *Dewey Decimated*. New York: Crown, 1977.

Gordons, the. *Power Play*. New York: Doubleday, 1965.

Gorman, E. J. *The First Lady*. New York: Forge, 1995.

Grady, James. *Hard Bargains*. New York: Macmillan, 1984.

———. *Runner in the Street*. New York: Macmillan, 1984.

———. *Six Days of the Condor*. New York: Norton, 1974.

Greenberg, Martin H., and Ed Gorman, eds. *Danger in D.C.: Cat Crimes in the Nation's Capital*. New York: Ivy Books, 1993.

Greene, Douglas G. *John Dickson Carr, The Man Who Explained Miracles*. New York: Otto Pensler, 1995.

Greenfield, Jeff. *The People's Choice*. New York: Putnam, 1995.

Greenlee, Sam. *The Spook Who Sat by the Door*. New York: Bantam, 1969.

Grisham, John. *The Pelican Brief*. New York: Dell, 1992.

Hallahan, William H. *Catch Me, Kill Me*. New York: Avon, 1977.

Hammett, Dashiell. *The Complete Dashiell Hammett*. New York: Knopf, 1942.

———. *The Glass Key*. New York: Vintage Books, 1972.

Hart, Carolyn G. *Something Wicked*. New York: Bantam, 1992.

———. *Southern Ghost*. New York: Bantam, 1988.

Hatvary, George Egon. *The Murder of Edgar Allan Poe*. New York: Carroll & Graf, 1997.

Haywood, Gar Anthony. *Bad News Travels Fast*. New York: Putnam, 1995.

Healy, Jeremiah. *Rescue*. New York: Simon & Schuster, 1995.

———. *The Staked Goat*. New York: Pocket Books, 1986.

Heidish, Marcy. *The Torching*. New York: Simon & Schuster, 1992.

Himmel, Richard. *Lions at Night.* New York: Delacorte, 1979.

Holton, Hugh. *Chicago Blues.* New York: Forge, 1996.

Hynd, Noel. *Truman's Spy.* New York: Zebra Books, 1990.

James, Leigh. *The Capitol Hill Affair.* New York: Manor Books, 1975.

Johnson, Haynes, and Howard Simons. *The Landing.* New York: Villard Books, 1986.

Johnston, Norma (Nicole St. John). *Carlisles All.* New York: Bantam, 1986.

———. *Carlisle's Hope.* New York: Bantam, 1986.

———. *To Jess, with Love and Memories.* New York: Bantam, 1986.

Keating, H. R. F. *Crime & Mystery, The 100 Best Books.* New York: Carroll & Graf, 1987.

Kimball, Stephen. *Death Duty.* New York: Dutton (Penguin), 1996.

King, Nina, and Robin Winks. *Crimes of the Scene.* New York: St. Martin's, 1997.

Knebel, Fletcher, and Charles W. Bailey II. *Seven Days in May.* Harper & Row, 1962.

Kraus, Krandall. *The President's Son.* Boston: Allyson, 1986.

Law, Janice. *Backfire.* New York: St. Martin's, 1994.

———. *The Big Payoff.* Boston: Houghton Mifflin, 1976.

Lee, Barbara. *Death in Still Waters.* New York: St. Martin's, 1995.

———. *Final Closing: A Chesapeake Bay Mystery.* New York: St. Martin's, 1997.

Lee, John. *The Ninth Man.* New York: Dell, 1976.

Lerner, Preston. *Fools on the Hill.* New York: Pocket Books, 1995.

Ludlum, Robert. *The Chancellor Manuscript.* New York: Bantam, 1977.

———. *The Osterman Weekend.* New York: Bantam, 1972.

MacInnes, Helen. *I and My True Love.* New York: Harcourt Brace, 1952.

MacLeod, Charlotte. *Had She But Known, A Biography of Mary Roberts Rinehart.* New York: Mysterious Press, 1994.

McCarry, Charles. *Shelley's Heart*. New York: Random House, 1995.

McGerr, Pat. *Pick Your Victim*. New York: Dell, 1946.

Marlowe, Stephen. *The Lighthouse at the End of the World*. New York: Dutton (Penguin), 1995.

Mason, Van Wyck. *The Washington Legation Murders*. New York: Lippincott, 1935.

Michaels, Barbara (aka Elizabeth Peters). *Ammie, Come Home*. New York: Meredith Press, 1968.

———. *Patriot's Dream*. New York: Berkley, 1976.

———. *Shattered Silk*. New York: Berkley, 1986.

———. *Smoke and Mirrors*. New York: Berkley, 1989.

———. *Stitches in Time*. New York: HarperCollins, 1995.

Michelin Washington, DC. Greenville, SC: Michelin Travel Publications, 1994.

Mikulski, Barbara, and Marylouise Oates. *Capitol Offense*, New York: Dutton (Penguin), 1996.

Moody, Susan. *Penny Black*. New York: Fawcett Gold Medal, 1984.

Moore, William. *The Last Surprise*. New York: St. Martin's, 1990.

Morice, Anne. *Murder in Mimicry*. New York: Detective Book Club, 1977.

Moyes, Patricia. *Black Widower*. New York: Henry Holt, 1975.

Nessen, Ron, and Johanna Neuman. *Knight and Day*. New York: Forge, 1995.

O'Brien, Patricia. *The Ladies Lunch*. New York: Simon & Schuster, 1994.

Olshaker, Mark. *The Edge*. New York: Bantam, 1994.

O'Toole, G. J. A. *An Agent on the Other Side*. New York: Dell, 1973.

———. *The Cosgrove Report*. New York: Dell, 1979.

Patrick, Keats. *Death Is a Tory*. Indianapolis: Bobbs-Merrill, 1935.

Patterson, James. *Along Came a Spider*. New York: Time Warner Books, 1992.

Patterson, Richard North. *The Lasko Tangent*. New York: Ballantine, 1980.

Pelecanos, George P. *The Big Blowdown*. New York: St. Martin's, 1996.

———. *Down by the River Where the Dead Men Go*. New York: St Martin's, 1995.

Peters, Elizabeth. *The Murders of Richard III*. New York: Mysterious Press, 1974.

Perry, Anne, ed. *Malice Domestic 6*. New York: Pocket Books, 1997.

Pierson, Eleanor. *Murder Without Clues*. New York: Novel Selections, 1942.

Plum, Mary. *State Department Cat*. New York: Doubleday, Doran, 1945.

———. *Susanna, Don't You Cry*. New York: Doubleday Crime Club, 1946.

Poe, Edgar Allan. "Murders in the Rue Morgue" in *Edgar Allan Poe Selected Tales*. Oxford: Oxford University Press, 1980.

Protopappas, John J., and Alvin R. McNeal, eds. *Washington on Foot*. Washington, D.C.: Smithsonian Institution Press, 1992.

Quayle, Marilyn T., and Nancy T. Northcott. *The Campaign*. Grand Rapids, MI: Zondervan, 1996.

———. *Embrace the Serpent*. New York: Crown, 1992.

Randisi, Robert, and Marilyn Wallace, eds. *Deadly Allies*. New York: Doubleday, 1992.

Revell, Louisa. *The Men with Three Eyes*. New York: Macmillan, 1955.

Richman, Phyllis. *The Butter Did It*. New York: HarperCollins, 1997.

Ripley, Ann. *Mulch*. New York: St Martin's, 1994.

Rinehart, Mary Roberts. *The Man in Lower Ten*. New York: Holt, Rinehart and Winston, 1909.

Roberts, Carey. *Pray God to Die*. New York: Avon, 1994.

———. *Touch a Cold Duck*. New York: Pageant Books, 1989.

Roberts, Kelsey. *Legal Tender*. New York: Harlequin Intrigue, 1993.

Roosevelt, Elliott. *A First Class Murder*. New York. Avon, 1991.

———. *Murder and the First Lady*. New York: St. Martin's, 1984.

———. *Murder in the Blue Room.* New York: Avon, 1990.

———. *Murder in the Executive Mansion.* New York: St. Martin's, 1995.

———. *Murder in the Oval Office.* New York: Avon, 1989.

———. *Murder in the Rose Garden.* New York: St. Martin's, 1989.

———. *Murder in the West Wing.* New York: St. Martin's, 1993.

———. *The White House Pantry Murder.* New York: Avon, 1987.

Roudybush, Alexandra. *A Sybaritic Death.* New York: Doubleday Crime Club, 1972.

Safire, William. *Full Disclosure.* New York: Ballantine, 1977.

———. *Sleeper Spy.* New York: Random House, 1995.

Sanders, Lawrence. *Capital Crimes.* New York: Putnam, 1989.

Schafer, Edith Nalle. *Literary Circles of Washington.* Washington, D.C.: Starrhill Press, 1993.

Schutz, Benjamin M. *All the Old Bargains.* New York: Bantam, 1985.

———. *Embrace the Wolf.* Bluejay Books, 1985.

———. "Mary, Mary, Shut the Door" (Edgar Winner), in Robert J. Randisi and Marilyn Wallace, eds. *Deadly Allies.* New York: Doubleday, 1992.

———. *Mexico Is Forever.* New York: St. Martin's, 1994.

———. *A Tax in Blood.* New York: Bantam, 1987.

Serling, Robert J. *The President's Plane Is Missing.* New York: Doubleday, 1967.

Sheldon, Walter J. *Rites of Murder.* New York: St. Martin's, 1984.

Stern, Aaron Marc. *Death Takes a Paying Guest.* New York: Doubleday Crime Club, 1947.

Stout, Rex. *The Doorbell Rang.* New York: Bantam, 1965.

Sucher, Dorothy. *Dead Men Don't Give Seminars.* New York: St. Martin's, 1988.

———. *Dead Men Don't Marry.* New York: St. Martin's, 1989.

Swanson, Jean, and Dean James. *By a Woman's Hand.* New York: Berkley Books, 1994.

Thomas, Ross. *Ah, Treachery!* New York: The Mysterious Press, 1994.

———. *The Brass Go-Between.* New York: Mysterious Press, 1969.

———. *Cast a Yellow Shadow.* New York: Mysterious Press, 1967.

———. *If You Can't Be Good.* New York: William Morrow, 1973.

———. *The Pork Choppers.* New York: Perennial Library, 1984.

———. *Twilight at Mac's Place.* New York: The Mysterious Press, 1990.

Titchener, Louise. *Homebody.* New York: HarperPaperbacks, 1993.

———. *Mantrap.* New York: HarperPaperbacks, 1994.

Travers, Robert. *The Apartment on K Street.* New York: Popular Library, 1972.

Truman, Margaret. *Murder at the FBI.* New York: Fawcett Crest, 1985.

———. *Murder at the Kennedy Center.* New York: Fawcett Crest, 1989.

———. *Murder at the National Cathedral.* New York: Fawcett Crest, 1990.

———. *Murder at the National Gallery.* New York: Random House, 1996.

———. *Murder at the Pentagon.* New York: Fawcett Crest, 1992.

———. *Murder in Georgetown.* New York: Fawcett Crest, 1986.

———. *Murder in the C.I.A.* New York: Fawcett Crest, 1987.

———. *Murder in the House.* New York: Random House, 1997.

———. *Murder in the Smithsonian.* New York: Fawcett Crest (Ballatine Books), 1983.

———. *Murder in the Supreme Court.* New York: Fawcett Crest, 1982.

———. *Murder in the White House.* New York: Fawcett Popular Library, 1980.

———. *Murder on Capitol Hill.* New York: Popular Library (Arbor House), 1981.

———. *Murder on Embassy Row.* New York: Fawcett Crest, 1984.

———. *Murder on the Potomac.* New York: Fawcett Crest, 1994.

Valentine, Paul. *Crime Scene at "O" Street.* New York: St. Martin's, 1989.

Viorst, Judith. *Murdering Mr. Monti.* New York: Fawcett Crest, 1994.

Weeks, Christopher. *AIA Guide to the Architecture of Washington, D.C.* Baltimore and London: The Johns Hopkins University Press, 1994.

Wilson, F. Paul. *The Select.* New York: Morrow, 1994.

Zencey, Eric. *Panama.* New York: Farrar, Straus & Giroux, 1995.

INDEX

© 1994 Rosemary Herbert

ABOUT THE AUTHOR

During 1996–97, Alzina Stone Dale led two Chicago mystery tours, taught a seminar on East Coast crime for the Newberry Library, and appeared on the Newberry's Mystery Weekend panel with Bostonian Jane Langton. She also took part in the Dorothy L. Sayers Society's annual meeting at Wheaton College and contributed essays to a Festschrift for Madeleine L'Engle's eightieth birthday and to a C. S. Lewis companion. She is currently working on a mystery about Chicago's South Side during the 1960s.

Dale is a Regional Director of Mystery Writers of America, a board member of the Ngaio Marsh Society, and on the editorial board of *GILBERT*, the quarterly journal of the American Chesterton Society. She is also a member of the British Crime Writers Association, the Society of Midland Authors, and the Authors Guild.